SERENITY
MEDITATION™ SERIES

DAY BY DAY
LOVE IS
A CHOICE

Devotions for Codependents

Richard & Jerilyn Fowler
Brian & Deborah Newman

❖ *A Janet Thoma Book* ❖

THOMAS NELSON PUBLISHERS
Nashville

❖ *A Janet Thoma Book* ❖

Copyright © 1991 by Richard Fowler, Jerilyn Fowler, Brian Newman, Deborah Newman

Published in Nashville, Tennessee, by Thomas Nelson, Inc.

Scripture quotations are from the NEW KING JAMES VERSION of the Bible. Copyright © 1979, 1980, 1982, Thomas Nelson, Inc., Publishers.

Library of Congress Cataloging-in-Publication Data

Day by day love is a choice / Richard Fowler . . . [et al.].
    p.   cm.—(Serenity meditation series)
   ISBN 0-8407-3317-8
   1. Codependents—Prayer-books and devotions—English.
 2. Devotional calendars.   I. Fowler, Richard A., 1948–
II. Series.
BV4596.C57D39   1991
242′.4—dc20
                                    90–49581
                                      CIP

Printed in the United States of America
7 — 96 95 94 93

An Overview of Codependency

To many, *codependency* is the current buzz word, the popular term to use when discussing addictive behavior. For millions, however, it's more than a classification . . . it's a painful reality.

The term *codependency* finds its roots in alcohol treatment. Specialists in this field realized that family members and friends played a significant role in perpetuating or enabling the disease process. Even though therapists continued to focus primarily on the patient or addict, they began to bring in family and friends as part of the program.

What therapists found was that these significant others had also adopted dysfunctional behavior patterns in an attempt to adapt to the patient's personality and life-style.

In the book *Love Is a Choice*, the authors define codependency as an addiction to people (by assuming the role of rescuer or victim), behavior (such as work, anger, sex, perfectionism), and things (including alcohol/drugs, money, food). Codependency arises from the fallacy of trying to control inner feelings by manipulating other people and circumstances.

The following ten points can identify a codependent:

1. A codependent is driven by one or more compulsions.
2. The codependent is bound and tormented by the way things were in the dysfunctional family of origin.

3. The codependent's self-esteem (and often maturity) is very low.
4. A codependent is certain his or her happiness hinges on others.
5. Conversely, a codependent feels inordinately responsible for others.
6. The codependent's relationship with a spouse or Significant Other Person (SOP) is marred by a damaging, unstable lack of balance between dependence and independence.
7. The codependent is a master of denial and repression.
8. The codependent worries about things he or she can't change and may well try to change them.
9. A codependent's life is punctuated by extremes.
10. A codependent is continually looking for the something that is lacking or missing in life.

Any addiction, including codependent addiction, will ultimately take its toll on our lives, because an addict will do anything, or give up anything, to satisfy his or her addiction. Frustration and misery are the only results.

The apostle Paul wrote (Rom. 12:2) that we are to have renewed and transformed minds. The process of recovery thus begins with God's Word. As you read and meditate on the following devotionals, our prayer is that the process of recovery from codependent relationships will begin in your life.

Our soul waits for the LORD;
He is our help and our shield. . . .
Let Your mercy, O Lord, be upon us,
Just as we hope in You.
—PS. 33:20, 22

Thanks to media and public attention, codependency has become a trendy topic. There are codependent treatment programs, books, and even jokes: How many addicts does it take to unscrew a light bulb? None. The codependents will do it for them.

But the men and women struggling to recover from allowing themselves to be affected by other people and their past are not laughing. They are searching for help and hope.

Help and hope are available through our Lord Jesus Christ. The Bible is a book about hope—hope for all people who are attempting to overcome sin's destructive influence in their world and in their hearts. As you read and apply God's truth, through God's power, you can find balance and health and love for your life.

And the God of love will be with you. God cares for you, and he can help you learn to properly care for yourself. God will help you recover. He will give you help for today and hope for the future.

Thank you for being with me, even now as I begin this new year. Give me insight and understanding each day as I read, and help me to apply what I learn as I work toward recovery. I praise you for the power you have to work in and through me, and I commit myself to your care.

> *Be doers of the word, and not hearers only,*
> *deceiving yourselves. . . . he who looks into the*
> *perfect law of liberty and continues in it, and is not*
> *a forgetful hearer but a doer of the work, this one*
> *will be blessed in what he does.*
> —JAMES 1:22, 25

Codependent people are people. And most people would rather do anything except change. When we identify a problem area, we become creative. We might analyze it. Worry about it. Read about it. Talk about it. Rationalize it. Cry about it. And pray about it. All before we *decide to do something* about it!

Don't be discouraged if you struggle to bridge the gap between desiring to change your codependent behavior and doing it. Lasting change takes time and work as you learn to intercept the cycle of codependency.

Make your goal applying the truth of God's Word as he reveals it, and God himself will come to your aid. Ask God to show you appropriate action steps and to give you courage to change. Keep a journal to mark your progress through the year. Documenting your desires, goals, plans, and follow-through can help you on the road toward lasting behavior change as you apply God's Word to your life.

Lord, I'm aware of some self-defeating behaviors and compulsions that need to be changed, but I often feel stranded, unable to do much about it. Please forgive me and help me. Show me step by step what and how to change. I want to obey your Word. Please empower me through your Spirit and give me the desire to be a doer of the word, and not a hearer only.

If you love Me, keep My commandments. And I will pray [to] the Father, and He will give you another Helper, that He may abide with you forever, even the Spirit of truth.　　　　　**—JOHN 14:15–17**

Have you ever tried to fly a kite without any wind? Of course, it doesn't work that way. And if you left the kite on the ground, could the wind fly it? Just as the person who flies a kite cooperates with and depends upon the wind, the Christian cooperates with and is helped by the Holy Spirit.

A parent wouldn't ask a child to fly a kite when the wind wasn't blowing. And God would never ask us to obey without making sure we had the help we need to do so. He sends a Helper, a Comforter, the Spirit of Truth to live in us and be with us. Just as the wind will not fly a kite by itself, the Holy Spirit will not carry on your life without you. It must be a joint effort.

What is your part? To be willing and obedient. What is God's part? To teach, enable, and direct you. That may be oversimplification, but remember that you are not alone in this adventure called living. God has given you a Helper.

Lord, thank you for your Holy Spirit. Give me a heart that feels his comfort, ears that listen to his words of truth, and a mind that accepts his instruction.

> *He who gets wisdom loves his own soul.*
> —PROV. 19:8

Let's take a moment to consider an overview of wise living. Here are seven building blocks, drawn from the book of Proverbs, that will help you construct a godly strategy for daily living. The wise man or woman is one who:

1. Respects God (Prov. 9:10).
2. Walks uprightly (Prov. 14:15).
3. Thinks ahead (Prov. 22:3).
4. Plans well (Prov. 16:9).
5. Utilizes the counsel of others (Prov. 15:22).
6. Realizes God is in control (Prov. 3:5–6).
7. Has a teachable attitude (Prov. 9:9).

By carefully reading the book of Proverbs, and the selected readings in this book, you will be able to add to the list. Write out your own list and review it often as you make your additions.

Wisdom is at the heart of all proper self-care. Wisdom provides protection, security, and satisfaction in life and in relationships. Gaining wisdom is in your own best interest, for "he who gets wisdom loves his own soul."

Dear Lord, I want to learn wise ways to treat myself and others. I ask for wisdom, and for the diligence to study your Word to seek it. I know wisdom is from you and pleases you.

I am the Lord your God and there is no other. My people shall never be put to shame.

—JOEL 2:27

If you're dealing with codependency issues, you've probably been profoundly influenced by shame. Appropriate shame can be a valuable tool for shaping behavior. But inappropriate shame is cruel and overwhelmingly painful. This misguided shame can convince you that it's not okay to be who you are, that you don't deserve love or nice things. You may feel chronic shame for having disappointed a loved one, even if his or her demands were unreasonable.

If you feel ashamed because you've done something that violates God's commands, simply admit you're guilty. Confess and repent. God will wash away your shame. You are free in Christ!

But if you feel a deep-rooted, toxic shame that is sending unhealthy messages to your mind, then you should acknowledge shame's presence and ask God to remove your sense of shamefulness. Destructive shame is not of God, and you shouldn't allow anyone to impose it upon you. God says, "My people shall never be put to shame."

Dear Lord, at times I feel stained and unworthy of anyone's love, especially yours. Help me see myself as you see me—cleansed and pure in Christ. Make me aware of shame-based thoughts and help me replace them with your loving truth. Great Physician, please heal my shame.

> *If it is possible, as much as depends on you, live*
> *peaceably with all men.*
> —ROM. 12:18

It is not always possible to do the right thing and to get along with everyone at the same time. The Bible does not encourage peace at any price. Denial, manipulation, or enabling others to indulge in sinful or irresponsible behavior are not biblically acceptable ways to keep the peace.

It's good to do your part to seek peace, as Paul instructs, "Let us pursue the things which make for peace and the things by which one may edify another," (Rom. 14:19). But conflict, reproof, or loving confrontation may be needed to "edify another" and work toward peaceful relations. Biblical love always desires the ultimate best for another within the confines of God's Word—even if it temporarily disturbs the peace.

You do not need everyone's approval or acceptance. Because we live in an imperfect world, once in a while the best way to reconcile a problem between two people may be simply to part ways as agreeably as possible. (The only time this is definitely *not* an option is in marriage, which carries specific scriptural directives of its own.)

Sometimes holding your piece promotes peace, but not always. Sometimes you must speak your piece as well.

Father, help me to risk rocking the boat when constructive conflict is called for. Don't let me throw away my integrity for the sake of maintaining false serenity.

I can do all things through Christ who strengthens me. Nevertheless you have done well that you shared in my distress.   —PHIL. 4:13–14

Cathy was petite and capable. Her husband's childhood had been miserable thanks to an alcoholic father, and Cathy was determined to make things better for him now. When he left on business trips, she looked after their two little girls and managed things at home. When her husband returned, Cathy looked after him, too. "All my energy was focused on pleasing him. Protecting him. Solving his problems," she explained. But the tensions in the marriage grew.

Through independent reading and marriage counseling, Cathy came to realize that Christ could give her husband the strength to face life. She resolved not to take responsibility for his feelings, not to shelter him or enable him to be irresponsible. But instead, to view him as "capable in Christ."

Cathy affirmed that Christ could give her the strength to "share in [her husband's] distress" without compulsively rushing in to take care of him and fix everything. In her notes, Cathy jotted this concise reminder in bold letters:

1) I can.
2) He can.
3) Let him!

Dear Lord, help me to see myself and those I love as you see us— capable in Christ.

> *See then that you walk circumspectly, not as fools*
> *but as wise, redeeming the time. . . . do not be*
> *unwise, but understand what the will of the Lord is.*
> —EPH. 5:15–17

Healthy time management is not a matter of how much you are doing. It's *choosing* to do the things you are doing, instead of feeling you have no choice. It's choosing to use your time doing God's will. But many people are shamed into taking on tasks God never intended for them. Dick, for example, worked from the moment he woke up until he went to bed. Any time he was tempted to let up, he heard his mother's voice from his childhood, "Can't you see there's work to be done? You ought to be ashamed of yourself for being so lazy!" Dick was driven to take care of everyone's needs—except his own.

Dick desperately needed rest. But it was hard for him to learn to say "no" without feeling guilty. Choosing to take care of yourself is not sin. Wisdom requires a healthy balance between work and rest, giving and receiving.

Take control of your schedule; don't let it control you. In doing so, you may not be doing everything others expect of you. That's okay. Jesus didn't heal every sick person, provide for every poor person, or solve everyone's problems. Yet he could say that he had finished the work God had given him.

Lord, don't let me be a puppet on the strings of other people's expectations.

*And above all things have fervent love for one
another, for "love will cover a multitude of sins."*
—1 PETER 4:8

Some situations call for sympathetic and perhaps sac-
rificial love, not for discarding the feeling of compassion. However, Satan can twist the truth of this verse
so that it seems to support a characteristic codependent response of tolerating serious sin or ignoring abusive offenses. But that is not what loyal love is about.

Noted theologian R. C. Sproul comments that this
verse:

> . . . assumes a context of forgiven people who struggle
> daily to improve their obedience to God though frustrated
> by fervent failures. It speaks of a love which is tolerant and
> patient, the kind which is willing to absorb minor sin. It is
> aimed at the avoidance of pettiness, or picking at minute
> faults or weaknesses. This covering is not a form of indul-
> gence of the serious sin or the criminal act. . . .
>
> Love demands excellence, and it affirms people by expect-
> ing responsible behavior from them.*

Don't let Satan twist the truth about true love.

*Lord, fill my heart, my consciousness, and my subconsciousness with
a true understanding of love. Guide my thoughts to the place where
love becomes love.*

*In Search of Dignity, R. C. Sproul (Ventura, CA: Regal Books, 1983), p. 48.

*In all things showing yourself to be a pattern of
good works; in doctrine showing integrity,
reverence, incorruptibility.*
—TITUS 2:7

An adult Sunday school class was discussing love and
the question was raised, "Do you think reading the
Bible can teach you how to love?" Immediately
George, a man who was recovering from a divorce,
answered, "Reading by itself isn't enough. If you've
never seen it, you won't have it. If you've never seen
healthy love modeled, you don't have a clue what to
do!"

The Bible recognizes the importance of role models.
Ideally parents should pass on to their children the
knowledge of how to deeply love and be loved. But if
intimacy and love weren't modeled in your family, reparenting is necessary. To some degree, you can re-
parent yourself. But the church family is also instructed
to fill the gap.

Older men can set the example for younger men.
Older women can teach younger women how to love.
Seek out people who maintain strong, loving relationships. Learn by example the patterns of good communication, problem solving, and conflict resolution.
Don't surround yourself only with those struggling
with the same issues you face, but also spend time with
those who can sharpen your relationship skills and
demonstrate wholesome love.

———————

*Father, please draw me to people who can help me learn how to love.
And help me become a good example for others also.*

But you are a chosen generation, a royal priesthood,
a holy nation, His own special people . . .
—1 PETER 2:9

You belong to Jesus. To those who believe in Jesus, God has given the right to become children of God. You are his own special child. Cherished. Cared for. God has chosen you to proclaim His goodness.

In your self-talk, what do you call yourself? Whom do you identify with? Do you call yourself an adult child of an alcoholic? A recovering codependent? These, and other labels, may indicate your circumstances, but you should not allow yourself to identify only with problems connected with a dysfunctional person.

You are most deeply associated with the Person of complete health and love. You are God's own special child. You can call yourself a child of God. You are one of the chosen, the faithful, the royal family! Identify yourself with God, with hope, with light and love.

Repeat to yourself: I am a child of God. I am a special person, cherished and cared for by God. I am precious in God's sight and worthy to be treated with respect and dignity. I am loved.

Heavenly Father, thank you for adopting me into your loving family. Thank you for choosing me, for being willing to trust me with your friendship and your name.

Lord, Satan sounds so truthful when he tells me I'm bad, undeserving, and dirty. On the days when the negative inner voices are loudest, let your truth ring out louder still!

All things are lawful for me, but all things are not helpful. All things are lawful for me, but I will not be brought under the power of any.

—1 COR. 6:12

We are called to glorify God in body and spirit. This means we must take care of our bodies: eat good foods, get proper rest, maintain balanced relationships—do things that help us stay healthy.

Beyond that, we must not be mastered by or addicted to anything. If you are chemically dependent, that addiction must be ended. One word of caution: Breaking the substance abuse cycle is most effectively and safely done under medical supervision. Seek professional help.

But there are many addictions and compulsions, in addition to drugs or alcohol, that are destructive to our bodies. Eating disorders, sleep disorders (too much or too little), using medications to cope, dependence upon caffeine or nicotine, and many other behaviors are abusive to our bodies.

If you are under the control of bad habits or compulsive behaviors, willpower alone will not be enough to help you regain emotional and physical health. You will need God's power to help you. Ask for God's help to exercise self-control in all areas that he might be glorified in your body.

Father, please free me from the grip of all addictions. Help me recognize trigger events that draw me into compulsive cycles, and retrain my responses.

With my whole heart I have sought You,
Oh, let me not wander from Your commandments!
—PS. 119:10

Following our feelings can cause us to wander away from God's Word. One young man who struggled to find a balance between not denying his feelings and being irrationally controlled by them commented, "Sure we acknowledge what we feel, but we shouldn't let our feelings sway us. We have to be more rigid about what God says and let the feelings fall where they may. I've got to remind myself to lighten up—to take myself less seriously and take God more seriously."

Seeking God with your whole heart means that you are emotionally, intellectually, and willfully building a relationship with him. God's Word provides the boundaries in which this relationship can thrive. If you wander away from God's Word, your relationship with him and others will suffer.

Learn how to combine emotion with reason to make your decisions. Your feelings are important—they should be recognized, not ignored. But feelings can't be allowed to dictate your decisions or thinking. Follow God's commandments, not your emotions, opinions, or self-protective inclinations.

God, I'm totally dependent upon your power to heal my heart and mend my damaged emotions. Please help me to accept my feelings and still do what you say is right.

> *Now salvation, and strength, and the kingdom of*
> *our God, and the power of His Christ have come,*
> *for the accuser of our brethren, who accused them*
> *before our God day and night, has been cast down.*
> —REV. 12:10

The messages that are played in your mind, your self-talk, generally fall into one of two broad categories: accusations or affirmations. Accusations are counter-productive. Affirmations are instructive.

For example, suppose you lost your temper with your kids. You could tell yourself, "I made a mistake. I've confessed it, apologized for it, and learned from it. Next time I'll remember to set a limit rather than allow them to speak disrespectfully until I'm angry and blow up." Or you could condemn yourself, "I should have known better. That was a stupid way to respond. I'm such a lousy parent. I can't even get along with the kids—much less discipline them correctly!"

Accusations can come from Satan, our past, or our sinful nature. But God never resorts to vague accusations. God may convict us of specific sin, but he does not cast a slur of condemnation and accusation. In Christ we are no longer accused!

Dear Lord, help me replace the accusations and destructive messages in my mind with messages of affirmations that positively assert my ability to change my worth in your eyes and my potential in Christ. Thank you so much for being a God of grace, who frees me from guilt and shame.

Speaking the truth in love, [we] may grow up in all things into Him who is the head—Christ.
— EPH. 4:15

I used to keep quiet no matter how strongly I felt. At work, home, church—wherever—even if people upset me or took advantage of me, I'd just put up with it," Marc said as he looked at the floor. Then he straightened and looked another member of his support group in the eye. "But I'm learning that you've got to stand up for what you are and not let yourself get run over. God has made me a somebody, and it discredits him when I lack the courage to speak up and say what I truly feel— in a loving tone of voice, of course."

Marc is growing into a clearer understanding of his value and worth. His struggle to say what he honestly feels is a common one. Everyone has, at times, failed to speak up because they lacked confidence, feared rejection, or felt intimidated. But speaking the truth in love paves the road to healthy relationships.

Keep in mind the two key guidelines when you speak. First, it must be the truth. No lies, deception, or fantasies. Second, you must speak in love. No controlling, manipulating, or retaliation allowed. As you do, you will grow in Christ and in love for yourself and others.

Dear God, sometimes I wish I could fade into the wall and become invisible rather than try to express what I think or feel. Give me the courage and confidence to stick up for myself in the proper way and to confront others when necessary.

> *. . . add to your faith virtue, to virtue knowledge,*
> *to knowledge self-control, to self-control*
> *perseverance . . . For he who lacks these*
> *things is shortsighted.* —2 PETER 1:5–6, 9

Did you hear about the psychologist who went to see a colleague for counseling? He explained the problem, "I make enemies because I just have no self-control around people. I compulsively talk sense to them."

It's impossible to be compulsive about solving other people's problems and to exercise self-control at the same time. Self-control is setting limits on your life and exercising control over your choices—not trying to control others or their behavior. God holds each of us accountable for our words and actions, not someone else's.

You can exercise self-control even when someone else isn't. You can control your response even when the other person in the relationship isn't behaving responsibly or rationally. Self-control is a minute-by-minute process, not a blanket New Year's resolution.

Here are some effective ways to increase self-control. Have a plan for situations where your control will be tested. Avoid situations you know you can't handle. Set reasonable boundaries and limits before you face a challenging situation. Reduce fatigue and stress to increase your ability to respond wisely. And pray specifically about areas of weakness.

Lord, teach me how to control my tongue, my physical appetites, and my thoughts so that I can live the self-disciplined life that pleases you.

Hear another parable: There was a certain landowner who planted a vineyard and set a hedge around it . . . —MATT. 21:33

In New Testament times landowners who planted a vineyard on choice ground would set a hedge around it to protect their valuable property. The hedge served as a boundary to mark off the territory and prevent others from trespassing, unlawfully eating of the fruit, or damaging the vines by trampling on them.

In the same way, setting a hedge or personal boundary is an effective way to protect the valuable person you are. Hedges are an appropriate way to keep others from trampling over you. Maintaining a sense of private territory, and boundaries for interpersonal relationships, is healthy. Hedges or boundaries help you protect your integrity as a person.

Hedges are also a healthy means of proper self-protection. For example, specific verbal and physical abuse boundaries maintain safety and reduce intimidation. Strict guidelines or limits help us nurture ourselves, curb addictions, and build self-esteem. Setting and sticking to reasonable boundaries are essential in relationships. Plant a hedge!

Lord, help me establish some healthy limits and set personal boundaries—then give me the strength to patrol the borders! Show me where to plant the hedges necessary to protect integrity.

My voice You shall hear in the morning, O LORD;
In the morning I will direct it to You,
And I will look up.
—PS. 5:3

One pastor remarked, "The person who constantly has an inner focus lives in a pretty small world."

There is a fine line between self-centered introspection and necessary self-evaluation. Glossing over your present feelings or the effects of the past is not wise. Being honest with God requires a careful inside look at our problems. Our inner sanctuary must be kept right with God.

But your eyes should not be focused on yourself. If you gaze just at your problems and only glance at God from time to time, you will lose sight of the purpose and power for living. Instead, fix your eyes upon Jesus, your Leader, Counselor, and Instructor. Look intently into his finished work on the cross on your behalf rather than dwelling on your sinful condition.

Identify and pray about your problems. Then ask God to open your eyes to his vast horizons of hope.

Lord, help me look beyond myself and my problems to your goodness and grace. Let me meditate upon the perfection of your character, not stew about the flaws in mine. Lift me beyond myself that I might serve you with a thankful heart.

The end of a thing is better than its beginning.
—ECCL. 7:8

No one can sustain the pressure of unfinished business. A universal need is for closure, for the sense of having completed one task or phase of life before moving into another.

Look back at your family of origin. Are there unresolved issues in your past that haven't been dealt with? You must come to terms with your past before you can let it go. Acknowledge your past, then put it behind you and move forward with a fresh start.

The best recovery process is a series of beginnings and endings, not a never-ending hassle! Set a goal—and achieve it. Make a promise to yourself—and keep it. Break down problems into steps that lead to the solution. And follow each step in the solution to completion. Finishing a task, however small, brings satisfaction and builds self-esteem.

Unending "to do" lists to reform yourself or your life are overwhelming and discouraging. Look for ways to bring things to a natural close. A healthy pattern of beginnings and endings offers security and satisfaction.

Father, I don't want to wrestle with the same problems forever. Provide the guidance I need through your Word, an outside observer, or support group, to effectively end the cycle of self-sabotaging behavior. Help me feel a healthy sense of completion and pride as I advance through each stage of my recovery program.

> *And He said to them, "Take heed and beware of*
> *covetousness, for one's life does not consist in the*
> *abundance of the things he possesses."*
> —LUKE 12:15

God is direct and frank. He requires that we face our problems directly. In this verse he puts his finger on a common problem. Materialism.

Money cannot satisfy our inner needs. But how we handle money is often a reflection of deeper issues— issues of power, self-worth, discipline, and nurturance. Money is almost always a factor in recovery from co-dependency.

Money can be used to reward or control others. It can be used to meet needs or withhold them. Money can be compulsively hoarded. Or spending can be an addiction. Regardless of the specific symptoms, in nearly every case, money is a significant issue in recovery.

Ask God to help you identify your attitudes toward money and any unhealthy tendencies in money management. Then ask for God's strength to rethink your beliefs about money and how to handle it in wise and healthy ways.

———————

Father, I know that happiness is not found in the things I have, or wish I had, no matter how appealing they seem. Wealth would not solve my problems; only you can help me work my way through them. Help me establish a right relationship with money. I commit my finances to you.

And whatever you do in word or deed, do all in the name of the Lord Jesus, giving thanks to God the Father through Him.

—COL. 3:17

Why do you do the things you do? Why do you say the things you say? To gain someone's approval? To keep the peace? Because you feel you have no choice?

The Bible encourages us to "do all in the name of the Lord Jesus," seeking to obey and demonstrate our love for him. Doing things in order to gain approval and avoid confrontation, or doing things by default because you haven't taken control of your life, will not bring fulfillment.

Jesus set the ultimate example. He could say that honoring God was his life's purpose. Jesus told his disciples, "He who sent Me is with Me. The Father has not left Me alone, for I always do those things that please Him" (John 8:29).

Whatever you do in word or deed, make your purpose to please God.

———————

Lord, you can see my heart and discern my motives. You know that I don't always want to do the right things for the right reasons. I'm utterly dependent upon your grace to do the things that please you. Give me a more consistent desire to please and honor you in all circumstances, that your name may be glorified in me.

> *God is our refuge and strength,*
> *A very present help in trouble.*
> *Therefore we will not fear.*
> —PS. 46:1–2

Jacob and Susan are struggling to overcome codependent behaviors. They say they are surrendering to God because he is with them and can help them. What they don't say is that they don't believe it. Because God has refused to do what they demanded, according to their time schedule, they have pronounced him powerless. They've written off the true God because they wanted a genie—someone who would instantly grant their wishes and make their dreams come true.

But God is too big to fit any tiny bottled images. We must worship God as he is revealed in the Bible. Majestic. Sovereign. Holy. We worship God on his terms. God is great and powerful. He wants to be our refuge and strength, our help. God is to be greatly exalted. His glory and power far exceed our puny perceptions!

As we go in the strength of the Lord, we make progress on the journey to Christlikeness. We need not fear failure because we are weak. Our God is so mighty, a very present help in all our trouble.

Lord, reveal yourself to me in your splendor and your power that I might worship you as you really are, and commit my life to you. Let my tongue talk of your greatness. Let my heart surrender to your strength. Let my sinful ways melt before the white heat of your holiness. Remold me, Lord, to reflect your glory!

You shall not be terrified of them; for the LORD your God, the great and awesome God, is among you. And the LORD your God will drive out those nations before you little by little; you will be unable to destroy them at once, lest the beasts of the field become too numerous for you.

—DEUT. 7:21–22

Looking at your problems will be overwhelming at times. Then you must set the whole codependency carton aside and look at God instead. Change perspective. Change your focus.

When you hold a blue balloon up to your face and look through it, the whole world looks blue. But you can't believe the distortion. If you take a God's-eye view from a mountaintop and look down on the balloon, you see only a small speck of blue.

Don't be terrified by your problems; the great and awesome God can deliver you. And the Lord your God will help you drive out—little by little—the fears, lies, and pain that have governed your life. You will be unable to conquer your problems all at once. Sanctification is a process. Recovery is a process. Growth is a process. There are no quick fixes or magic answers.

But fantasy aside, God is greater than your problems. The Lord your God is the great God, mighty and awesome. And God is with you.

Lord, you are the great and awesome God, mighty in power and glorious in strength. Please fight on my behalf, be with me, Lord, as I seek to escape from the lies that hold me and to cling to your truth.

> *Casting all your care upon Him, for He cares for you.*
> —1 PETER 5:7

An honest young woman gave this humorous description of her struggle to overcome worry: "When I'm at the end of my rope, I can usually loosen my grip and lay down my problems to the Lord. But then about thirty minutes later, I catch myself picking up the rope again and trying to play tug-of-war!"

Have you ever cast your cares upon God and then checked in every fifteen minutes to see how they're getting along? We've all done that on occasion. As we get to know God better and trust him more fully, we become strong enough to surrender control with less anxiety. Acknowledging that there is Someone greater than ourselves—who is in control—Someone we know and trust—brings us comfort and peace of mind.

But you can not trust a make-believe God. To be truly willing to relinquish control and commit ourselves to God, we must be willing to commit ourselves to reality: to face ourselves, our problems, and our God as He has revealed himself in the Bible. Trust must be based upon truth. The truth is God cares for you.

Dear God, I've been hurt by so many people I've allowed myself to trust. I've been let down enough times that it's hard for me to drop my guard, even with you. But you understand me. You know all about me. Enlarge my heart so that it can hold a true knowledge of you. I want to cast all my cares upon you in complete confidence.

*Do not lie to one another, since you have put off
the old man with his deeds.*   —COL. 3:9

A Bible study group had grown increasingly frustrated with one member's codependent behaviors. "Alan claims he needs help, doesn't know what to do, needs more time, and wants us to be more supportive," the group leader commented. "But what more can we say? The first step is clear: make a commitment to quit lying! Even if he'd just decide to do only that *one thing*, and stick with it, he'd have something."

Telling the truth is a basic ingredient in the Christian life and in all good relationships. Lies destroy trust. Caring friends were trying to give Alan the message, "You've got to be honest with yourself and others. Love and lies don't mix."

Telling the truth takes courage and confidence, especially when it means risking rejection or owning up to our failures or insecurities. Sometimes we lie to look good or gain other people's approval. Being completely honest isn't easy. But the boundary is clear-cut. Do not lie.

God, I'm tired of the excuses and lies I sometimes hide behind. I want to tell the truth, but I know I lack the courage and confidence. Give me the inner strength to be honest with myself and you and others. And forgive me, Father, for the many times I haven't been completely honest.

All Scripture is given by inspiration of God, and is profitable for doctrine, for reproof, for correction, for instruction in righteousness, that the man of God may be complete, thoroughly equipped for every good work.
　　　　　　　　　　　　　　—2 TIM. 3:16–17

A person working through recovery issues needs support. The Scriptures provide a place for help with the pain of codependency. Unique from any other recovery material, the Bible is inspired by God!

The Bible presents truths that are profitable for teaching, for reproof, for correction and for training in righteousness. No one wants you to heal from codependency more than God. His words will encourage and help you be adequately equipped for every good work.

The Bible is a reliable source for direction, and you should not neglect its power. Tremendous benefits come as a result of using biblical truths in the recovery process.

These are God's words to you. Words are precious, but even more when they come from the heart of an almighty God.

_____

Father, your Word is precious to me. Let it be a source of strength and encouragement to me while I work through recovery issues.

Greater love has no one than this, than to lay down one's life for his friends. —JOHN 15:13

What is love? Today the answer can be different depending on who is answering. Jesus has given us a definition of true love. True love is a person's willingness to lay down his life for his fellow man.

The term used here for *life* is not only referring to a living, breathing body, but to the inner life. The inner life is your personality, your true self which can be known by others. Codependents find it almost impossible to reveal themselves at the beginning of their journey to recovery. They have denied themselves for so long that their true self is repressed. But knowing who you are is an important part of understanding true love rather than codependency. Discover yourself, and then allow others to get to know you as you really are. This in fact is the greatest form of love.

Jesus, help me be willing to open up to others and to show them who I truly am.

> *And Jesus increased in wisdom and stature, and in*
> *favor with God and men.*
> —LUKE 2:52

As we work through codependent issues, we must be willing to grow in wisdom. We need to gain insight into ourselves and into our defenses. Developing a personal relationship with God is part of developing wisdom. Our understanding of Jesus' life demonstrates how to relate in healthy ways to those around us.

Information alone is not wisdom. We can gain knowledge about codependency issues, but that will not give us strength to break addictive cycles. What we need beyond information is wisdom to apply this information in our lives. Wisdom is demonstrated in a personal relationship with God and in healthy relationships with our fellow men.

Insight alone is not enough to break addictive cycles. God, be my source of power to overcome addictive behaviors.

Hear, O Israel: The LORD our God, the LORD is one! You shall love the LORD your God with all your heart, with all your soul, and with all your might. And these words which I command you today shall be in your heart.

                                            —DEUT. 6:4–6

Our total love and commitment should first be toward God. We are to love the Lord with all our heart, soul, and strength. However, codependents invest that kind of energy into unhealthy relationships. As a result, we struggle with issues that cannot be solved. We have God-needs that people, behaviors, or substances cannot fill.

By making God a priority in our lives and by loving him with our whole being, we can establish a relationship which will free us. We can enter into healthy and profitable relationships. We will no longer look for something else to supply our God-needs. People cannot relate to us as we need God to relate. People cannot be available to us twenty-four hours a day; God can. People cannot love out of a pure heart; God can. People do not always have your best interests at heart; God does. When we try to make people (or behaviors or substances) fill our God-needs, we devote our energy and strength to a hopeless cause. This produces great pain in our lives.

Lord, I want my relationship with you to be the priority relationship in my life.

> *The way of a fool is right in his own eyes,*
> *But he who heeds counsel is wise.*
> —PROV. 12:15

When we are consumed by codependent relationships, we often don't understand why the relationship is unhealthy. Denial keeps unhealthy codependent relationships flourishing. If we trust in our own wisdom, we can use logical-sounding explanations for our codependent behavior. Foolishly, we think that others can make our lives right. Foolishly, we also believe that our acceptance by significant others will make us acceptable. These beliefs seem correct to us.

A wise man is a person who listens to advice. As you deal with codependent relationships, you receive advice from counselors, friends, or significant others. Sometimes their advice conflicts. The challenge is to listen, to evaluate, and to see how the advice might be helpful in your life. Don't trust your own wisdom alone.

It is wise to listen to the advice of others. Help me to evaluate whether or not that advice is pertinent to my situation.

It is the glory of God to conceal a matter,
But the glory of kings is to search out a matter.
—PROV. 25:2

We must open ourselves up and look at the underlying issues of our codependency. Sometimes we can do this work on our own, but many times the issues are too deep and require someone else who is trained to draw them out.

As you look at your own life, be willing to seek help and to allow another to help you reveal hidden parts. You may have many painful events deep inside your heart. These issues are festering and causing pain that you may not understand. Allow each one to come out, and look at it as an adult, fully loved by God. He will help you face the pain of your wounded heart. He will help you recover from your path of codependency.

I must be willing to allow others to penetrate the deep parts of my life. God, help me face what lies hidden and guide my recovery.

Apply your heart to instruction,
And your ears to words of knowledge.
—PROV. 23:12

Openness is a necessary feature of recovery. Open your heart to listen to the guidance and instruction of others. Open your ears to the knowledge of those around you. Humble yourself and develop a teachable spirit in order to understand the issues within your soul.

Gaining knowledge and understanding about how these issues developed is the beginning of knowledge. Be open and willing to face yourself and look at your past behaviors. Have the courage to deal with the pain in your life.

God, I want an openness to instruction and a heart to grow in knowledge.

Biblical Commands for Codependency

What are appropriate behaviors and attitudes for relationships? How do I relate to other people? Are there rights and wrongs? And if so, what are the rules that govern the dos and don'ts? Those of us who are codependent may shy away from reciprocal rules because they represent a threat to our freedom and our need to be in control. At least subconsciously, we want to make up our own rules for relationships so that we can use others to fill the voids we have in our own lives.

As Christians, however, God expects us to use his Word as our rule book. To follow his commands will ultimately lead to peace, harmony, and self-content. Following God's rules for relationships also takes the guesswork out of personal and corporate expectations.

Solomon was the richest and most influential person in his day. Yet, with everything going his way, he still concluded life was vanity for him. The closest Hebrew meaning of the word *vanity* is "soap bubbles." And the more he strove after his own desires and to live life "his way," the more he felt like a soap bubble. After a life full of struggles, Solomon finally concluded in the last chapter of Ecclesiastes that obedience to God is the only path to true freedom and for lasting, meaningful relationships.

We begin this section on the Biblical Commands for Codependency, or the Relational Dos and Don'ts, as a foundation for recovering codependents. If we intellectually and emotionally adhere to the following commands in Scripture, given by God for us to follow in our relationships, we will be well on our way to victory.

Yet do not count him as an enemy, but admonish him as a brother.
—2 THESS. 3:15

Every day while driving our automobiles, we see signs like: "Slow—Sharp Curve Ahead," or "One Way—Do Not Enter." What are these signs designed to do? They are put there to warn us of a possibly harmful situation while driving.

In much the same way, God in his love and wisdom has designed road signs in his Word which warn us of possible harm on the road of life. God has asked us not only to heed these warnings ourselves, but also to warn others whom we see straying from the truth. Those people who enjoy controlling others use the instruction to admonish others with an air of great superiority and satisfaction. However, three key points must be kept in mind.

First, any admonishing must take into consideration the best interests of all involved. Second, our warnings must be grounded firmly in the commands of Scripture rather than merely reflecting a personal prejudice. Third, as we correct a brother or sister, we must do so in a spirit of genuine humility, love, and gentleness, realizing that except for the grace of God, we could be in the same situation.

Lord, if I am called on to correct or warn a brother of a potential danger, may I have the wisdom to exhort him in love. Thank you for the road signs in your Word that keep me on track.

> *Now I myself also am confident concerning you,*
> *my brethren, that you also are full of goodness,*
> *filled with all knowledge, able also to admonish*
> *one another.*
> —ROM. 15:14

To those who have a strong desire to be in control, admonishing or correcting another can be a real ego boost. However several parameters define the extent and conditions under which we can admonish another. First, we must be "full of goodness" and second, "full of knowledge" in order to effectively warn or correct another. The first character quality implies that our intentions are noble and we are truly concerned for the best interest of the brother or sister we feel led by God to admonish. The second quality indicates that our insight is aligned with biblical truth.

Thus, our inner being becomes the key to effectively administer a warning to a brother or sister in Christ. We must not come across in a superior "better-than-thou" manner. Instead, we must demonstrate humility, brotherly love, and genuine sorrow over the wrong path the brother or sister has taken.

Finally, remember that we should confront the problem, rather than the straying person's self-worth. If we prayerfully do these things, our brothers and sisters will see God's love and concern for them manifested in our lives.

Lord, if called upon to admonish another, may my spirit be pure, may my love be evident, and may I be granted wisdom in what to say so that the relationship will become even stronger than before.

*Bear one another's burdens, and so fulfill the
law of Christ. For if anyone thinks himself to be
something, when he is nothing, he deceives himself.
But let each one examine his own work, and then
he will have rejoicing in himself alone, and not in
another. For each one shall bear his own load.*
—GAL. 6:2–5

This passage is difficult for codependents because relationships are many times based on the need to "rescue" or a need to "be rescued." These verses, however,
provide us with wise boundaries when we discover
that helping another or receiving aid from another is
conditional. There are definite guidelines for each situation. "Bear one another's burdens" carries the idea of
helping one who is weighed down by "excess" weight.
"Bear his own load" means that each person must
carry his "own normal weight." There are times in life
when we must march ahead, carrying our own backpack as a good soldier of the cross. However, there will
be other times when we find we have much more than
just a backpack to carry. At these times it is good and
right for others to help us with our "overload."

*May I be willing, Lord, to slow down and help the one who is carrying
excessive weight, and may I have discernment to know when a
brother needs to carry his own weight.*

> *And in these days prophets came from Jerusalem to Antioch. Then one of them, named Agabus, stood up and showed by the Spirit that there was going to be a great famine throughout all the world, which also happened in the days of Claudius Caesar. Then the disciples, each according to his ability, determined to send relief to the brethren dwelling in Judea. This they also did, and sent it to the elders by the hands of Barnabas and Saul.*
> —ACTS 11:27–30

Several other implications can be made today concerning this command to bear another's burdens. First, true believers do have problems, too! Often it is popular to teach the false notion that if we are in tune with God, we will not have struggles. This passage shows us otherwise. Second, once we become aware of a genuine need (as had the believers in Antioch), God wants us to be willing to do our share. Third, most excess burdens are of a fairly transient nature and once the crisis passes, it's no longer necessary for us to continue carrying the weight of another. And finally, the degree to which we can help another is contingent on our own financial, emotional, or family situation. If an individual is in need of both emotional and financial support, we may be able to supply one, but not the other. God knows each of our situations completely, and he will give us the privilege to help others in some way.

Lord, may I have the same determination to help others as those in the early church had in assisting famine victims.

Therefore let us pursue the things which make for peace and the things by which one may edify another.

—ROM. 14:19

Lately, I have been able to fulfill one of my lifelong dreams. I am taking flying lessons. But all those responses, which look so easy when performed by a seasoned pilot, have proven very difficult for me. But I keep going and making progress because I have such a good flight instructor. In the early stages of my training after a frustrated hour spent learning how to land the aircraft, he would say something such as, "You fly the traffic pattern well, your ground reference manners were right on the money, and hey, we'll continue to work on the landings—they were difficult for me to learn as well."

Now that's a good example of encouragement! My instructor didn't overlook my areas of difficulty, but he motivated me to continue by relating his past experiences and focusing on what I did well. With each lesson he has given me hope and the courage to continue. This is the same kind of "building up" God tells us to *pursue* in Romans 14:19. When we pursue something, we are determined to lay hold of it and make it our own. Let's be that determined to keep encouraging each other to be and do all we can for the Lord Jesus.

Dear God, may my motives be right as I uplift and encourage others today. Help me to look for the good, instead of looking for the faults in others.

> *Therefore comfort each other and edify one*
> *another, just as you also are doing.*
> —1 THESS. 5:11

The early church was quite a mixed lot. Some believers were Jews, some Gentiles. Some were slaves while others were free. Some were well educated and there were those who were poorly educated. But the common bond of this diverse group was the love they shared for Jesus Christ and, thus, for one another. The same focus should bind and direct the interaction among believers today. Each of us should be doing our part to build up the faith of our brothers and sisters in Christ. We should be praising the strengths we see in others, as well as encouraging them to overcome their weakness and continue to grow in the Lord.

God wants us to take the time and care to build up others because He knows we will find ourselves needing this same kind of encouragement to pull us through difficult times.

Finally, God wants us to build up others because realistically, we can't make it on our own. If we keep in mind that we all have strengths and weaknesses, we will do a wiser and more cheerful job of building up and encouraging one another.

Lord, give me the wisdom to build someone up today. May I also accept from others their encouragement in all humility.

But our presentable parts have no need. But God composed the body, having given greater honor to that part which lacks it, that there should be no schism in the body, but that the members should have the same care for one another.
—1 COR. 12:24–25

One of the constant struggles of a codependent personality is the tendency to take advantage of another person in order to fill the void in our own lives. This tendency may take many forms, depending on our personality type. We may shrink back from responsibility or try to take control or become jealous easily. In this passage, however, the apostle Paul tells us that we should have genuine love and care for each member of the body. This means that instead of using others to gratify our needs, we will be responding to the needs of individuals and the body of Christ as a whole.

Unhealthy competition, self-exaltation, or self-debasement all keep us from enjoying the unity God wants us to have with our fellow Christians. Each of these attitudes keeps our attention focused on ourselves rather than others. But we can stay on track in our relationships if we are daily asking God to take our eyes off our own troubles and concerns and to focus them on others.

Dear Lord, help me to realize that I have flaws and weaknesses which make me rely on others in healthy ways that you have ordained for your body. Thank you for seeing all of us on an equal and impartial basis.

> *Confess your trespasses to one another, and pray for one another, that you may be healed. The effective, fervent prayer of a righteous man avails much.*
> —JAMES 5:16

Confessing our sins to another person when we have been in the wrong is a powerful demonstration of love. The act of confession signals a desire to change as well as a desire for reconciliation.

Many codependents who need approval from others to validate their self-esteem may, however, be hypercritical of themselves, confessing imagined shortcomings or blowing trivial oversights out of proportion. This kind of confession to the extreme can be overwhelming for everyone. True confession does not imply that every negative thought or act must be articulated to another. When we dwell on our negative thoughts or commit deliberate, hurtful acts out of selfishness, we then are obligated to confess those shortcomings to another in order for healing to take place and spiritual growth to occur.

A wonderful peace comes over individuals as they confess sins that have weighed them down for years. Right and true confession will always bring true peace.

God, I realize that confession is your method of ridding me of that weight which keeps me from winning the race of life. Help me be prompt in my confession to you and when necessary, in my confession to others as well.

*Therefore if you bring your gift to the altar, and
there remember that your brother has something
against you, leave your gift there before the altar,
and go your way. First be reconciled to your
brother, and then come and offer your gift.*
—MATT. 5:23–24

The hardest two words to say in the English language
are "I'm sorry." When a relationship goes sour, it is sel-
dom the fault of only one party. More often than not,
the truth is that both parties are somewhat to blame
for a problem.

Reconciliation and unity with our brothers and sisters in Christ are more important and indeed preempt
any other act of service to God. Yet, many people attempt to fool God and even themselves by becoming
wrapped up in "doing good" in order to cover up or
justify a heart that stubbornly refuses to be reconciled.

Jesus would want us to go to our brother or sister
and say, "If I have offended you, I'm sorry." God will
honor this act of confession in ways we never imagined
for the good of others as well as ourselves.

Once I learned to say "I'm sorry," especially to my
children, the best by-product that emerged for me was
a sensitivity I had never known before. Doing things
God's way with God's priorities reaps untold dividends.

*Lord, by mastering the two hardest words in the English language,
"I'm sorry," may I thus receive the gift of sensitivity.*

Beware, brethren, lest there be in any of you an evil heart of unbelief in departing from the living God; but exhort one another daily, while it is called "Today," lest any of you be hardened through the deceitfulness of sin.

—HEB. 3:12–13

When I was a youngster, basketball was my life. Our coach would not give us the privilege of playing, however, unless we had gone through pre-season "boot camp." During this time we never touched a basketball—we just ran, ran some more, and lifted weights. I hardly ever looked forward to pre-season. In fact, I dreaded it. My mind continually argued with my body, "Why are you killing me?" "It's really not worth the price." But when any team member really felt that he was about to quit, the other team members would encourage him to "hang tough" and remain faithful to the goal we, collectively, had set.

It is much the same in our relationships within the body of Christ. There will be times when a brother or sister's desire to continue obeying the Lord will falter. They may question if the Christian life is worth the price. Each of us as believers has the duty and privilege to exhort our "teammates," to urge them to continue a strong and steady walk with the Lord.

When done in a spirit of humility and love, exhorting others helps them to renew their desire to serve Christ and live for him.

Lord, help me be the best cheerleader or exhorter a friend could have.

> *I, therefore, . . . beseech you to walk . . . with all*
> *lowliness and gentleness, with longsuffering,*
> *bearing with one another in love.*
> —EPH. 4:1–2

I can't stand _____! He drives me crazy! Have you ever caught yourself saying that? Surely all of us have from time to time. Codependents are especially prone to statements like this because their relationships tend not to be founded on commitment and mutual equality, but on unmet needs and inequality. So, when people act and think the way we want them to, life seems rosy. But when others choose to respond in ways that expose our emotional weaknesses, we may explode or find a corner in which to sulk. Even when we are well into recovery, we may find ourselves upset and shaken by others who seem able to magnify our weaknesses.

This is why Paul speaks to us about "putting up with" other people. God, of course, does not ask us to put up with sin or to overlook definite wrongdoing. But many times we will be called upon to accept others and put up with their irritating habits or frustrating ways. It is always good to remind ourselves that we too might irritate others. We would want them to forbear with us just as God wants us to forbear with them. Forbearance preserves the oneness Christ wants us to have.

May I be able to discern, Lord, the difference between preference and principle and put forbearance into practice.

> . . . *endeavoring to keep the unity of the Spirit in the bond of peace.*
>
> —EPH. 4:3

Just as today, the early church was comprised of many different ethnic and social backgrounds, as well as people who were at different levels of spiritual maturity.

"Endeavoring to keep the unity" simply means we are to put up with, or tolerate, the differences of those on our team as long as the basis of our faith and doctrine is not jeopardized. If I practice unity of the Spirit in the bond of peace, I will not be quick to judge or rebuke. Instead, I will seek to put myself in that person's shoes and see the situation through his eyes.

I pray for patience, Lord. Forgive me for being too quick to judge the motives of others. Help me see how important unity and peace are to your cause.

*For if you forgive men their trespasses, your
heavenly Father will also forgive you. But if you do
not forgive men their trespasses, neither will your
Father forgive your trespasses.*

—MATT. 6:14–15

Forgiving another is not an option. Failure to forgive,
Jesus says, is a violation of his specific instruction to
us. In other words, lack of forgiveness is sin. Why is
there such importance placed on forgiveness? Primarily, we are to forgive others because God forgave us.
When we accepted the death of Jesus as payment for
our sins, God forgave our sins—past, present, and
future—and declared us to be justified in his sight. Now
as believers who are growing in him, we are to be constantly becoming more like him. God wants us to reflect the image of Jesus Christ, and the essence of that
image is unconditional love and forgiveness.

We are obligated to forgive even when the other
person is not interested in restoring harmony. Nor
should our forgiveness be contingent upon a reciprocal
act of repentance by the other person. Actually, forgiveness frees us from being slaves to the offending
person's potential power over us. By relinquishing
those real or perceived wrongs, through total forgiveness, the slate becomes clean, and we grow stronger
because we are reflecting Christ.

May I obey you, Lord, by forgiving those who have wronged me.

> *Put on tender mercies, kindness, humbleness of*
> *mind, meekness, longsuffering; bearing with one*
> *another, and forgiving one another, if anyone has a*
> *complaint against another; even as Christ forgave*
> *you, so you also must do.*   —COL. 3:12–13

In these two verses, the act of forgiving those who have wronged us is strongly linked with being kind, meek, gentle, and patient. The willingness to let others off the hook by forgiving completely is more a sincere act of our will, rather than a response to a feeling.

Years ago, five missionaries lost their lives trying to make contact with the Auca Indians in Equador. They were brutally murdered by the tribes people. But since that time, almost the whole tribe has come to know Christ as Savior because the wives of those men chose to live with the tribes people and forgive them unconditionally, without expectation of repentance. True forgiveness can make a positive impact, but without forgiveness, bitterness, hatred, and hurt feelings become magnified. Forgiving another individual does not necessarily mean that the hurt from the wrong is eliminated immediately. But when that particular hurt is brought to mind, the decision to practice the act of forgiveness keeps us from building up resentment or demanding revenge, which could not only destroy others but ourselves as well.

Dear Lord, when wronged, may I have the power to forgive—even if I don't feel like it. Help me to let go and not demand revenge, realizing you will ultimately judge each of us in your way.

Greet one another with a holy kiss. The churches
of Christ greet you.
                                        —ROM. 16:16

When we meet an aquaintance on the street, the conversation usually goes like this. "How are you?" and
the response "Fine, thank you." Even if we are sick or
sad, or both, we probably will say, "I'm fine." And to be
honest, few people would really care to hear if we
were feeling otherwise. One interesting study concluded that the average American lies over 100 times a
day. No wonder our relationships are shallow.

When we greet other believers, however, God would
have us be honest in our concern and in our response.
In doing so, we are communicating our own worthiness and the worthiness of the other believer. That in-
herent worthiness stems from the fact that we both
belong to Jesus. And the more we practice showing
genuine concern when we greet others, the easier and
more fulfilling it will become.

Dear Lord, it is difficult for me to greet others with my mask off.
Please give me the desire and ability to show genuine warmth and
concern for fellow believers each day.

> . . . *distributing to the needs of the saints, given to hospitality.*
> —ROM. 12:13

Hospitality refers to the act of giving rest and refreshment in a loving manner to another, especially to a stranger, who cannot reciprocate with an equal act of kindness.

When the apostle Peter wrote these words of exhortation, he was encouraging Christians to entertain, feed, and house traveling evangelists and missionaries. The command also referred to assisting someone who was physically abused because of the gospel.

How easy it is to assist someone when we can expect the favor to be returned. It may be more difficult, on the other hand, to show hospitality to those we don't know or to those who can in no way return our efforts. In our society today, we can respond to this exhortation by inviting families who are new to our community to come with us to church or over to our house for a meal. We can help individuals and families who suffer emotional or physical pain with our time and our emotional support. We can house missionaries who need a place to stay. We can show hospitality to the widows and orphans—those who can't meet their needs on their own.

Lord, I want to actively pursue this command to be hospitable. I realize as I serve others with no strings attached that I am pleasing you. Thank you for allowing me to be a blessing to others.

Let all bitterness, wrath, anger, clamor, and evil
speaking be put away from you, with all malice.
And be kind to one another, tenderhearted,
forgiving one another, just as God in Christ
also forgave you.
                                    —EPH. 4:31–32

To be kind means we are to exhibit mercy and compassion to others out of genuine love. Kindness is a concrete demonstration of care and concern.

Being kind to someone is easy when that person is also kind. However, it is quite another matter to be kind when the other party despises you! When Jesus was on trial, he did not return evil for evil; rather he showed kindness and gentleness to his accusers.

We must not forget that our acts of kindness are noticed by God. And, because we belong to him, God wants us to demonstrate to others the kindness he has bestowed on us. Before we were saved, each of us lived for himself and in hostility toward God. But still he loved us enough to send his Son down to earth to die for you and me so that through his kindness, we might have eternal and abundant life.

Thank you for showing your kindness to me even when I didn't deserve it, Lord. May I reflect your kindness to all those who come my way.

> *Be kindly affectionate to one another with brotherly love, in honor giving preference to one another.*
> —ROM. 12:10

What is love? Very practically speaking, love is kindness. And oh, the power of kindness! If we are kind, we will not be arrogant or jealous, but rather we will exhibit patience. Lovingkindness grows strong in a climate of genuine humility and a meekness that doesn't keep score.

How can we express kindness in a tangible way? First, we can show kindness by not reminding another of his or her faults, especially when we are in a debate. Second, we can demonstrate kindness by practicing the art of toleration. Scripture points out that love covers a multitude of sins. This doesn't mean we are to compromise the principles of our faith, but rather that we will be generous in overlooking the shortcomings of other human beings, accepting them as they are. Third, we can express kindness by giving graciously to those who cannot give back in return. And finally, we can live out kindness by verbally encouraging the less fortunate, the sick, the widows, and those who face difficult situations.

Can you think of any additional ways you can personally express kindness today?

Dear Lord, as I put myself in the shoes of others today, may the power of kindness do your work in the lives of those I meet.

*He who does not love does not know God, for God
is love. In this the love of God was manifested
toward us, that God has sent His only begotten Son
into the world, that we might live through Him. In
this is love, not that we loved God, but that He
loved us and sent His Son to be the propitiation
for our sins.*   **—1 JOHN 4:8–10**

Love is something inward which manifests itself in
actions. *Love* is a word that almost defies definition because of the magnitude of meanings it carries. In our
culture, *love* is used to refer to a hamburger, a car, or a
relationship. The word has come to generally denote a
degree of liking rather than a statement of commitment.

The passage read for today, however, gives us some
insights into God's definition of true love. First, love
originates from God, which means I can't really sustain
it on my own power, nor can I adequately express it
apart from my relationship with God. Second, love is
an inward attitude that seeks God's best for another.
True love does not love for selfish reasons. Its main
motivation is not "what can I get from this relationship?" Finally, Christ's example through his life and
death should be our standard for defining and practicing love.

---

*Dear Lord, thank you for loving me so much that you sent your son
Jesus to die in my place. May the commitment, wisdom, and compassion of your love be mine through the Holy Spirit's power.*

> *Love suffers long and is kind; love does not envy;*
> *love does not parade itself, is not puffed up; does*
> *not behave rudely, does not seek its own, is not*
> *provoked, thinks no evil; does not rejoice in*
> *iniquity, but rejoices in the truth; bears all things,*
> *believes all things, hopes all things, endures all*
> *things.* —1 COR. 13:4–7

After reading these verses most of us (if we are honest with ourselves) feel woefully inadequate. We may even find ourselves saying, "There is no way I can fulfill that criteria! I may as well quit!" But just because the goal is lofty, it need not overwhelm us.

When I was in college and graduate school, I learned one trick to help me achieve my academic goals. Instead of dwelling on my ultimate degree objective, I broke down the degree plan into manageable chunks and concentrated on doing my best on those less intimidating goals. Finally, my ultimate goal was reached, and the degree was mine. The same can be said of learning how to love. On a scale of one to ten, write down how you measure up on each description of love found in the passage today. Then, make a simple, reachable (and measurable) goal in each area. Finally, acknowledge your list to God.

———   ———

Dear Lord, because of my fallen nature I realize that I cannot love others as you would have me to love them. Help me to keep growing each day. Keep me from feeling guilty when I do not achieve perfection and help me to strive in the power of your Holy Spirit.

Epaphras, who is one of you, a servant of Christ, greets you, always laboring fervently for you in prayers, that you may stand perfect and complete in all the will of God.
—COL. 4:12

For some reason, one of the things which should come easily and most naturally to us as believers is often very difficult. Praying for others requires perseverance and determination. It's hard to be an Epaphras—always striving in prayer for others. Why is it hard to pray?

It's hard to pray because prayer is hard work! To pray, we must not let our minds wander—and even Jesus' disciples had problems in this area! When Jesus asked them to "watch in prayer" at the Garden of Gethsemane, they went to sleep instead. To effectively pray, we must have self-discipline and be determined to stay on target, even when our minds want to wander.

I have found the following ACTS prayer formula to be very helpful.

A—Start your prayer by giving **A**doration to God for who he is. Rejoice in his wonderful attributes.

C—Second, **C**onfess your sins to God.

T—Third, **T**hank God for what he has done in your life.

S—Present your **S**upplications or requests to God.

Today take the ACTS formula and use it in a personal prayer to your Heavenly Father.

Yes, we had the sentence of death in ourselves, that we should not trust in ourselves but in God who raises the dead, who delivered us from so great a death, and does deliver us; in whom we trust that He will still deliver us. —2 COR. 1:9–11

God has ordained prayer as a means to accomplish His work on this earth, but God may not grant us every request. However, he wants us to bring our petitions to him as a son would talk to his earthly father.

As a child, I learned the essence of faith and prayer from my parents. My folks were missionaries at the time in Central America, and for some reason our income check had not made it through the mail. Over a period of a week our food had depleted steadily to almost nothing. I will never forget that evening when we three boys and my folks sat down to an empty supper table. Instead of begging God for food, my dad began giving thanks for the food we were about to eat! I said, "Dad, there's no food in the house. What are we praying for?" His reply, "Son, God knows we have need of food, and he has promised to supply us with our needs." At that moment there was a knock on the door. We opened the door to find two bags of groceries—but no one was in sight! God does answer prayer. And it's also exciting to know that he will use people like you and me to fill the needs of his sheep when we are listening to his voice.

Lord, may I never cease to pray to you, and may I also listen to you so I can be a willing and faithful worker for you.

Therefore receive one another, just as Christ also received us, to the glory of God. —ROM. 15:7

Many codependent relationships are built upon one-upmanship or superior-inferior games. Because of the widely varied social strata of the early believers, the apostle Paul was careful to give instruction in how to respond toward those whom the world looked down upon. He encouraged the believers to take to themselves other like-minded individuals without reservation.

What keeps us from accepting another person? In the early 70s when the hippie movement was at its height, many Christians had the attitude, "A hippie can't be a true believer because he doesn't look like one." Such views kept many young people from becoming and staying involved with established churches. I have developed a strategy to combat these tendencies; I have learned to place an imaginary *E* on the forehead of everybody I meet. The *E* stands for *Equal* in Christ Jesus. In Christ no one is superior or inferior to me. Each is my brother or sister and my peer. Each is worthy of my complete acceptance because God himself accepts them completely.

Dear Lord, let me never forget that you loved me when I was unlovely. Help me receive others without hesitation, because you received me in that way.

> *For perhaps he departed for a while for this*
> *purpose, that you might receive him forever, no*
> *longer as a slave but more than a slave, as a*
> *beloved brother, especially to me but how much*
> *more to you, both in the flesh and in the Lord. If*
> *then you count me as a partner, receive him as you*
> *would me.*
> —PHILEM. 15–17

A memory forever etched in my mind was one as a freshman in a large high school. It was an unfortunate tradition at the school that upper-class boys played cruel pranks on the lowly freshman boys, making life miserable.

However, I was very fortunate. I had a 6'7" brother who was a senior the year I was a freshman. He made it clear that anyone who harassed me would have to answer to him. I was saved from all the torture awaiting me as a freshman. While other freshmen cowered in fear at approaching upperclassmen, I strolled confidently by, secure in the knowledge that my older brother's name gave me security and acceptance.

In the same way, the name of Jesus should be a precious covering of security and acceptance among believers. We accept one another because we all have the same Lord Jesus, "the first-born among many brethren." Because he is precious to us, so are our brothers and sisters in Christ.

———————————

Dear Lord, thank you for friends. Thank you for the security, vulnerability, and comfort you allow me to have through my relationship with others.

A new commandment I give to you, that you love one another; as I have loved you, that you also love one another. By this all will know that you are My disciples, if you have love for one another.
—JOHN 13:34–35

Jesus made it very clear that loving others is an act and attitude of obedience. He also stressed that this was a sign to the world that we belong to Him. The apostle John, under the guidance of the Holy Spirit adds, "If someone says, 'I love God' and hates his brother, he is a liar" (1 John 4:20).

What then can we conclude? First, loving one another is not optional. We love not out of a codependent need, which is our attempt to fill our empty love tank, but we love because we want to please God. And second, truly loving one another is not easy and can only be accomplished through the supernatural strength of the Holy Spirit.

Dear Lord, help me to obey your command to love those whom you put in my path each day. Thank you for giving me the power and strength to love the unlovely as well as to enjoy the reciprocal love of others who love me.

*And do not be drunk with wine, in which is
dissipation; but be filled with the Spirit, speaking to
one another in psalms and hymns and spiritual
songs, singing and making melody in your heart to
the Lord.*
—EPH. 5:18–19

Did you know it is almost impossible to be depressed and sing songs of praise at the same time? Praise to our God is so therapeutic! A good example of this is found in the book of Acts, chapter 16. In this passage we find Paul and Silas in a dungeon, praising God and singing hymns, even though their backs were torn and bleeding and their feet were in stocks. Can you imagine the encouragement that they passed on to their fellow prisoners! Praise is contagious! Singing indicates we are making the best of life, that we have chosen to accept our circumstances as those wisely picked for us by a good and sovereign God. Our trust and hope expressed through praise can lift not only ourselves but others.

But how do we begin to change our perspective if we are the kind of person who naturally sees the glass as half empty instead of half full? One way is to practice praising God in the good times and earnestly seek to know him better when times are good. Then, these learned responses will stay with us through the hard times, and we will find that we can even "sing in the dungeon."

Lord, you are worthy of our praise. Thank you for putting a new song in our hearts.

. . . submitting to one another in the fear of God.
—EPH. 5:21

When I conduct seminars for business groups, I often conduct a team exercise entitled "Moon Survival." Initially, the participants are given a list of fifteen items they will have in their space survival kit on the moon. They are asked to prioritize each item as to its value. The second part of the exercise then has the group rank the items in terms of importance. About 80 percent of the time, the group score will come closer to NASA's official priority list than each individual arrived at on his own. Why? Since the group had to come to a unified consensus, mutual submission evolved and the final product was better because of it.

One biblical scholar indicates that the verse we read in Ephesians means "individually, I'm weak; together, with you, I'm strong." As we couple this with Ecclesiastes 4:12, which states that a strand of three cords is not easily broken—God, me, and you—we discover God's plan to make us all the best we can be through mutual submission to one another.

Lord, I realize you created me with imperfections so that I will need others. Help me learn to accept help and strength from others as well as to give of myself in areas where I am strong.

> *Likewise you husbands, dwell with them with understanding, giving honor to the wife, as to the weaker vessel, and as being heirs together of the grace of life, that your prayers may not be hindered.*
> —1 PETER 3:7

When my wife and I met over twenty-three years ago, codependent needs drew us together. She was attracted to me because I would rescue her. On the other hand, I was drawn to her because I could control her. As a result, I began to demand that she submit to me. It took ten years of marriage and a degree of mental stress before I realized that God never told me to force my wife to submit. As I came to realize later, my demand for her to submit reflected a deeply insecure feeling I had. I found that by controlling her I could cover up this insecurity.

According to this passage, God's message to me was to honor and understand my wife in order to have my prayers heard. The beautiful conclusion I came to was this: The more I served, honored, and loved my wife, the more fulfilled we were as a couple.

Thank you, Lord, for letting me realize that honor, understanding, and love represent the highest goals for a relationship, and that submission to another becomes easy when placed under this umbrella.

*Likewise you younger people, submit yourselves to
your elders. Yes, all of you be submissive to one
another, and be clothed with humility, for "God
resists the proud, But gives grace to the humble."*
—1 PETER 5:5

As recovering codependents, we may find ourselves
submitting to someone simply because our "life script
tapes" have dictated this response to us. However, our
submission should be governed by our submission to
God and his Word rather than by our old life-style.
And, if submitting to others requires us to disobey God
at some point, then we must choose to honor the Lord,
submitting to him rather than to man.

Once we learn the biblical pattern for submission,
the implication becomes clear. We will be "like-
minded, having the same love, being of one accord, of
one mind" (Phil. 2:2).

Mutual submission thus becomes the key to true
freedom. We will be truly free to love and be loved as
God intended.

*God, as I read your Word, may I learn how to submit to you totally.
And, thank you for the freedom you give me as I obey your mandate
of mutual submission.*

> *Therefore humble yourselves under the mighty*
> *hand of God, that He may exalt you in due time.*
> —1 PETER 5:6

To many codependents, the word *submission* implies strict obedience without the right to voice an opinion or have one's ideas and feelings considered. This kind of submission can be demanded overtly or coerced covertly, especially if the reward for obedience is meeting a void in the submitter's life.

True submission, however, is not created through power struggles, because the act of submission is self-imposed and given to another with no strings attached. True submission exemplifies that dimension of love that "does not seek its own" (1 Cor. 13:5) but rather, desires to serve others through love (Phil. 2:1–11).

Biblical submission then is an attitude that all Christians should possess. When two individuals totally and humbly respond to each other in the spirit of submission, a healthy, rather than codependent, relationship emerges.

Lord, I need to let go of my need to control others and take the risk of responding to my friends according to the principles you gave in Scripture. May a submissive life-style become a part of my attitude from this day forward.

That which we have seen and heard we declare to you, that you also may have fellowship with us; and truly our fellowship is with the Father and with His Son Jesus Christ. And these things we write to you that your joy may be full.

—1 JOHN 1:3–4

Many codependents, struggling with a low self-image, will shy away from sharing truth with a friend or acquaintance for fear of rejection. However, when we choose to do so, we will discover how very liberating it can be. One woman, recovering from this fear of rejection, came to my office very excited and wearing a T-shirt with an environmental message on it. She stated to me that all her life she could not bring herself to take a position on anything. After months of therapy, she finally concluded that she had a right to share her views and speak her beliefs on important issues. She had taken a giant step toward emotional and spiritual growth.

Sharing truth is often the springboard of real change in our own lives as well as others. When we are willing to leave the results to God and simply share his message with others, we discover a joy that cannot be matched.

Lord, thank you that someone shared with me your love and forgiveness through Christ. Give me the courage and opportunity to share it too.

> *Let the word of Christ dwell in you richly in all wisdom, teaching, and admonishing one another in psalms and hymns and spiritual songs, singing with grace in your hearts to the Lord.* —COL. 3:16

But I'm not cut out to be a teacher," you say. It may be true that most of us will never be teachers of large groups, yet all of us, whether introverts or extroverts, are exhorted to teach and admonish others. Teaching one another mainly means imparting knowledge or insight to another. It is quite comforting to realize that we don't have to have seminary or academic degrees to impart truth. God's desire for us is basically "As I learn, I share" and he holds us accountable for our willingness to share the truth we've received.

Since the role of the Holy Spirit is to direct us into all truth (John 16:13), the closer we get to the Lord through Bible study and prayer, the more insight we will be able to share. And we can teach others by our own life-style as well as by our words. When we live daily in the truth of God's Word, others will see Christ in us, and our teaching will be the most effective.

Lord, help me to be the proper role model to others today. May I be able to impart to others what you have taught me. Thank you for your Holy Spirit who is my source of truth.

> *For all the law is fulfilled in one word, even in this:*
> *"You shall love your neighbor as yourself." But if*
> *you bite and devour one another, beware lest you*
> *be consumed by one another!*
>
> —GAL. 5:14–15

In this passage, the words *bite and devour* mean to "tear apart piece by piece." Picture in your mind a television nature film of Africa. Predatory animals patiently, determinedly stalk a herd of antelope or zebra. At a precise moment the predator strikes, dropping its victim and devouring it, piece by piece. What a gruesome sight!

The apostle Paul uses this same vivid idea to help us understand what we are capable of doing with our words. As the Galatian church debated the issue of the law and grace, some believers had begun to tear each other apart with their words.

Often we shift our focus from a problem at church or home and attack the person or persons involved instead. The apostle Paul warns that this tendency results in the breakdown of love and may ultimately destroy relationships. But avoiding the issue is not the answer either. We are not to shy away from important issues, but must ensure that the conflict we tackle is indeed necessary. Truth, peace, and the good of all concerned come through treating others as we ourselves would like to be treated.

Lord, forgive me for the times I attacked the person over the problem. May I obtain the wisdom necessary to discern and practice wise conflict resolution.

> *Therefore, laying aside all malice, all guile,*
> *hypocrisy, envy, and all evil speaking . . .*
> —1 PETER 2:1

To envy is "to pine after," "to aspire to have what is not ours," "to be jealous." Envy used to be considered one of the seven deadly sins. Now it is culturally accepted, even applauded. We are taught that to be successful we must "grab for all the gusto we can." Television ads play on envy—"Look what your neighbor has. Shouldn't you have that too?"

It must be noted that to strive for a betterment of our circumstances is not wrong. However, when that drive becomes obsessive, it turns to envy; our motives become distorted, and we hurt people in the process.

Contentment is the antidote for envy. As we walk with the Lord Jesus daily, his contentment and peace will fill us. We will trust in his leading and provision, and we will be able to express true love for others, relating to others without envy.

I desire to follow your example, Lord, as I strive to appreciate what you have given me. May I not be jealous of those who have more than I, and may I be generous with those who have less.

*Do not speak evil of one another, brethren. He who
speak evil of a brother and judges his brother,
speaks evil of the law and judges the law. But if
you judge the law, you are not a doer of the law
but a judge. There is one Lawgiver, who is able to
save and to destroy. Who are you to judge another?*
—JAMES 4:11–12

Kids can be very cruel to each other. I was walking
by a playground recently and overheard two boys
hurling anathemas at each other. They ended up in a
fist fight, and each battled for his integrity. To speak
evil of another means we discredit or defame somebody in an attempt to make ourselves superior. Children seem to learn this response easily and take great
pleasure in it.

But wait. Before we come down too hard on children, who tend to openly reveal their true feelings,
perhaps we should scrutinize our own motives and responses. You see, we adults are not very different. We
simply camouflage speaking evil in socially acceptable
ways, such as gossiping and showing prejudicial behavior or even by "asking prayer" for a brother or sister involved in a certain situation.

Thus, whether we speak evil openly or through culturally accepted cover-ups, in God's eye it is still sin.
The best way to handle any problem we have with another person is to go directly to that person and speak
the truth with genuine love and humility.

*Dear God, forgive me for the times I have slandered others. Help me
to learn that you and you alone have the right to judge motives,
thoughts, and behaviors.*

*Therefore let us not judge one another anymore,
but rather resolve this, not to put a stumbling block
or a cause to fall in our brother's way.*
—ROM. 14:13

Many churches split because one or more parties begin to participate in needless judging. The same is true for marriages and other relationships as well. In too many instances, what one person holds to be an absolute may be nothing more than a personal prejudice or preference. If someone doesn't act or think in the way we deem appropriate, we make a value judgment which lowers our love and acceptance of that person. As a result, the preference takes precedent over the relationship. When we find ourselves caught in this negative and judgmental position, our energy shifts from handling the problem to destroying the person.

To judge another unjustly is to elevate ourselves at the expense of another. The antidote to judging is unconditional love. When we truly love we overlook the area where our preferences have been violated. Judgment must be reserved for the absolutes of Scripture and, even then, must be tempered with humility and love.

Lord, teach me to love others unconditionally, to remember that it is not my place to judge.

Judge not, that you be not judged. For with what judgment you judge, you will be judged; and with the same measure you use, it will be measured back to you. And why do you look at the speck in your brother's eye, but do not consider the plank in your own eye?

—MATT. 7:1-3

Ask several people to describe a quarter. One person may talk about George Washington's image or point out the word *liberty*. Another, however, may refer to the image of the American eagle and the inscription, *United States of America*. Both individuals may be adamant as to their perspective. Both may judge the other's description as wrong. Yet, both are correct.

When we judge others we assume the power of omniscience. This position leads us to adopt what is called all-or-nothing thinking. When I entered the counseling field years ago, I was very rigid and inflexible in the way I dealt with people and their problems. But through the years, I have come to realize that life isn't all black and white and that "knowledge puffs up, but love edifies" (1 Cor. 8:1). I have come to understand that when I judge, I replace God as judge and jury, which is sin (James 4:11–12). However, when I empathize, I listen with an open heart and state what I have learned and experienced (1 John 1:1–4). I have become a seed-planter, leaving the outgrowth and response up to God.

Lord, may I pray for others without condemnation. And, may I be granted the wisdom to plant the seed of truth with those in need, knowing that it is up to you to reap the harvest.

> *Judge not, and you shall not be judged. Condemn*
> *not, and you shall not be condemned. Forgive, and*
> *you will be forgiven.*
> —LUKE 6:37

I remember the day I was in a hurry for an important appointment. I grabbed my coat and went to the dresser where I generally keep my car keys. They were gone. Angrily, I accused my wife of misplacing them. After making some unkind and judgmental remarks about her memory, I stormed out of the house, using her keys. Four hours later I was still upset. "Why is my wife so careless?" I said to myself. When I arrived home, my godly wife calmly said, "I found your keys. They were on the mantel where you had left them!" She graciously accepted my pleas for forgiveness, and for that I'm thankful. But what a lesson I learned that day.

When those of us with a drive to be in control discover that a particular situation is beyond our control, we often respond by judging others. Judging is one way we make ourselves feel as if we are in control. When we use this tactic, however, we chip away at the relational building blocks we have established. And once the habit of judging becomes an unconscious response in our lives, change is very difficult.

I thank God that he taught me this valuable lesson, even though I had to "eat crow."

Lord, I know unrighteous judging is a result of an unhealthy need that I have. Instead, may I demonstrate mercy and insight, realizing that I have faults as well.

*Now I urge you, brethren, note those who cause
divisions and offenses, contrary to the doctrine
which you learned, and avoid them.*

—ROM. 16:17

One researcher has concluded that the average American lies over one hundred times a day. Is this possible? Let's think about it. When is the last time you were asked the question, "How are you?" You probably responded, "I'm fine," even if you felt rotten. "But," you say, "I was just being tactful."

When we lie, we distort the truth in such a way as to convey a false impression. It is an act of deceit. It is probably valid to say that tactfulness is different than lying, especially if deceit is not the intended message. However, in many situations deceit *is* intended, and we become used to wearing masks in order to camouflage our true intentions and feelings.

Types of lies include the embellishment of the truth for special effect, "trick" wording to give a false impression, false claims about ourselves, and not keeping our vows made to man and God. As we continue to wear the masks of deceit, we become easily addicted to its power and its false sense of security.

We must remember two points: first, in God's eyes a "white" lie is not little, and second, our "yeas" must be yea and our "nays" must be nay.

Lord, the reputation I desire is that I be known as an honest individual. May I learn how to be tactful, without being deceitful.

> *Do not lie to one another, since you have put off*
> *the old man with his deeds, and have put on the*
> *new man who is renewed in knowledge according*
> *to the image of Him who created him.*
>
> —COL. 3:9–10

The "old man" refers to our natural tendencies. And one of the things most natural for us to do is lie. Lying to others is one technique codependents use to try to be in control of their lives. But unless the folks around us are very naive, we can only carry this charade so far. Then we find that a lack of respect and mistrust begins to permeate others' attitudes about us. And when an atmosphere of mistrust is present, insecurity results. People start to second-guess us as they attempt to interpret what we say. In this environment, true relational intimacy is impossible to achieve.

Lying to ourselves is another way we might attempt to control our lives. This type of lying is called denial. If we perceive a situation to be too painful or if the truth hurts too much, we may choose to believe a lie we have told ourselves. For example, if we are addicted to a substance, we may lie to ourselves by saying, "I'm not addicted. I can quit anytime."

The pressure and stress of constantly skirting the truth becomes a great burden to the perpetual liar. Instead, as Scripture says, we should speak the truth in love. Make sure that what you say is truth and that you present that truth under the umbrella of love.

Lord, my heart's desire is to put aside lying and replace it with the truth. May I learn how to speak the truth in love. Keep me from lying to others and myself.

If we live in the Spirit, let us also walk in the Spirit.
Let us not become conceited, provoking one
another, envying one another.

—GAL. 5:25–26

To provoke someone is to agitate, belittle, and upset a person until an argument ensues. Some people seem to thrive on such conceited behavior by provoking one another. A husband and wife may challenge the limits of each others' patience. Then when the fire has been stoked to the boiling point, it is often too late to rethink the situation calmly.

Whenever we provoke others, we are essentially challenging the self-worth of another in order to gain power or status. People who enjoy provoking others usually have a grandiose estimation of themselves and thus are very weak spiritually. The habit of provoking others is lethal to any relationship. There is no possible benefit from agitating another for selfish reasons. These people usually end up extremely lonely because people learn that they are incapable of true friendship. Instead of stirring up strife, we can promote understanding and unity by realizing that other people are entitled to hold views that are different from our own.

Instead of provoking people to fight, let's commit ourselves to provoke and encourage others to do good (Heb. 10:24).

Lord, at times I'm selfish in my views and feelings and find myself provoking others to anger and frustration. Instead, may I provoke others to good works, through encouragement and love.

> *Now in those days, when the number of the*
> *disciples were multiplying, there arose a*
> *murmuring against the Hebrews by the*
> *Hellenists, because their widows were*
> *neglected in the daily distribution.* —ACTS 6:1

The word *murmur* means what it sounds like—low noises of frustration, spoken under our breath. And when there is a problem at church or at work or even in our homes, murmuring can easily magnify an already touchy situation. People murmur when they feel powerless, when they are impatient, or when they yield to their bad moods.

The New Testament has much to say about our attitudes and one principle is that we must be content in whatever situation we find ourselves. The Bible also says that it is God who is in charge of all things and events, not we puny mortals. So, when we wrestle with him through murmuring or by using other control tactics, the end result will be frustration and exhaustion, not peace and contentment.

Since we live in an imperfect world, a percentage of all the events in our life will have problems. Instead of murmuring about that part, let's determine to focus our attention on the positive and quietly trust our God who promised that ultimately "all things work together for good to those who love God."

Lord, keep my outlook positive. Give me the peace that comes with knowing you care about everything that happens to me and that you do all things well.

And if your hand makes you sin, cut it off. It is better for you to enter into life maimed, than having two hands, to go to hell, into the fire that shall never be quenched—where "their worm does not die and the fire is not quenched."

—MARK 9:43–44

I grew up playing basketball and tennis and other sports. In hindsight I now realize that many of my coaches equated winning with "success." Most of the world is trapped in this same false viewpoint. This hierarchal view of success, which measures a person's worth by position, power, or wealth, affects all areas of life—from the athletic arena to grades in school to promotions at work, even to the size of a church a pastor can expect to work in.

Jesus said we should not seek greatness and esteem from men. Christ's example of servitude is of course diametrically opposed to our world's formula for greatness and success. The truly spiritual man realizes his priorities should not be focused on power, position, and wealth, but rather on Christ's priorities revealed in Scripture. But how does this happen? Only when we wait on the Lord, obey him, and allow him to do the exalting according to his own time and choosing will this occur. As we serve others and submit in obedience to him, we are guaranteed a deeper security and peace than the world could ever hope to offer. Let's not conform to the world's standard on greatness. Instead, let's commit ourselves to Christ's standard who came to earth not to be served, but to serve.

Put someone in my path today, Lord, whom I can serve.

> *For you, brethren, have been called to liberty; only
> do not use liberty as an opportunity for the flesh,
> but through love serve one another. For all the law
> is fulfilled in one word, even in this: "You shall love
> your neighbor as yourself."*   —GAL. 5:13–14

An ingredient of true servitude is unconditional love.
As we seek to become the servants God intends us to
be, we should keep several thoughts in mind. First,
Jesus did not make any restrictions on who was to
serve. Therefore, *all* believers are to seek ways to
serve others.

The degree of spiritual maturity a person possesses
does not determine the kind of service he or she can
render to others. We should all be willing to perform
the lowliest jobs of servanthood when the Holy Spirit
reveals a need. We may serve the body as a whole by
mowing the church lawn, for example. Or we may
serve individuals by helping to care for the sick or elderly. When we serve, we are expressing true humility.
Thus, servitude dethrones self and elevates the body of
Christ.

---

*Lord, teach me humility so that I can learn to unconditionally love
another. Make me willing to serve you as I serve my fellow believers.*

Codependency: An Addiction to . . .

Certain behaviors and addictions often accompany codependency. The topics in this section include addictive behavior with people, sex, food, anger, work, materialism, alcohol/drugs, religion, perfectionism, and obsessions. Not every reader will find each of these areas troubling in their life; however, don't overlook the areas that you have not struggled with personally. Keep each of these areas in balance and perspective. You can benefit from addressing issues that develop into addictions for some people and try to keep them from becoming addictions in your life.

The devotionals will encourage you to fight the addictive behavior that destroys. They will offer you strength and hope when your days seem difficult and impossible. Use these meditations to focus on the positive results from the difficult choices you are making. Read them as motivations to begin each day fresh and ready to carry out your recovery process.

Therefore let no one glory in men. For all things are yours.
                                                    —1 COR. 3:21

God designed you to have mutually satisfying relationships. Relationships are essential to mental health, but you can get your human relationships out of perspective. Your God-created need for relationship can be misdirected.

You are important, valuable, and significant. Centering your life around other people to the degree that you become unbalanced in your relationships is a waste. When you focus on other people's needs, wants, or desires at the exclusion of your own, you are not functioning in a healthy manner. Codependents develop these unhealthy relationships to avoid facing the negative beliefs they hold about themselves.

You may identify with the codependent pattern of developing your worth from what significant others think of you. At the core of this behavior is the belief that you do not have value and worth. This is not how God sees you. He says that it is wrong to glory in men, because you have what all men have. You need to see yourself as a person worth "glorying" in.

The reasons for glorying in yourself may not be the same ones the world glories in people. You may not have fame and fortune, but in God's perspective you are just as valuable. Today think of three reasons you can glory in yourself.

God, I feel so worthless that I focus on others to avoid facing myself. Help me see the value, worth, and significance you created in me.

A sound heart is life to the body,
But envy is rottenness to the bones.
—PROV. 14:30

Can you look in the mirror and accept what you see there? Although you've discovered many areas for improvement in your life, accepting yourself is the catalyst for making the changes you desire for your life. Contentment in the fact that God didn't make a mistake when he created you is at the basis of those changes.

While contentment with oneself (a sound heart) brings life, envying others brings rottenness. When you focus on what others have and how God deals with them you are miserable inside. That type of focus draws you further away from contentment. Comparing your life to others will breed the opposite of a sound heart. When you focus on the reality that God created you—that he loves you, that he wants you—contentment and excitement about life follow.

Soundness of heart, or contentment about who you are, is built upon accepting yourself in Christ. The opposite of this is focusing on other people and envying them. It is amazing how destructive envy can be to mental health and a sound heart. Guarding your life from envy of others and believing in your personal worth and dignity will prevent this destruction.

God, you made me uniquely and personally. Help me discover and celebrate my uniqueness and not compare myself to others.

The king's heart is in the hand of the LORD,
Like the rivers of water;
He turns it wherever He wishes.
—PROV. 21:1

Your life will be frustrating and miserable if you make it your goal to change others. It is essential to your mental health that you learn this lesson. Others are not under your direct control.

Your life will be frustrating when you try to change others. This type of behavior frustrates the people you are relating to as well. You cannot change others, but you can change yourself. You will still want those significant people in your life to change and grow, but your goal should not be to change them, only to change yourself.

Ultimately, all change for good has God at its source. If there is a time that God chooses, he can make a person change. When you find yourself frustrated and agonizing over significant relationships, talk to God about them. Realize that you should not make it your goal to change others. Come up with ideas about how to relate to the person(s) in your life if they do not change. Don't stop hoping for these people to change, but don't make it your goal to change them yourself.

God, I realize that there are times when you do change men's hearts for your specific purposes. Help me face the reality that I do not have the power to change other people, but I can change myself. Help me make the changes I need to make in me.

> *Do not be envious of evil men,*
> *Nor desire to be with them.*
> —PROV. 24:1

Part of your recovery from codependency may involve changing friendships and adjusting relationships. Some of the people who have become significant in your life may have a damaging influence on you. Developing a healthy support group is essential to your continued growth away from codependency.

Breaking away from some of your friends will not be easy. You have developed an escape from loneliness and a sense of caring from these people, along with the unhealthy patterns. Maybe these old friends are disappointed in you for controlling your addiction. If they are still addicted, they will not like the fact that you are not. It's difficult to disappoint others, but your decision for healthy living demands changing your pattern of relating. You may have to disappoint others, so let that be okay. This is a step of growth away from codependency.

A healthy sign of recovery from codependency is when you feel free to choose friends who encourage you. The people you are closest to should be people who want the same kind of healthy relationship you are seeking. There are many cruel and evil men and women in this world. You need to learn to keep your distance from them.

God, show me the friends that you want me to have in my life. Help me find the kind of quality people who will help me become the person you and I want me to be.

Confidence in an unfaithful man in time of trouble
Is like a bad tooth and a foot out of joint.
—PROV. 25:19

Relationships are important in life. You will need friends and friends will need you. That is why it is important to develop healthy friendships. When you build your life around a few dysfunctional relationships, you will find yourself empty and abandoned at the time when you need friends most.

This is why it is important not to build your life around unfaithful friends. Realize the importance of building strong, healthy friendships. One characteristic that distinguishes between a healthy and unhealthy friendship is faithfulness. Is the person faithful in his/her friendship with you? Friends are important in the good times and the bad times. Unfaithful friends will be there for the good times, but they will abandon you in the bad times. The ultimate test of a true friend is their faithfulness to you in the hard times.

Are you a faithful friend? Faithfulness is an important characteristic for you to be developing in your life. A faithful friend is different from a codependent friend. A faithful friend's actions are based on legitimate concern for the friend, while a codependent's actions are based on a dysfunctional need for that friend. There is a subtle difference in the actions, but the motivations are very distinct.

God, I want to be a faithful friend. I want to have faithful friends. Help me be the kind of friend you desire.

For who in the heavens can be compared to the
  LORD?
Who among the sons of the mighty can be
  likened to the LORD?
                                            —PS. 89:6

Those codependent relationships you have had in the past cannot compare to the friendship you can experience with God. Can you imagine that God really is a friend to you? He desires to have a personal relationship with you. He doesn't want to use you or hurt you; he only wants the best for you. He isn't controlling. He is merciful to you and slow to anger. He is a friend who will be faithful during the hard times. He is the ultimate friend, and his relationship with you cannot be compared to your human relationships.

Human friendships are very important. But it is relationship with God that keeps them in perspective. You will never experience in human relationships sinless involvement, for all human relationships will be stained by sin. Therefore, the motivations for them will always be imperfect. Human relationships still meet legitimate, God-created needs, but human friendships are limited. Your friendship with God is infinite.

As you develop your friendship with God, you will gain wisdom for dealing with your human friendships. You need to relate to someone who will not fail you; only God can meet that need.

God, I can't believe that the God of the universe cares personally and intimately about me. I want to return that care and believe in your offer of friendship.

*With good will doing service, as to the Lord, and
not to men.*
                                        —EPH. 6:7

In the past you have developed unhealthy patterns of
codependency. Many of the things you have done for
people have been motivated by your low self-esteem
and fear of losing others.

Your new way of relating involves feeling accepted
in Christ, then being motivated to service and kindness
to others. You no longer serve people because you
need to avoid your self-hate; rather, you serve people
because you are already accepted in Christ.

It's a freeing experience to do things for people out
of goodwill, and not out of fear. You may find that
much of what you have done for others in the past is
not what you need to be doing in your recovery. You
will be able to see the desperation of your behavior.
When fear and desperation motivate you, the opposite
of goodwill results.

After recovery, there will be times to do things for
others. Doing things for others out of goodwill is a new
experience. Because your service doesn't define you
as good or bad, you will have the freedom to enjoy
what you are doing for others.

*God, I want to learn to relate to others the way you want me to. Help
me understand what it really means to serve others. Help me to believe that I am accepted already by you so I don't have to desperately
seek codependent relationships.*

> *For the love of money is a root of all kinds of evil,*
> *for which some have strayed from the faith in their*
> *greediness, and pierced themselves through with*
> *many sorrows.*   —1 TIM. 6:10

In general populations a higher incidence of suicide exists among affluent persons than among those of a lower socioeconomic income. The link between loving money and evil can lead to emptiness.

Money itself is not a source of evil. People who love money get off track. Money is not a good lover; it can breed obsessive and addictive behavior. When you love money to the exclusion of people, your life becomes unbalanced.

Some of the richest people in the world are the most miserable in their personal relationships. They become paranoid that people only want to be close to them because of their money. They have become so obsessed by money that relationships have little value. Love is an action that should be reserved for human relationships. When your loving actions center around belongings and money, your relationships will suffer and your life will be empty.

God, help me to see that money is not the answer to my troubled life. I need to focus on loving you and the people in my life. Money can never replace the priceless value of healthy relationships.

The Lord makes poor and makes rich; he brings
low and lifts up.
                                                —1 SAM. 2:7

When you set your whole ambition in life around money, you are pursuing an uncertain goal. You can work your whole life for more money and end up very unhappy.

Many people become addicted to money because they feel more of a sense of control over it than they do in their personal relationships. It is a false sense of control, however, for you cannot protect your riches. They can vanish in a moment without warning, as the many who have earned and lost fortunes can attest.

Money will also offer a sense of false security. When you trust in money, you cannot trust in God. Learn to trust in God. Recognize the reality that it is he who is in control of your financial standing. Trust him more than money and you will learn how to truly enjoy all that God gives to you. You won't be obsessed by money that cannot satisfy you ultimately.

Money has its place and purpose on this earth. When you realize that it is God who is ultimately in control, you will be free to enjoy its purpose.

God, help me find your perspective on money. I want to trust in you and not in my bank account.

*A little that a righteous man has
Is better than the riches of many wicked.*
—PS. 37:16

Character is more important than riches. Without character you will not be satisfied with riches. In the same way, without character you will have difficulty accepting and dealing with poverty.

Your attitude is important to whatever financial condition you find yourself. Money that is gained by wicked or malicious ways has hidden traps. It traps you into a life-style of secrets and shame, providing only temporary satisfaction.

When you earn money in legal and legitimate ways, your conscience is clean. You do not have a need for secrets. This is why the little that a righteous man has is worth more in terms of eternal value. Satisfaction and contentment in life cannot be measured by financial means. Its value is priceless.

God, help me accept my financial situation. Help me see that money is not the most important issue in life. Help me value the character of righteousness above financial gain.

Surely every man walks about like a shadow;
Surely they busy themselves in vain;
He heaps up riches,
And does not know who will gather them.
And now, LORD, what do I wait for?
My hope is in You.
　　　　　　　　　　　　　　—PS. 39:6–7

The more money you have, the more trouble you gain. You have to worry about how to keep it safe, how to spend it, how to save it. This is not to say that money is bad or that it is the worst kind of trouble to have. Just as there are troubles in trying to survive without money, there are also troubles in having a lot of money.

Money brings with it troubles of its own. This is why it is so important to focus on God rather than money. When you begin to hope in money, you find yourself without a true foundation. Having a lot of money will not solve the problems in your life.

Money provides a means by which you can enjoy the world you live in. It also provides a way to give back to the world. Having money provides ways to live in more comfortable environments. But money does not dissolve problems.

Enjoy your money and your financial gain—but not to the exclusion of God and other people. Don't seek after money as the solution to your problems. You will only end up empty and sad.

God, money isn't the answer. Help me realize this. Help me identify the lie that if I only had more money I could be happy.

> *There is one who makes himself rich, yet has*
> *nothing;*
> *And one who makes himself poor, yet has great*
> *riches.*
> —PROV. 13:7

True riches depend on how they increase the quality of one's life. Many times affluence brings emotional bondage. Affluence may provoke the paranoia that others only like you for your money. It makes possible choices to entertain the negative influences of drugs, alcohol, etc. Its obsession may alienate you from relationships, decreasing the quality of life rather than increasing it.

Money and things are meant to be secondary to inner peace and relational satisfaction. The disease of materialism is rampant in today's society, for it is encouraged and rewarded by society. The deceit is that money and power bring the ultimate satisfaction in this life. But in reality its victims are left lonely and empty.

Don't waste your life pursuing money. Pursue God and healthy relationships. Enjoy your money. Money and things are meant to be used and enjoyed, not obsessed over.

God, open my eyes to the reality of materialism. I don't want to waste my life pursuing something that is not meant to resolve my personal and relational problems.

Thus says the LORD:
"Let not the wise man glory in his wisdom,
Let not the mighty man glory in his might,
Nor let the rich man glory in his riches;
But let him who glories glory in this,
That he understands and knows Me,
That I am the LORD, exercising lovingkindness,
   judgment, and righteousness in the earth.
For in these I delight," says the LORD.
—JER. 9:23–24

Knowing and pursuing God can bring the needed balance for dealing with issues like materialism. The key to satisfaction is being centered and finding inner peace and contentment. It is then and only then that you can truly enjoy money.

Don't assume your riches will last forever. Don't assume you are safe and don't need God. When you realize how much you need God and don't believe that money will supply that need, you will begin to enjoy money. Don't put your confidence in anything but God, and you will find a center and place from which to truly enjoy your life.

People who pursue money as they need to pursue God lack fulfillment in their lives. There is never enough money, never enough belongings, never enough. The reason that there is never enough is because people are not created to find fulfillment in material belongings or money. These things are meant to be enjoyed, not supply inner peace.

God, I don't want to pursue materialism instead of relationships with you and others.

> _And the cares of this world, the deceitfulness of_
> _riches, and the desires for other things entering in_
> _choke the word, and it becomes unfruitful._
>
> —MARK 4:19

Materialism is a deceitful disease. The lie that says "If you only had that bigger house, that boat, that dream vacation—you could be happy" is very destructive. Real happiness and contentment doesn't come from things; it comes from inner peace and contentment.

The deceitfulness of materialism is very strong. An image of a wonderful, exciting life is never fully experienced with increased riches and things. The image of choking is a truer image of the quest for things.

Growth in life depends on being centered and directed. Materialism will not provide a healthy direction for positive growth. It will lead to obsessions and a lack of fulfilling relationships with others and God. Eventually it will choke out what is really important and valuable in life. Because what are really important—relationships—are priceless and cannot be bought.

God, help me break my addiction to materialism. Make me see the truth that money will not satisfy me. Help me see the value of relationships.

*Then I looked on all the works that my hands
    had done,
And on the labor in which I had toiled;
And indeed, all was vanity and grasping for
    the wind.
There was no profit under the sun.*
—ECCL. 2:11

Workaholism—the disease Americans praise—can destroy relationships. Being driven by power, money, promotions is a counterfeit to what you really long for. You will end up feeling the same way as King Solomon after you have achieved your goals. When you are at the top of the ladder, pursued by those who want your power and money, alienated from true and meaningful relationships—you will look at your work and find it empty also.

Your goals are incomplete if they do not include building healthy relationships. What comfort is it to know on your deathbed that you have cars, boats, money if you don't have family and friends to comfort you? All the promotions and belongings that you have acquired will be meaningless without true personal relationships.

Reevaluate your goals. Ambitions are good. Ambitions about work are satisfying, until you put these ambitions above God and others. What ambitions do you have for pursuing God and meaningful relationships?

God, help me develop ambitions that are healthy and include relationships with you and others. I want to keep my life full and balanced.

> *Man goes out to his work*
> *And to his labor until the evening.*
> —PS. 104:23

Work is a fact of life. It is both essential and fulfilling. But making work your life is both unhealthy and ultimately unfulfilling. Work can touch personal and relational needs in counterfeit ways if you use it to gain a sense of worth or value.

You need to develop worth and value in relationships. Because so many have found so much pain in personal relationships, most people retreat from intimately relating to others. Work is a means to not only meet physical needs for food and shelter, but to also meet emotional needs. Feeling good about the work you do and encouraged by the pats on the back you receive for a job well done is good. When you become compulsive about your work because you don't like yourself or to avoid relationships, you are exhibiting codependent behavior. Work can *touch* your needs for inner fulfillment and relationship, but it cannot *meet* those needs. Eventually you will come to the place where all your labor feels empty and unsatisfying.

You were created for relationship. First, you need to develop relationship with God. Then you need to develop healthy relationships with others. Work is a daily task. It can be fulfilling or difficult. When you make work your life, you miss out on life.

God, help me keep work in perspective. Help me see it as an avenue to developing relationships with others.

*Then God blessed them, and God said to them, "Be
fruitful and multiply; fill the earth and subdue it;
have dominion over the fish of the sea, over the
birds of the air, and over every living thing that
moves on the earth."*

—GEN. 1:28

You are designed to enjoy cultivating, subduing, and
having dominion over the earth. Most people do not
enjoy sitting around without anything to do. Even the
wealthy and retired have a need to continue producing. Humans are acts of God's creation and are designed with a desire to expand and develop God's
creation, to be creative as he is.

Working does increase the quality of life. Hard work
and determination are satisfying when you have
achieved a goal. The need to be productive is a healthy
drive. The reality of this God-created need is why
work can become so compulsive.

Workaholics are driven by legitimate, God-created
needs. Just as other addictions, the misuse of work to
meet needs it wasn't designed to meet creates the
struggle. When work becomes the highest priority in
one's life, other areas will suffer. Usually the area that
suffers most is the family and friends of the workaholic.

A proper balance between work and other relationships is very important. Ultimately work will let you
down if you are using it to meet relational needs. Don't
let it keep you from experiencing the relationships God
wants for you.

Thank you for work. Help me use it in the ways you desire.

> *Do not overwork to be rich;*
> *Because of your own understanding, cease!*
> —PROV. 23:4

Our society drives us to make the most money possible. Whether you use someone for it, work hard for it, receive a good inheritance—whatever you do, make a profit. Success is usually linked to the amount of wealth one has acquired. If you follow that kind of reasoning, ultimately you will find yourself burned out, dissatisfied, and empty in life.

Money, status, and ambition are good to have. They are meant to be enjoyed. They shouldn't be what defines or motivates you. Real understanding means not getting your value as a person from how much money you have. Rather, you measure yourself from how much character you have.

Don't accept the world's philosophy that the amount of money you have will bring you greater joy and happiness. Think about the wealthy people you know. You only need to know a few to find that those who have peace and satisfaction do not find it in their wealth alone. Wealth is a means by which their life is made easier in some ways, but it is not a substitute for relationships.

God, help me live my life by your standard of wisdom. I want to pursue wisdom and not riches.

*Therefore, whether you eat or drink, or whatever
you do, do all to the glory of God.*
—1 COR. 10:31

The key to changing workaholic patterns is to change
your motivation. You need to work, and it is not wrong
to have the nice things and belongings that work sup-
plies. The problem arises in your motivation for having
these things and your motivation for work.

Does your bank account or position in the chain of
authority define you? Are you defined by who you are,
or what you do? Cultivate an attitude of doing whatever you do to the glory of God. Avoid doing whatever
you do to make you feel acceptable as a person. Do
you lose your value and worth because people don't
recognize you as valuable?

Doing everything for God's glory brings a different
twist. You can begin to do things for him and not to
define yourself as good or bad by your work efforts.
You gain a freedom for the compulsiveness of workaholism. Work is an experience you have, not who you
are.

---

*God, help me keep my life in perspective. Help me get away from
allowing work to drive me.*

*And on the seventh day God ended His work which
He had done, and He rested on the seventh day
from all His work which He had done.*
—GEN. 2:2

We need to rest from work. You don't get ahead if you don't rest. You find yourself burned out, tired, depressed, and eventually you lose the ground you have made. Many of the confessed workaholics that come to our clinic have found this to be true.

God himself rested from his work. This rest must come on a weekly basis as in the example he sets. One day a week you need rest so renewal can take place. For true workaholics there is no good time to take a vacation or a day off. Therefore, it is best to plan far ahead for your rest and vacation. Then, when the time comes, take that vacation no matter what.

Are you in the habit of making time for rest and renewal one day a week? Make this time of rest a part of your weekly schedule. If you do not, ultimately you will lose your creativity. You were created to be productive and enjoy your creativity. You were also designed to need rest and renewal. It will catch up with you eventually.

———————————

*God, keep me from believing I must just finish this one project. Help
me trust in your design for rest and renewal and make it a part of my
life.*

Their land is also full of idols;
They worship the work of their own hands,
That which their own fingers have made.
                                        —ISA. 2:8

What a picture of despair—a land where the ultimate hope centered around what they had made. The work of man's hands cannot even compare with the work of God.

Man has done many amazing things in this world. Beautiful buildings and creations have been made. Wonderful medical technologies have been discovered. But they don't even compare to God, and that is why they are not worth being worshiped.

What an empty feeling to only have the work of man's hands to worship. It is so incomplete. The work of man's hands is at an all-time peak. Computer technology, medical breakthroughs, and scientific discoveries are awesome and exciting. The work of man ultimately helps us see the magnitude of God, the real Creator. It also helps us see the need for God. All the things that man has made has not made mankind any less brutal or resolved the problems that plague societies.

Worship belongs to God. The work of man's hands reveals the futility of man's efforts without the existence of a personal and real God.

God, without you my life is worthless. I may be capable of many wonderful creations, but the meaning comes from knowing you.

> *An angry man stirs up strife,*
> *And a furious man abounds in transgression.*
> —PROV. 29:22

Angry people aren't always able to see the fullness of their destructive behavior. This destructive behavior hurts them, but it also hurts others. Anger without control is very damaging to relationships. Anger itself is not wrong, but expressing it in ways that damage relationships is wrong.

Inappropriate anger expressed to others cuts deeply. It hurts others' self-esteem. Inappropriate expression of anger is expressing the anger only for yourself. Appropriate expression of anger is expressing the anger for the benefit of yourself and the person(s) to whom you express it. You need to face the impact of your anger with others. You need to take responsibility for your behavior when you have expressed inappropriate anger.

Unbridled expression of anger is very damaging. Expressing your anger by raging at other people is rarely appropriate. When you do this, you stir up strife and broken relationships. If your desire is to build relationships, you will express your anger in a way that will be best received by the other person.

God, help me see where I need to change in the expression of my anger. Help me face the fact that raw expression of anger does little to build a relationship and usually stirs up strife that is damaging to any relationship.

He who is slow to wrath has great understanding,
But he who is impulsive exalts folly.
—PROV. 14:29

Anger is not wrong, but too quickly raging in your anger can be very negative. A good way to control the expression of your anger so you don't express it in inappropriate ways is to be slow to express your anger.

Upon the immediate impact of your anger—keep your mouth quiet. Think through your anger and how you are feeling. Become fully aware of what is going on for you. Acknowledge your anger to yourself and God. Then decide what would be the most appropriate way to express your emotions.

For rageaholics it takes very little to provoke an unnecessary and unwarranted attack. Perhaps someone cuts you off on the highway, then your wife asks you to make a quick stop. Instead of raging at her, stop and think about what occurred. Recognize that you are angry at the man who just cut you off and that the stop she wants to make is a minor change of plans. Get things into perspective; then share your real anger with her. If you take the time to think when you feel rage about to flow, you may find many of the issues are really insignificant.

Learn to control your anger. A big step toward controlling anger is to be slow in expressing it. Don't react in your anger. Stop and think about how to express your anger appropriately.

God, help me recognize the rage I feel and acknowledge it to you and myself and not vent it on the people in my life.

> *Do not say, "I will recompense evil";*
> *Wait for the LORD, and He will save you.*
> —PROV. 20:22

Anger that sours turns to bitterness. Revengeful people suffer from intense bitterness. They have not been able to find an appropriate way to express their anger, and it has turned against them. George Washington Carver said, "I will not allow another person to ruin my life by hating them."

Are you that way? Are you driven by revenge so much that it robs you of the joy of life? That kind of rage and anger destroys you. It affects you physically and emotionally. God doesn't tell you to let go of your revenge for the other person's sake; it is simply the best thing you can do for yourself. Pursuing revenge will destroy you in the end.

Give your desire for revenge over to God. Fully acknowledge your anger to yourself, express it to people as appropriate, and leave the rest to God. Spending your life hating others robs you of the vitality of life.

God, these people have been so cruel. They have hurt and shamed me. But I don't want to sink as low as them. Help me work through my anger and trust you to take care of the revenge.

My son, if you become surety for your friend,
If you have shaken hands in pledge for a stranger,
You are snared by the words of your own mouth;
You are taken by the words of your mouth.
So do this, my son, and deliver yourself;
For you have come into the hand of your friend:
Go and humble yourself;
Plead with your friend.

—PROV. 6:1–3

It is very easy to rage at people inappropriately in your anger. Many have developed a lifelong pattern of inappropriate expression of anger. Often this is patterned in family systems and is a difficult pattern to break. However, you don't have to give up when you have failed to control your expression of anger.

Go to the person you have wronged and take responsibility for what you have done. Sometimes the issue that you are angry about is appropriate anger. To rage at people is rarely appropriate. Take their feelings into account, even when they haven't considered you. Even if you were right in the issue you are angry about, you can apologize for the inappropriate way you expressed your anger.

When you have been wrong in the way you expressed your anger, you should take responsibility for your behavior. This step helps many rageaholics change their behavior. Don't see it as a defeat, but as a victory over your emotions.

God, help me humbly acknowledge the ways I need to change in my expression of anger. Make me willing to go to the people I have wronged and make things straight.

> *For His anger is but for a moment,*
> *His favor is for life;*
> *Weeping may endure for a night,*
> *But joy comes in the morning.*
> —PS. 30:5

God himself is an example for us of being slow to anger. He does not rage, although he has many reasons to rage and be angry. This world is very sinful, and God has literally millions of reasons to rage at us—even destroy this world. He is slow to anger. There are times when he has expressed his anger fully and forcefully, but generally he does not rage at the millions of wrongs committed each day.

You are created in his image. You will be most content when you are in control of your anger rather than letting your anger control you. This is a sign of character and self-control. Many times when you put off expressing your rage at the moment, you will be glad later that you did. Sometimes you see things in a different light and find it would not have been appropriate to be angry in that situation.

Always acknowledge your anger to yourself and to God. Then choose the best expression of your anger. Don't become compulsive in your expression of anger. Give your anger time to be used for good in your life and others' lives.

God, thank you for being slow to anger. Help me use my anger in positive ways.

Cease from anger, and forsake wrath;
Do not fret—it only causes harm.
—PS. 37:8

Don't rage your life away. Being angry about insignificant issues takes a toll on your mind, body, and soul. To be angry all the time takes a great deal of energy. Anger robs you of life's vitality, and even of life itself. A significant number of heart attack victims have a pattern of rageaholism.

You are learning to always acknowledge your anger. Repressing anger creates the same kind of burden on you. Neither unbridled expression of anger nor repression of anger are healthy. Healthy anger is acknowledged and controlled anger. Wrath and uncontrolled anger are damaging and destructive both to yourself and others.

Don't live your life as an angry person or a repressed person. Don't let anger control your life. Learn to control your anger and to express it appropriately and you will grow in the quality and enjoyment of your life.

God, help me cease from anger. Don't let me get angry about insignificant things. Help me not repress the anger I feel. Show me appropriate ways to express what I feel inside.

But He, being full of compassion, forgave their iniquity,
And did not destroy them.
Yes, many a time He turned His anger away,
And did not stir up all His wrath.   —PS. 78:38

Anger can be properly balanced by compassion. Many times the people we are most angry with need the most compassion. You may have even developed a pattern of using compassion to cover up anger, a type of codependent behavior. You do need to consider others when you express your anger, however.

You may have valid reasons for anger with people in your life. God has valid reasons for anger with us, but he also has compassion and forgiveness for us. Learning to control your wrath and forgive others feels good. Avoid unhealthy patterns of avoiding the conflict in your relationships by forgiving too easily.

Balance is the key. There is a need for compassion toward others in the healthy life. Learn to balance your anger toward others with compassion for them. See them as valuable, significant people when you express your anger.

God, help me see people as you see them. Help me see when and where it is appropriate for me to express my anger at others.

The Lord is merciful and gracious,
Slow to anger, and abounding in mercy.
—PS. 103:8

Have you ever been merciful? How did it feel? Mercy is purposely letting someone off the hook for what they have done without regret. It is giving someone kindness when they deserve much less. Being merciful for healthy reasons, not codependent reasons, is very rewarding.

It takes character to be merciful to others when your feelings at the moment tell you to lash out at them. Mercy is a characteristic of God. When you are merciful, you are motivated to deeper love.

You have opportunities to express mercy in your anger and mercy instead of anger. When you feel angry today, think of a way to be merciful to that person. The world tells you to be aggressive when you are wronged to keep it from happening again. Mercy is the opposite of aggression. It has amazing power in your life as well as in the lives of those to whom you are merciful.

God, thank you for your mercy. Help me to be merciful to others.

> *Fathers, do not provoke your children, lest they*
> *become discouraged.*
> —COL. 3:21

Angry tempers rage in family situations. Parents should especially think of the ways they provoke their children to wrath. Some rageaholics are the calmest people on a job site, but their rage is lashed out on their family. Usually people feel a greater degree of safety in their family and express themselves more freely; rage can be very damaging to the family relationships.

You can be a good example to your children and your other close relationships when you demonstrate appropriate expressions of anger. It is a refreshing experience to relate to someone who neither represses nor expresses anger inappropriately.

Relationships will provoke anger. Living in close proximity as a family does increases the situations and occurrences of angry feelings. This is why it is especially important to consider your expression of anger with your children and with your family. Teach them how to express anger appropriately and how to deal with their anger with you. Don't teach them to vent or repress their anger.

God, help me consider my anger in my closest relationships. I really need to concentrate on using anger appropriately so that I am teaching my children this also.

Let your fountain be blessed;
And rejoice with the wife of your
*   youth.*
As the loving deer and graceful doe,
Let her breasts satisfy you at all times;
And always be enraptured with her
*   love.*
                              —PROV. 5:18–19

God designed sex. He designed it to be wonderfully pleasurable. He also designed it to be a part of monogamous, committed relationships. The world has misused sex. One of the biggest misuses of God's gift of sex is to pursue pleasure only. The pursuit of sex for pleasure disregards the feelings of the person and depersonalizes the intimate relationship that the two should be experiencing.

A beautiful, unspeakable experience is available to those who will follow God's design for sex. In his design sex does not become an addiction but remains a wonderful experience. When sex becomes an addiction, the complete satisfaction and fulfillment is abandoned. The pursuit for pleasure only creates a destructive cycle that leads to emptiness. There is never enough pleasure to fill the need for relationship.

God's design for sex is wonderful and beautiful. It involves enjoying satisfying pleasure in the context of relationship. The relationship sustains the pleasure long after the sexual experience is over.

God, I don't want to misuse sex. I want to experience it the way you designed. You created sex to be a wonderfully pleasurable experience. Help me obey you and use sex appropriately.

> *You have ravished my heart,*
> *My sister, my spouse;*
> *You have ravished my heart*
> *With one look of your eyes,*
> *With one link of your necklace.*
> —SONG 4:9

Many think that enjoying their own sexual dynamic is sinful or wrong. This can not be more false. God chose to include in his written communication to us—the Bible—a love story that includes all the passion that love exudes. The Song of Solomon dispels the images of God despising sex.

The Bible encourages responsible and beautiful sex. God created you as a sexual being. Sexual fulfillment is an important aspect of healthy living. However, getting out of balance with sexuality is destructive to self and others.

Sexual fulfillment can become a counterfeit to a meaningful relationship. When sex becomes an addiction, relationships and lives are destroyed. Sexual addiction creates a compulsive need for more and more sexual stimulation. The relationship between monogamous, committed lovers doesn't matter at this point. The emptiness a person feels inside drives him or her to sexual addiction and away from a relationship. Only in the context of a relationship can the emptiness that drives the sexually addictive person be filled.

God, I want to know meaningful sexual intimacy the way you designed me to experience it.

*Therefore God also gave them up to uncleanness,
in the lusts of their hearts, to dishonor their bodies
among themselves.*
                                                —ROM. 1:24

What God created to be an important aspect of your life can turn into a destructive den of compulsion and emptiness. The cycle of sexual addiction leads to torment. The fulfillment lasts but a moment, and the emptiness reigns on and on in your life.

If left to the lusts of our own hearts in total disregard to others, sexual expression evolves into more and more dishonoring ways. Gone is the desire for relationship, love, and intimacy. What remains is the pursuit of pleasure for pleasure's sake.

The person is left in an empty but desperate state. They have long abandoned what they really need, love and relationship. They are left with a need for pleasure that can never be satisfied. The real need underneath the sexual addiction is the need for relationship. God gives us over to the futility of our own lusts, so once we have tasted of the emptiness awaiting there we might come back to him.

God, help me journey your way. I want to follow your wisdom. I want to adhere to your plan for my sexual expression. I don't want to get in a destructive, sexually addictive cycle.

> *But put on the Lord Jesus Christ, and make no*
> *provision for the flesh, to fulfill its lusts.*
> —ROM. 13:14

Unbridled lusts quickly lead a person away from peace and satisfaction in life. When you set your life on fulfilling your own lusts, you will end up empty and trapped. The trap of following the lusts of the flesh is a destructive cycle. The pursuit of sexual pleasure to avoid the painful reality of this world will result in feeling lost and abandoned.

When sexual pleasure controls your life, it will lead you to a way of evil and wickedness, away from relationship and character. Your sexual pleasure will become your god, and you will be compelled to worship yourself through sexual fulfillment. The fulfillment will last shorter and shorter, so you will never get enough to manage the pain and agony that is in your heart. Your life will be one of pain and hell, separated from what will really fill you.

God, I want to control my sexual drives in a way that brings glory and honor to you. I don't want to be driven by my sexuality. I want to enjoy it as you created me to enjoy it.

*Flee also youthful lusts; but pursue righteousness,
faith, love, peace with those who call on the Lord
out of a pure heart.*
                                        —2 TIM. 2:22

There is nothing like the contentment of a pure heart.
It leads to a more fulfilling and satisfying enjoyment of
sex. Growing in character and concern for others creates an atmosphere for the greatest appreciation of
sexuality.

Sexuality in a meaningful relationship is the kind of
sexual relating you were created for. Allowing your
lusts to be fulfilled without concern for others leads to
sexual expression that becomes compulsive and meaningless.

Purity is not the opposite of sexuality; it is the opposite of lust. Sexuality is part of your being. God created
it and it is good. Sexuality can be experienced in pure
ways. Lust is the misuse of sexuality and cannot result
in purity.

You need to develop purity in the expression of your
sexuality. This means that you control your sexual
drives; you are not controlled by your sexuality. You
express your sexuality in the context of monogamous,
committed relationships. Your concern in your expression is not only for your own sexual fulfillment, but also
for the partner that you love. This is purity in sexuality.

---

*God, I want what you have designed. I am a sexual being. I can either
use my sexuality to dishonor myself and others or I can use it in pure
ways. Help me find your way.*

> *Knowing this first: that scoffers will come in the last*
> *days, walking according to their own lusts.*
> —2 PETER 3:3

Being controlled by and walking after your own lusts leads to emptiness. Sexual pleasure can only provide temporary relief, becoming a diversion from personal and relationship pain. Used in this way, sexual pleasure is very self-centered and not at all as it was intended. This is why it becomes addictive and self-destructive.

Sex experienced the way God designed will always remain undeniably pleasurable, never lead to an addiction, and remain one of the most physically satisfying experiences. A biochemical reaction in your body during sexual expression decreases depression. An essential part of healthy living, it can become destructive if it is not used properly.

If you let your lusts drive you, they will lead you to despair. Dissatisfaction and addictive behavior are the result of living for your lusts. You have a choice to walk in God's wisdom or after your lusts.

God, I don't want to be a scoffer. I don't want to ignore your wisdom. I want to express my sexuality in ways that I was created for.

Nevertheless, because of sexual immorality, let each man have his own wife, and let each woman have her own husband. Let the husband render to his wife the affection due her, and likewise also the wife to her husband.

—1 COR. 7:2–3

In marriage the union created sexually is a giving of oneself. The physical representation of this giving is the act of sex. It should be a voluntary giving of oneself for the purposes of oneness and pleasure.

You are a sexual being, created to develop and enjoy sexual intimacy. The ultimate enjoyment of sexual intimacy is experienced in a loving marital relationship. In such a relationship you do not use sex to bring self-centered pleasure. Sex becomes an expression of love, an avenue from which to please your spouse. You give and receive pleasure in the context of a growing, loving, committed relationship.

Marital sex is the ultimate expression of sex, but it is just as misused as worldly sex. Many partners don't realize its healing power. Many remain self-centered and use sex for pleasure alone. You can be misusing your sexuality in the context of marital sex. The purpose of sexuality is to express the oneness you should be growing toward. Your sexual expression with your partner should be out of love and respect for him or her.

God, help me experience what you desire for me. Help me come to experience and know the intimacy in my marriage that you created it to fulfill.

*And they were both naked, the man and his wife,
and were not ashamed.* —GEN. 2:25

This verse not only refers to the nakedness of their physical bodies, but the nakedness experienced in their relationship also. The man and his wife—Adam and Eve—experienced something that we will not experience again until heaven. They experienced their sexuality in the context of total acceptance.

There was nothing in Eve that Adam did not accept and likewise nothing in Adam that Eve didn't accept. Therefore their experience of sexuality never left either feeling vulnerable or used. It was a mutually satisfying experience.

Sin has perverted sexuality and sexual intimacy. Vulnerability and feeling used are the strongest detours from the intention of sex. Sexual addictions develop because people are drawn to the pleasure and escape found in sex. People who use sex for the pleasure of giving and receiving and as an expression of commitment and love will find themselves satisfied sexually. The endless quest for sexual pleasure alone will lead to despair.

God, I often am naked and ashamed emotionally and physically. I want to grow into the person you want me to be. Help me learn to understand myself sexually.

Have you found honey?
Eat only as much as you need,
Lest you be filled with it and vomit.
—PROV. 25:16

Food is a necessary and enjoyable experience in your daily life, important for nourishment and also for pleasure. Food is not a counterfeit for relationships. When used as an anesthesia for personal pain, chaos develops in your life.

If you are a compulsive overeater, you know this personally. When you eat more than is appropriate, you make yourself sick. The sickness becomes more emotional than physical. The behavior of compulsively overeating poisons your view of yourself. You believe you are weak and unlovable. You see yourself out of perspective and believe you don't have value or worth unless you can stop your compulsive behavior. Eventually you forget that you felt so unlovable before you even began to overeat.

The key to enjoy food, but not indulge in it, is in your heart. Let your stomach be your measure for when food is enough, not your heart. Food does provide legitimate pleasure and nourishment, but it only provides limited pleasure. When it is used to deal with loneliness, anxiety, etc., it is very negative and destructive.

God, show me when food is enough. Help me face the reality that the pleasure of food won't cure my relational pain.

> *Slothfulness casts one into a deep sleep,*
> *And an idle person will suffer hunger.*
> —PROV. 19:15

Hunger is a painful sensation. In many countries it can be easily remedied because there is food available. The reason food addiction is such an epidemic is that when hungry, most people could easily stop their hunger with food. When people try to use food to satisfy their relationship hungers, the temporary and short pleasure food provides cannot fix the relationship pain.

Food becomes a quick fix, a way to distract you from the pain in your personal life. Your compulsive need creates new unhealthy patterns and deeper pain in other areas of your life. You may begin focusing on your eating problem as the reason for your self-hate. Now you aren't facing the reason you feel so compelled to eat at all. You get on a destructive cycle of binge eating and hate, followed by more compulsive eating. On some levels you think you hate yourself because of your compulsive overeating. In fact, the hate goes much deeper. Your food addiction is not a problem with physical hunger, but a problem of personal pain.

Food will resolve the pain created by physical hunger. Food will only temporarily soothe the personal and relational pain in your life. You can resolve your personal and relationship pain. Your hungers can be filled, but not with food.

Teach me how to resolve my emotional hunger for intimacy and relationship without going to food.

They shall neither hunger anymore nor thirst
anymore; the sun shall not strike them, nor
any heat.
—REV. 7:16

Hunger and thirst are powerful drives. When these drives are unfulfilled, a person will go to many extremes to get them filled. Emotional hunger drives people in the same way, but emotional hunger will never be satisfied by food. Food functions as a diversion temporarily; afterward the emotional pain is more poignant.

There will come a time, for those who believe in Jesus Christ, when there will neither be physical hunger nor emotional hunger. These drives will be completely fulfilled. Until then, you must deal with your emptiness for food by proper daily nourishment and with your emotional needs by proper emotional responses.

Imagine a day when your physical and emotional hunger pains won't exist. On earth your physical and emotional hungers will not be filled perfectly, yet there are appropriate and balanced ways to have your hungers satisfied. Part of your journey to recovery is to observe the ways you can meet your emotional needs.

Thank you for providing for my hungers. Help me learn to accept the limited satisfaction I will receive on earth.

> *For the drunkard and the glutton will come*
> *to poverty,*
> *And drowsiness will clothe a man with*
> *rags.*
> —PROV. 23:21

When food takes over your life you will lose the enjoyment of life. Your soul becomes impoverished because of your compulsive behavior of overeating. Food becomes your best friend, your counselor. This separates you from the richness of life found in relationships.

Most compulsive overeaters believe no one will accept them because they are fat or out of control. They avoid relationships for this reason. So many believe that they have to lose weight or get control before they are lovable. If this is what you believe, you are wrong. The answer isn't to lose weight and then get into a relationship. The answer is to get involved in meaningful relationships and thus deal with the pain of relating without food.

Overweight people are referred to here as gluttons. Not all overweight people are gluttons. It is only when your stomach is your god that you are gluttonous. God wants to be your God. He is a jealous God and he doesn't want to be replaced by food. He is a loving God and he knows you will never be satisfied with food as your God. Don't settle for less and make food your God.

God, help me not put food ahead of you. Forgive me of my gluttonous behavior. Help me see it's not only my body that needs to change; it is more important to change my heart.

*The Son of Man has come eating and drinking,
and you say, "Look, a glutton and a winebibber, a
friend of tax collectors and sinners!"*

—LUKE 7:34

Jesus Christ himself enjoyed the fruits of this earth. As a physical and spiritual being, he partook of food in relationships. He enjoyed the taste and nourishment it provided. Although he was accused of being "ungodly" for this behavior, food was a part of his daily life and completely sinless.

He always remained balanced in his enjoyment of food. Food did not take over his life, but it was used for spiritual symbolism, enjoyment, or nourishment. Balance is the key to your life. You need to learn how to use food for its pleasure and nourishment. Since it will always be a part of your daily life, you must break your addiction to food by breaking its power over you. Food gains power over you when it becomes your life, rather than a part of your life.

Recognize the power food plays in your life today. Become aware of the urge to eat when you are feeling lonely or under pressure. Acknowledge your feelings and the reality that food will not resolve your emotions. Find better ways to deal with your emotions.

God, help me to have food as a part of my life as Christ did when he was on the earth. Help it not be my life. There is so much more you desire for me to experience.

Who gives food to all flesh,
For His mercy endures forever.
—PS. 136:25

God is the ultimate provider of your food. He provided manna for the Israelites each morning as they traveled to the promised land. Jesus fed thousands with small portions. He also cooked fish for the disciples after he was crucified and before he returned to heaven. Most of the time God provides food by sending rain, sunshine, and seeds, the tools by which food grows.

God wants you to have adequate nourishment. He wants your hunger to be provided for. The provision of food and nourishment that you have enjoyed in your life has come from him. As you get food in perspective, see God as its provider. Learn to trust in him to provide for your other needs also. Stop trusting yourself to meet your needs by food. Food will only meet nourishment and limited pleasure needs. It cannot fill the void from the rest of your needs.

God provides your food. He also provides for your emotional and spiritual needs. Learn to trust his wisdom and not run to food for your comfort. He alone is trustworthy.

Thank you for being my provider. Help me trust you more to provide my needs.

Remove falsehood and lies far from me;
Give me neither poverty nor riches—
Feed me with the food You prescribe for me;
Lest I be full, and deny You,
And say, "Who is the LORD?"
Or lest I be poor and steal,
And profane the name of my God.
                    —PROV. 30:8–9

King Solomon—the wisest king—speaks of the deceitfulness of food, the false sense of fullness. At the moment of bingeing the pleasure seems all-consuming. Later the pleasure is gone and you sink deeper into despair. You hate yourself more for being so out of control that the use of food actually increases your pain.

Food will lead you to vanity and lies. You begin by believing the lie that just one more of this or that will satisfy you. When it doesn't fill you, you think you need more and more. You become compulsively addicted to food in order to meet needs only God and relationships can touch.

King Solomon's prayer is very wise. He asks for his physical needs to be met, but that he will always enjoy them in the context of his relationship with God. When food is used to replace your relationship with God, you feel lost and lonely.

Recognize the limitation of food. See the real unlimited provider in God, not food. Put God back on the throne; don't be deceived by your full stomach.

God, help me realize the emptiness and the lies my obsession with food has created. I want to turn to you for fullness and truth.

> *And do not be drunk with wine, in which is*
> *dissipation; but be filled with the Spirit.*
> —EPH. 5:18

Chemical addiction, such as alcoholism or illegal drug usage, is diagnosed as either dependence or abuse. Dependence is diagnosed when the user has a physical and psychological addiction to the substance. A person abuses drugs and alcohol when he or she uses substances in inappropriate ways and allows them to impair judgment, although a physical or psychological dependence may not be apparent.

Both are troublesome ways to use alcohol and drugs. Both will destroy lives—the abuser and those who love the abuser. The excessive use of drugs and alcohol leads to addiction and self-destructive behavior. It eventually results in despair and loss.

When you are filled with the Spirit, you can never be filled to excess; with alcohol you can be filled to an inappropriate amount. The Spirit will not lead you astray, for you just can't get negatively addicted to the Spirit. Every human has spiritual needs that can only be met in relationship with God through Christ. However, excessive use of alcohol and drugs reflects a spiritual despair that may lead to chemical dependency. Only relationship with God can provide the real answers needed by the abuser.

God, help me find my highs by being filled with the Spirit.

*The LORD has mingled a perverse spirit in her
midst; and they have caused Egypt to err in all her
work, as a drunken man staggers in his vomit.*
                                                —ISA. 19:14

The disease of alcoholism takes over your entire life.
In the midst of your own despair, you stagger through
life. Many alcoholics hit bottom so hard that they are
not able to help themselves. Perhaps you started on
your path to recovery with the help of family members
who would not sit idly by and let you die.

The misuse of alcohol will lead to pain and despair.
The hole created is so deep that there seems to be no
way out. You make many damaging decisions that
results in loss of businesses, finances, and relationships. The wonder of this disease is that it is self-
inflicted. Can you picture the despair of a drunken man
staggering in his own vomit? It is not an appealing
sight. The misuse of alcohol eventually strips a person
of his or her dignity.

Nothing is hopeless with God. Alcoholics and drug
addicts can recover from despair with his higher
power. Most drug and alcohol abusers won't receive
help fully until they have hit bottom. Staggering in
vomit may be the way your life feels right now. Help is
available to you through the power of a loving God.

*God, I often feel trapped. There doesn't seem to be anything for me
but despair. You promise a way out, a way to live on this earth in
peace in relationship with you. Help me find that.*

> *Do not enter the path of the wicked,*
> *And do not walk in the way of evil. . . .*
> *For they eat the bread of wickedness,*
> *And drink the wine of violence.*
> —PROV. 4:14, 17

Often a part of recovery from codependency with alcohol and drugs is changing friends. Many times codependent, unhealthy friends have contributed to the problem of alcohol. Someone who has the same weakness can easily bring you down.

Your pathway to recovery from chemical dependency will include changing friends and readjusting relationships. You need to develop healthy friends who understand your problem with chemical dependency and want to encourage you to get on a new path.

Don't think you can go back to your old friends. Some people feel they have to prove they are strong enough to face those old friends. This black-and-white thinking is not very helpful in changing your behaviors. Present abusers cannot be in your intimate circle of support, because they will sabotage your efforts. You can still love them and pray for them, but you must recognize their destructive influence against your recovery.

_____

God, help me find the support and relationships that will encourage me in my pathway to recovery.

Wine is a mocker,
Intoxicating drink arouses brawling,
And whoever is led astray by it is not wise.
—PROV. 20:1

No one who develops codependency and chemical dependency wants to be mocked and deceived. But, ultimately, these behaviors lead to just this—deception and mockery. By the time the problem has progressed to the point of dependency or abuse, the person is caught in a lie.

The lie is that just one more high is worth the pain. In reality one more hit clinches you tighter in the jaws of hell. You feel lower than you felt before the "one more" experience. Still the deception persists that you need your substance in order to live on this earth. You are caught in a cycle of destruction and despair, and your life becomes a mockery.

Wisdom is realizing the mockery and deception that accompanies chemical dependency. Recognize the reality of what that high really does to you. See how hard and low you crash. The high really wasn't very high after all. Don't be mocked and deceived by chemical dependency.

_____

God, help me see the deception and mockery of the life I am living. Help me trust you that my future can be different.

> *He who loves pleasure will be a poor man;*
> *He who loves wine and oil will not be rich.*
> —PROV. 21:17

Alcohol and drugs are not good lovers; they do not love back. In fact, they do not give anything to the person but heartache. They take away dignity and control; they deceive and destroy lives and relationships.

Often love issues motivate the chemical dependency. Unmet love needs often lead a person to the trap of chemical dependency. An individual who has a low self-esteem and lack of strong interpersonal relationships is much more susceptible to developing chemical dependency than someone whose love needs are met.

Alcohol and drugs are not the answer to lack of love. When you love your substance, you cannot have meaningful relationships. Having a chemical dependency makes you act in ways that are similar to love. You think about your craving, wonder when you can do it again. But this really has little to do with true love. True love would not destroy your life.

Being loved can be a tremendous motivation in life. Who are you going to love—people or drugs and alcohol? God says love him first, your neighbor, and yourself. Alcohol and drugs don't make very good lovers.

God, help me realize my legitimate need for love. Show me how to meet my needs for love in legitimate ways.

Who has woe?
Who has sorrow?
Who has contentions?
Who has complaints?
Who has wounds without cause?
Who has redness of eyes?
Those who linger long at the wine,
Those who go in search of mixed wine.
—PROV. 23:29–30

Do you know anyone with a chemical dependency whose life is full and satisfying? More likely you know individuals whose lives are full of woe, sorrow, contentions, complaints, red eyes, and wounds. The description of chemical dependency has not changed very much since this one was written over three thousand years ago.

When you abuse drugs and alcohol, you are inviting sorrow and woe into your life. People can't see themselves as they really are when they are in the midst of chemical dependency. Most people don't begin to change until they have what Alcoholics Anonymous calls "hit bottom." Usually hitting bottom means facing yourself for the first time in a long time. Often it happens when things have gotten so out of control the abuser cannot use the hiding tricks from the past. Freedom comes in seeing yourself as you really are and making the appropriate changes. Come out of hiding and into God's presence where you are safe.

God, show me I can face myself with you because you will not reject me.

> *Let him kiss me with the kisses of his mouth—*
> *For your love is better than wine.*
> —SONG 1:2

King Solomon describes something that chemical dependent persons may not know. Much in life is more fulfilling and satisfying than drugs and alcohol. Not just reserved for a few, it is available to each human being on this earth. Relationships that are healthy and strong are more fulfilling and satisfying than the pleasure of drugs and alcohol.

Chemical dependency becomes addictive because we are pleasure-seekers. Humans in pain are desperate to find solutions to resolve their personal pain. Chemicals provide immediate, though brief, pleasure. The crash from the high then takes you lower than you felt before you used the drug or alcohol.

Many pleasures in life can be enjoyed free of addiction and destruction. Alcohol and drug abuse provide only short and temporary conscious relief while destroying your body, mind, and relationships. When you consider the whole picture, the pleasure isn't really worth it.

God, I want to believe that there is life out there for me. Help me find the kind of relationships that make life seem worth living.

*For I say to you, that unless your righteousness
exceeds the righteousness of the scribes and
Pharisees, you will by no means enter the
kingdom of heaven.*
                                    —MATT. 5:20

Humans need a sense of security in their environments. They have this same need in their religious environment. The Pharisees devised a plan by which to feel secure in their religious standing. Rituals and laws defined a person as in good standing before God; the rules were so extravagant they opposed Jesus healing a blind man on the Sabbath. They were so busy obeying God according to their standards, that they missed what God really wanted for them.

It was impossible to exceed the righteousness of the Pharisees, yet even with their degree of righteousness, they were not righteous enough to enter the kingdom of heaven. Many people are codependent on religion in the same way. They define themselves as good or bad based on the degree of righteousness in their lives.

This is a false sense of security. Just as the Pharisees had a false sense of security, Christians today use religion to make themselves feel good and avoid pain. The key to avoiding this codependency is to make a personal relationship with God the focus of your religion.

*God, help me understand the relationship you offer to me. Help me
learn to trust and depend on you in healthy ways.*

> *Blessed is the man to whom the LORD does not*
>   *impute iniquity,*
> *And in whose spirit there is no guile.*
> —PS. 32:2

Religion itself can become addictive. People can use seemingly healthy avenues to meet needs illegitimately. Religion is one of those healthy areas that can be misused and lead to codependent behavior.

King David, the man after God's own heart, understood God's belief about his behavior. Relationship with God cannot be measured by the amount of religious activities one participates in. God desires for your religious expressions to be demonstrations of your relationship with and trust in him.

Codependent religious behavior seeks acceptance and approval from God in much the same way you did in your dysfunctional family. The difference with God is that he accepts you in Christ. This acceptance is not based on what you do, but on the worth and value he created in you.

God doesn't want you to use religion to cover up your pain from your dysfunctional family. He wants to welcome you to a relationship with him where you have the freedom to face the pain from your family of origin and the pain from living in a fallen earth. He wants you to worship him and realize that only in a relationship with him can you be free of your past.

Help me not use religious behaviors to make me feel good about myself. Help me experience a true relationship with you.

*And in vain they worship Me, teaching as doctrines
the commandments of men.*   —MARK 7:7

Why do people use religion in codependent ways?
The abuse of food, drugs, or alcohol is easier to understand. People turn to religion for acceptance, yet their
grid of acceptance is only through conditions. They
cannot comprehend the doctrine of God—he accepts
you completely in Christ. Instead they act out family
systems whereby men's doctrines are preached and
guilt and shame are imposed.

Relationship with God is the true context of religion.
Are your religious activities performed to get God's approval? Or, are you in a real relationship with God? Do
you sit still to hear his voice?

Think about your relationship with God. How much
of the trouble you have believing him is linked to your
relationship with your parents on earth? Do you find
yourself having trouble believing and accepting God's
love? Can you see parallels between this and your natural pattern of relationship? God's love is totally radical
to the experiences most of us have had in this life. His
love is real and unconditional, but often difficult to understand. In your growing experiences of God, realize
the trauma from your past and how it has disguised
him from your eyes.

---

*God, help me grow to see you as the true and loving parent you tell
me you are. I don't want to make you into what I believed from my
parents.*

> *But the hour is coming, and now is, when the true worshipers will worship the Father in spirit and truth; for the Father is seeking such to worship Him.*
>
> —JOHN 4:23

We were created for relationship with God, and we have a need to worship. Just like the many other needs, this need can be misdirected. Worship can become a means to inflict self-hate and pain.

True worshipers realize they are totally unworthy of any relationship with God. They worship God because he made relationship with himself possible through Christ. This is different from worshiping out of guilt and fear. It is worshiping from excitement and freedom because someone really loves them and desires the best for them. Although they have hurt this someone, the hurts aren't held against them. They want to worship out of freedom.

Many worship out of guilt and fear. They see themselves as unworthy, and they look to their religious behaviors to make them valuable as humans. This is false worship and the essence of codependency. It burdens a person under a cloud of despair. This is not what God desires for us to experience.

God, help me find excitement in true worship of you. Open my eyes to the reality of how great a love you have. This feeling of love motivates true worship, not doubt and fear.

God, who made the world and everything in it, since He is Lord of heaven and earth, does not dwell in temples made with hands. Nor is He worshiped with men's hands, as though He needed anything, since He gives to all life, breath, and all things.
—ACTS 17:24–25

God does not need our worship in a desperate, codependent way. He enjoys our worship. He is delighted when we obey him; but he does not need it to validate himself.

God desires that we worship because we were created by him to fellowship with him. Unlike God, we need to worship him. In relationship with him we are validated. We do not worship God so he can feel good about being God. Rather, we worship God and recognize at once our value and worth from being created by one such as him.

God doesn't need us; we need him. We need to enter into relationship with him. When we do this, our religious behaviors become more than rituals. They are events where meaningful relationship and fellowship are enjoyed. True worship brings balance and peace and understanding into our existence. This is nothing like being codependent on religion. Codependency on religion brings burdens and fear and self-righteousness.

God, I worship you because it is in worshiping you that I can find peace and understanding in this life.

> *For by grace you have been saved through faith,*
> *and that not of yourselves; it is the gift of God, not*
> *of works, lest anyone should boast.*
>
> —EPH. 2:8–9

Many people judge their works to understand their faith. They need to be seen as worthy by the religious behaviors they do. This misuse of religion is a sign that one's religion has developed into codependency.

God does not invite relationship with himself in codependent ways. He invites us, unacceptable though we are, and accepts us through Christ. His grace saves us. At the bottom of codependency is the fear of unacceptability. In true Christianity there is no room for codependency. The truth of Christianity is the reality that we are unacceptable to God, but that God sent his perfect Son to die for us so we could be acceptable to him. We are accepted through his grace. We could never be good enough to be invited to relationship with God. He does not invite us based on our worth alone; he invites us in Christ. You don't have to try to prove yourself to God—he saves you through faith.

———————

God, help me accept the ways you love and accept me. Help me not bring my old codependency styles into a relationship with you.

*Be anxious for nothing, but in everything by prayer
and supplication, with thanksgiving, let your
requests be made known to God; and the peace of
God, which surpasses all understanding, will guard
your hearts and minds through Christ Jesus.*
                                        —PHIL. 4:6–7

Obsessive and anxious behaviors are often associated with codependency. The obsessions and anxiety function as a means to avoid dealing with personal pain. In a way, the obsessions build a wall of safety. The person may be miserable obsessing and worrying, but in a sense they are safe from facing the real issues that they fear the most. The most painful issues in their lives are locked deep inside, covered by their obsessive and anxious behavior.

Avoiding personal pain is the source of the anxious thoughts. The cure for anxiety and obsessiveness is trust in God. When you find yourself obsessing and feeling anxious, think of the worst thing that could happen to you in that situation. Realize that you could survive that with God's help. Accept what you can and cannot control. The key is to trust God with your heart. The source of the pain that is causing the obsessive behaviors is hiding in the heart. Take a step of trust today.

*God, help me to trust you just as you tell me I can. I am afraid I have
developed futile ways to protect myself. Help me find your ways and
live by them.*

Rest in the LORD, and wait patiently for Him;
Do not fret because of him who prospers in
his way,
Because of the man who brings wicked
schemes to pass.
—PS. 37:7

Trust in God is the antidote needed for the pain that has been caused in relationships. Many have developed obsessive behavior to divert themselves from the personal pain caused by painful relationships. They feel anxiety and anger when they cannot control other people or change them into the persons they want them to be.

You have been hurt by relationships, or you may be frustrated to see evil men prosper. You may wonder why God would allow such a thing to happen. When you spend your life worrying about why God would allow certain people to live seemingly unmarked by the pain they have caused others, the quality of your life decreases. God's response to you is to wait patiently on him. He will take care of those people in his time.

Usually the waiting is most difficult, and God not only tells us to wait but to do so patiently. Patience depends on trust in God. He cares about you and your personal relationships. He promises to take care of those evil person(s) in your life. You may never see how or why, but you must trust just the same.

God, the evil people in my life have crushed my soul. Help me see how they still have power over me as long as I worry or think about them. Help me trust that you can take care of them for me.

The foolishness of a man twists his way,
And his heart frets against the LORD.
—PROV. 19:3

At the core of obsessive behavior is fretting against the Lord. It is not enough to simply say, "Trust and stop obsessing." Just like any other addiction or codependent behavior, obsessions develop because you haven't learned how to trust; you've rarely found people in your life who are trustworthy.

Trust in God probably goes completely against your experiences in life. This is why the obsessive behavior develops into such a compulsive drive. You were not designed to love without trust; therefore you build trust into your obsessions. They help you avoid the lack of trust in your life. In a strange way, they become your protector and guide and even develop into your best friend.

It won't ever work. You were designed for relationship with God and with others. Your obsessive behavior keeps you safe to a certain degree, but it also keeps you lost and lonely. You can trust God. When you trust God, you are beginning your path to recovery. Trusting in his existence and his love is the beginning of changing your obsessive and anxious behavior.

God, my heart is so full of fear that trust is the last thing I think I can do. I want to trust you; I want to believe you. Trust goes against my experiences in this life. You are trustworthy. Help me believe this today.

> *Therefore do not worry about tomorrow, for*
> *tomorrow will worry about its own things.*
> *Sufficient for the day is its own trouble.*
> —MATT. 6:34

Growing in relationship with God involves growing in trust and appropriate dependency. So many issues in your life may seem confusing when it comes to God. You may wonder where He was when certain things happened to you. Verses like this may seem very impossible. You can trust in God and experience his trustworthiness.

Your obsessions and anxiety keep you from trusting. The energy for trusting is put into your obsessive behavior. When you find yourself anxious and obsessing, ask yourself, What am I trusting right now? Am I trusting God? The answer is most likely no. You are trusting in yourself and your ability to ward off the evil that might come to you. As you already know, the evil in this world is much more than you can handle. Your obsessions and anxiety only give you a false sense of security in how to deal with them.

Relationship and trust in God give you true security to face and accept the evil you face each day. Begin today by focusing on God when you obsess or feel anxious. Talk to Him about what is in your soul and the fears you have.

_____

God, help me trust you to help me deal with the evil I must face today.
Help me stop my destructive cycle of obsessive and anxious thoughts
so I can live fully and freely.

Keep your heart with all diligence,
For out of it spring the issues of life.
—PROV. 4:23

Obsessions are a symptom of a troubled heart. Many people's troubled hearts are caused by unconscious fear and pain. The real issues in your heart are locked deep inside of you. You are afraid to face the pain in your life, so you avoid it by obsessive behavior.

Avoidance doesn't work very well. Those issues in your heart remain, fighting for a way out. Dealing with your anger and pain requires daily attention. When you do this, you "keep your heart." This stifles the power beneath your obsessive behavior.

Keep your heart. Face what is in there. Don't let your obsessive behavior keep you from enjoying life and walking in trust with God.

God, help me trust you and believe you can handle all that is in my heart.

Because it is written, "Be holy, for I am holy."
—1 PETER 1:16

Scripture like this seems to encourage perfectionism. One might wonder what is wrong with perfectionism. It is not all bad to be concerned about doing a job to the best of one's ability. The problem with perfectionism evolves in relationships. Perfectionistic tendencies often build barriers in relationships.

Perfectionists are never satisfied with themselves or with others. This of course makes a relationship with a perfectionist difficult, since the relationships are constantly in tension and pressure.

Perfectionists will never achieve satisfaction because being perfect is not attainable. You cannot make anything in your life perfect. You might ask, why would God include such a statement as this in his Word if he did not want to provoke dissatisfaction and perfectionism? God is perfect and holy and when he exchanges our lives in heaven, we will be like him. Still, on earth he encourages us toward holiness. Holiness is intrinsically different from perfection in that perfectionism is a defense against feeling insignificant. Holiness is a state of being filled with God's love and acceptance and allowing this quality to be played out in your life.

God, help me understand holiness and the difference between that and perfectionism. Help me desire holiness and relationship with you, and not perfectionism.

And God is able to make all grace abound toward you, that you, always having all sufficiency in all things, have an abundance for every good work.
—2 COR. 9:8

There is a unique and destructive difference between perfectionism and doing good work. Perfectionism is a self-protective means to avoid facing and dealing with personal and relationship pain. Perfectionism leads to disgust and pain because it is impossible to attain. At the bottom of perfectionism is fear of unacceptability, so you will try as hard as possible to prove your worth. Good work is motivated by God and abounds from one's feeling of acceptability. Doing good work is a positive aspect of perfectionism. This should not be abandoned in your quest to become a whole person.

Perfectionism is done by human power. Doing your best means accepting the reality that you are limited and weak. The perfectionist is not able to face this reality. Freedom comes in allowing God's power to move in you to overcome your addictive personality and codependency. You don't need to be a perfectionist anymore because unacceptability is OK.

Acknowledging powerlessness and yielding to a higher power is essential. When that higher power is the Lord Jesus Christ, yielding opens even more power over perfectionism and other codependency issues.

God, help me find in you motivation to do my best based on your acceptance, not on my fears.

The integrity of the upright will guide them,
But the perversity of the unfaithful will destroy them.
—PROV. 11:3

Integrity is an essential element of mental health. One must develop the integrity to face oneself openly and honestly. It requires integrity to be honest about the pain going on underneath the perfectionism and other codependency issues.

Perfectionism is often rewarded in many ways, but it gets in the way of relationships. It builds walls and barriers and distances you from your feelings. The Pharisees were perfectionists. They concerned themselves so much with looking right on the outside that they missed the truth that God wanted them to know. They missed out on deep and satisfying relationships. They missed out on the joy of salvation; even in their own unacceptability, Christ died for them.

What is perfectionism doing in your life? How does it keep you from truly enjoying life?

God, help me not use perfectionism to keep me from facing my feelings and from enjoying my relationship with you and others.

A desire accomplished is sweet to the soul,
But it is an abomination to fools to depart from evil.
—PROV. 13:19

Perfectionism compels because accomplishment is good. To a true perfectionist, the accomplishments are never quite good enough, only to a certain degree. You were created to be an active, creative member of this world to do something and see it fulfilled.

The joy of accomplishment is shown to us first by God in his acts of creation. Everything he made was very good. He enjoyed its goodness. He wasn't too proud or falsely humble. We should feel good when we accomplish a goal.

Perfectionism takes away the good feeling when something is done. A perfectionist always feels that it could have been better, if there were only more time. God was able to see what he made and enjoy what he did. At the same time he rested and did not have to get everything done in one day. You can replace your pessimistic perfectionism with true enjoyment of a job well done.

God, help me see the goodness in what I do. Help me fight the urge to discount my work.

Commit your works to the Lord,
And your thoughts will be established.
—PROV. 16:3

One way to deal with perfectionistic tendencies is to commit your works to the Lord. Let him show you how to relax and accept your life. The energy behind perfectionism is that unless this is done perfectly and everyone who sees it agrees, including myself, I am not worthy.

The lack of worth is the motivation behind unhealthy behavior. When you commit your works to God, you accept his acceptance of you and whatever your works may be. In this way your works do not define you as good or bad; rather, they are an expression of who you are. Your standing before God is not better or worse based on what you do.

You are accepted even as a perfectionist. Recognize this. Let the freedom of God's acceptance penetrate into your works. See them as expressions of yourself, not definitions of yourself.

God, help me see myself through your eyes. Help me see that all my works are to glorify you, not define me as acceptable or unacceptable.

Do you see a man who excels in his work?
He will stand before kings;
He will not stand before unknown men.
—PROV. 22:29

Perfectionist personalities need to realize the fears that are going on beneath their behavior. They need to face their relationships and the pain caused by expecting others to relate to them by their perfectionistic standards. But they need to accept part of their personality as good and appropriate.

I would hate to think what this world would be like if there were no perfectionists in it. The diligence and determination to get a job done and to get it done in the most accurate way possible is very noteworthy. As you face yourself and your relationships, don't become so overcome with change that you get rid of all of your positive qualities too. Accept part of your perfectionism. Don't become so desperate in it. Learn to enjoy your works and enjoy other people. Learn to enjoy people who are not as driven as you and imitate them in some ways.

Thank you for the driven, perfectionist tendencies you have gifted me with. Help me learn to use them in positive ways to enhance myself and my relationships.

A little sleep, a little slumber,
A little folding of the hands to rest.
—PROV. 24:33

Rest is one of the areas a perfectionist might ignore in order to attain his or her unattainable goals. We all need rest. Perfectionists need to learn how to rest. Balance is a key in life, and rest is an important part of a balanced life.

Mental health is greatly affected by physical health. Proper physical health in terms of exercise, diet, and rest are important. Perfectionists need to accept their limitation and need for rest.

Jim Henson, the creator of the Muppets, was a workaholic and perfectionist who suffered premature death due to not responding to bodily symptoms. God created your body with unique signals to alert you when you need rest. You need to listen to those signals on your path to mental and emotional health.

God, help me realize my need for rest. Help me not keep perfectionistic standards that rob me of the enjoyment of life.

Codependency Issues

As we study the various family situations, problems, and personalities which lead to codependent relationships, issues will surface that need to be addressed. How do we address our weaknesses? What place do honesty, self-assessment, confession, fellowship, accountability, and forgiveness have in becoming healthy? How do we move from dependence to independence in our relationships? Can we become intimate with another person without becoming codependent again? How can we base our self-esteem on truth if we have never experienced value? The following devotionals will prepare our hearts for recovery.

God is faithful, by whom you were called into the fellowship of His Son, Jesus Christ our Lord.
—1 COR. 1:9

Many recovering codependents hesitate to get involved with other people, even other believers, for fear that old styles of relating may resurface. Yet the Bible teaches us that healthy interaction, or fellowship with others, is an integral part of true contentment.

Fellowship can be defined in ways such as seeing my friends at a church gathering or going out to eat with loved ones. The biblical definition, however, goes beyond the realm of activity. True fellowship implies a close, personal relationship with people who share a common bond. For Christians, that common bond is Jesus Christ.

My work as a Christian therapist has taken me to many places around the world. On one such trip to Malaysia, we had the opportunity to attend a national church service. I recall the body of believers singing praises to the Lord Jesus in their native tongue. Even though I could only understand the tune, I indeed felt a oneness with them. This oneness which results from our common bond in Jesus Christ is the foundation for all healthy relationships between believers.

Dear Lord, help me to realize that the more I learn to know you, the better I can relate to my fellowman.

> *But do not forget to do good and to share, for with
> sacrifices God is well pleased.*   —HEB. 13:16

Why do we share? For many codependents, sharing is a way to receive positive affirmation, a way to get a deeply needed message that says, "You're worth something." We should share with others not for those reasons, but because the act pleases God. When God was pleased with a sacrifice in Old Testament times, he declared it to be a "sweet savory aroma" to his nostrils. For sharing to be a sweet aroma to God, we must eliminate all strings that we have attached to the act. Only then can we be blessed. Also the word *share* is the same Greek word for fellowship. Thus a good test for true fellowship involves not only sharing what we have, but also doing such sharing from the pure motive of love for the Lord Jesus instead of self-promotion.

Dear Lord, please give me an opportunity today to share selflessly with others, so that my actions will be accepted by you as a sweet aroma.

. . . fulfill my joy by being like-minded, having the same love, being of one accord, of one mind.
— PHIL. 2:2

Several years ago I watched the U.S. Olympic basketball games. To get ready, the team played different N.B.A. greats. It was remarkable to watch as the college All-Star team, made up of younger and less experienced players, won every game. Why? Because they experienced true fellowship and oneness of purpose. By virtue of their closeness as a team and their unity of direction, this college team was able to overcome normal deficiencies and defeat stronger and more experienced opponents.

As recovery codependents, we will benefit from constantly reminding ourselves that the Lord Jesus and fellow believers are our "team." And we are in the winner's circle when we are able to glorify the Lord Jesus and edify our precious teammates. We can't win the game of life alone, but we must always be willing to give 100 percent for Christ and His team.

Dear Lord, keep me from becoming self-centered and so preoccupied with my own needs that I forget I'm on the most important team of all. Help me keep on reaching out to edify others and to glorify you.

> *Now all who believed were together, and had all
> things in common.*
> —ACTS 2:44

Perhaps the main difficulty we have in understanding the ramifications of true fellowship is in understanding what its outward expressions really are.

In the passage we are studying (Acts 2:41–47), five outward expressions of fellowship are presented. As we summarize these five, we should ask ourselves the question, "How can we demonstrate the following examples in our life today?"

First, true fellowship involves spending time together in the study of God's Word and in prayer (Acts 2:42). Second, true fellowship involves a willingness to make our assets of time and money available to others who have a genuine noncodependent need (Acts 2:45). Third, true fellowship involves a common purpose and goal (Acts 2:46). Fourth, true fellowship involves sharing the everyday concerns of life with others without fear of rejection (Acts 2:46). And finally, true fellowship involves more "doing" than "receiving" (Acts 2:46–47).

True fellowship is its own reward because genuine fellowship with other believers always results in unity, joy, and praise.

Dear Lord, may I learn from the Christians of old who understood the true meaning of fellowship. Help me to develop a life-style of fellowship as I commit to others and you all that I am and all that I have.

Then Peter came to Him and said, "Lord, how often shall my brother sin against me, and I forgive him? Up to seven times?" Jesus said to him, "I do not say to you, up to seven times, but up to seventy times seven."

—MATT. 18:21–22

The story Jesus tells Peter in the verses that follow the passage read today (Matt. 18:23–38) is a good lesson on the subject of forgiveness. The King and Master in the story is God himself. Jesus is reminding Peter that God had already forgiven him an inestimable debt (ten thousand talents would be equal to at least several million dollars). Peter, Jesus said, should not be like the servant, who, after forgiven for his huge debt, then refused to show mercy and compassion toward the person who owed him a much smaller debt.

God in His mercy forgave us and saved us when we deserved nothing but condemnation and eternal punishment. Now we must become willing "from the heart" (v. 35) to forgive and to be reconciled and to overcome the tendency to retaliate.

If we are, on the other hand, in the position of needing to make amends for wrongs we have done, the underlying attitude must still be the same—"from the heart." When God sees such a heart—totally willing to obey regardless of the human outcome—he will move and work and bless far above our ability to ask or even think.

———————

Without your forgiveness, Lord, I would not have had a chance to really live. May I extend that forgiveness to others today.

Have mercy on me, O Lord, for I am weak;
O LORD, heal me, for my bones are troubled.
My soul also is greatly troubled;
But You, O LORD—how long?
Return, O LORD, deliver me!
Oh, save me for Your mercies' sake!

—PS. 6:2–4

It is human nature to want to be (and to believe that we are) in control of our circumstances and our lives. But truly fortunate people come to a point in their lives when they realize this is not always possible or even desirable. These people are the fortunate ones because they have come to the end of themselves just as David had come to the end of his physical and emotional resources. "My bones are troubled" is a Hebrew way of saying "I'm wracked with pain." David, the valiant warrior, admits his weakness, his emotional collapse. But instead of being defeated by this admission, David has actually placed himself in the strongest position possible. He now is free to quit scraping the empty barrel of his own resources, ever trying to manage things in his own strength. Instead, he is now able to begin dipping into God's unlimited resources!

Give me wisdom, Lord, to discern when I need to assume control and when I need to relinquish control to you.

Jesus said to him, "If you can believe, all things are possible to him who believes." Immediately the father of the child cried out and said with tears, "Lord, I believe; help my unbelief!"

—Mark 9:23–24

When we have been held captive by damaging habits or behaviors, it is sometimes hard to believe that we will ever be free of them. We may have even accepted Christ as Savior, and yet the chains of our past still seem to bind us. These words need to take root deep in our hearts right now: "For with God *nothing* shall be impossible" (Luke 1:37, emphasis added).

A frightened and doubting father discovered the truth of these words as Jesus descended the Mount of Transfiguration. The father's precious son was demon-possessed and had nearly died several times because of his evil tormentor. The child's father had asked the disciples for help, but they were unable to heal the child. With all hope nearly gone, he petitions Jesus, "If you can do anything, have compassion on us and help us."

Instead of giving him a sermon on his lack of faith, Jesus shows the man that the point is not *his* ability to heal the boy, but the father's ability to trust in God who can do what is humanly impossible. The father's cry echoes the cry of each of our hearts, "Lord, I believe; help my unbelief." He declared his faith but was honest about his weakness.

Lord, help me to let go of my doubt so I can begin to trust your power.

I have come as a light into the world, that whoever believes in Me should not abide in darkness.
—JOHN 12:46

If as a child you had been hidden away in the dark recesses of a cave, it is possible that you could grow to maturity never having seen the light or observed yourself in that light. Because you had always dwelt in darkness, the light and what it revealed would be foreign and incomprehensible.

In somewhat the same sense, those of us who have struggled with disabling conditions since childhood may actually be totally unaware of the extent of our problems. Because of our traumatic childhood experiences, we may be defiant, resentful, self-deluded, or controlling without ever realizing it.

But when we come to the light of God's power and love, we no longer have to abide in that crippling darkness. In the light of his love we can accept ourselves as we truly are, and then in the light of his power we can walk out of the darkness for good.

Lord, thank you for turning on the lights of your truth and allowing me to see myself for who I really am.

> *"Come to Me, all you who labor and are heavy
> laden, and I will give you rest. Take My yoke upon
> you and learn from Me, for I am gentle and lowly
> in heart, and you will find rest for your souls. For
> My yoke is easy and My burden is light."*
> —MATT. 11:28–30

These verses are among the most beloved in the New Testament and for good reason. A compassionate Savior holds out his hands to all mankind in these verses. His invitation is freely given, and his promise is more to be desired than gold.

Some of us have been bowed down with burdens of guilt, shame, bitterness, fear, and discouragement since childhood. We are weary of trying to even stand, let alone walk, under such a heavy load. Jesus is saying, "Come to me and I will take that load off your back." As we allow God's healing love to take over in our lives, for the first time we will experience true rest.

Yet, just when we have first come to know rest, the Lord Jesus tells us to take his yoke upon us and learn from him. Why? In Bible times a farmer would yoke a young ox with an older, capable one so that the young one could learn to plow the right way. Jesus is saying that we no longer have to try to pull the plow ourselves. He will be in the yoke with us now, and we will be his disciples, learning from him. Because he is always in that yoke with us, whatever we have to face becomes easier because he is the strong one, pulling us through and guiding us to keep the furrow straight.

Help me to run life's race free of unnecessary or painful burdens.

> *For the lips of an immoral woman drip honey,*
> *And her mouth is smoother than oil;*
> *But in the end she is bitter as wormwood,*
> *Sharp as a two-edged sword.*
> *Her feet go down to death,*
> *Her steps lay hold of hell.*
> *Lest you ponder her path of life—*
> *Her ways are unstable;*
> *You do not know them.*   —PROV. 5:3–6

Not all of us have a problem with adultery. But we can all learn from the type of behavior described here.

When we first begin to develop harmful habits, we do so because it seems pleasant or at least easier than an alternative behavior. Unfortunately, in the end those habits become as bitter as wormwood. Only long after the chains are forged can we see how destructive our behavior has become to ourselves and those around us. How important it is for us to begin to seriously "ponder the path of life." Up until now, many of our ways and reasons for doing things were "unstable." Perhaps even the adultress of Proverbs 5 used denial to avoid scrutinizing her own life. But now, we have determined that with God's help we will begin making an honest personal inventory. We will courageously seek out and accept our weaknesses knowing that God is there to impart to us both his wisdom and his unconditional love.

Dear Lord, help me to realize that my desires for the present may lead to my downfall in the future. Give me wisdom to understand what my true needs and motives should be.

Beware of the leaven of the Pharisees, which is
hypocrisy. For there is nothing covered that will not
be revealed, nor hidden that will not be known.
—LUKE 12:1–2

Leaven or yeast is used throughout the Bible to represent sin.

Here Jesus is warning his disciples to beware "of the leaven of the Pharisees which is hypocrisy." We are hypocritical when we pretend to be something we are not. Sometimes as codependents we are so good at pretending that we even fool ourselves.

Recovery, however, demands that we evaluate our lives and accept the truth of our personal history. Why? First, God already knows everything about us anyway. We might be good at fooling others and even ourselves, but we can never fool God.

Second, we must acknowledge our fears in order to set our priorities straight. Fear of what others will think or of facing the truth about ourselves keeps us emotionally unable to deal with the most important issue in our lives—our relationship with God.

And finally, God cares about us very deeply. This is the most important reason for honestly evaluating our strengths and weaknesses. If God cares about every little bird, think how much more important we are to him. Now that we trust him, he is right here to help us uncover our real self. We don't have to be afraid, because that real self is the person the Lord Jesus loves.

Lord, help me to honestly evaluate my life without hiding behind the mask of self-denial.

All the ways of a man are pure in his own eyes,
But the Lord weighs the spirits.
Commit your works to the Lord,
And your thoughts will be established.
—PROV. 16:2–3

Several years ago a young friend flew me to a speaking engagement in Florida. En route, we encountered a thick layer of clouds. After we had been in the midst of these clouds for what seemed an interminable time, I began to feel as if the plane was actually flying on its side! I felt compelled to voice this concern to my friend, but he assured me that our plane was positioned exactly as it should be. He was positive of this, he said, because he was using an instrument called an artificial horizon indicator. He explained that it is normal for our senses to become confused in the murky thickness of a cloud bank, but the horizon indicator is never fooled.

How well this illustration relates to our own natural wisdom versus God's heavenly wisdom. All our ways seem right to us, but our omniscient God knows what direction is best for us to take as we go through the storms of life. Trying to run our own lives is like trying to fly a plane through a cloud bank without a horizon indicator.

But when we decide to open our lives honestly to his scrutiny and accept what we find revealed there, we have taken the first step toward righting our plane and keeping it off a collision course.

When I feel you are not near, help me to rest in the fact that you are indeed close by.

And do this, knowing the time, that now it is high time to awake out of sleep; for now our salvation is nearer than when we first believed. The night is far spent, the day is at hand. Therefore let us cast off the works of darkness, and let us put on the armor of light. Let us walk properly, as in the day, not in revelry and drunkenness, not in licentiousness and lewdness, not in strife and envy. But put on the Lord Jesus Christ, and make no provision for the flesh, to fulfill its lusts.
—ROM. 13:11–14

Many codependents are unaware of the deepest reasons for our attitudes and actions. We are a bit like a sleepwalker moving through scenes and events, yet unaware of how we did so. God calls us now to awaken. The night of our emotional imprisonment is ending. The day of our recovery is at hand. But we cannot cast off the "works of darkness" until we are completely aware of what those sins and weaknesses are. We must accept reality instead of denying or excusing or becoming angry or fearful.

On the positive side, however, Paul tells us to put on the Lord Jesus Christ. We do this by drawing on his strength, aligning our thoughts with his Word and by yielding our wills over to him.

Help me to see myself as you see me, and grant me insight to know how to become more like you.

> *Confess your trespasses to one another, and pray for one another, that you may be healed. The effective, fervent prayer of a righteous man avails much.*
> —JAMES 5:16

Our isolated, me-centered society has developed a strong repugnance for the word *accountability*. We no longer want to be accountable to and for our families, our churches, or even ourselves. Although the idea of accountability is out of vogue, the Bible has much to say about it.

God says we are not only accountable to him, but we are accountable to our brothers and sisters in Christ as well. And far from being an odious burden, this is in fact a major source of joy and healing.

When we find the courage to confess our sins to a fellow believer, we open ourselves to a new energy and capacity to change our lives. Our confession actually strengthens our commitment toward spiritual growth since we now have a companion interceding in prayer for us, encouraging and sharing with us. And even though we may have times of weakness when we fall back into our old ways, we also will have the love and support of the Lord Jesus and our fellow believers to pick us up and help us back onto the path of life.

May I have the courage to seek someone out who will agree to be my accountability partner.

> *Therefore gird up the loins of your mind, be sober,*
> *and rest your hope fully upon the grace that is to*
> *be brought to you at the revelation of Jesus Christ;*
> *as obedient children, not conforming yourselves to*
> *the former lusts, as in your ignorance; but as He*
> *who called you is holy, you also be holy in all your*
> *conduct, because it is written, "Be holy, for I am*
> *holy."*
>
> —1 PETER 1:13–16

In order for recovery to take place, codependents must "gird up the loins of your mind." We must prepare for action, get ready to let Jesus do some serious work in our minds. Self-control and resting your hope upon Christ Jesus are necessary for what lies ahead.

When you turned your life over to Jesus, he gave you a new nature, created in him. As you consciously refuse to be controlled by your past habits and attitudes, your new nature is more and more able to control your thoughts and actions. The natural consequence of these wise choices is an obedient, holy life. Sometimes we think of holiness as a very pious, abnormal way of living. But being holy simply means that we have a fully integrated personality. God wants us to fully enjoy and delight in the life he has given us. Our time of ignorance has passed. We no longer have to conform to those former lusts and habits. We are ready for God's holiness to make us whole.

It's hard to break old habits, Lord, but it is encouraging to know if we sincerely desire to change, you will give us the energy that will lead to ultimate victory.

> *There is no fear in love; but perfect love casts out*
> *fear, because fear involves torment. But he who*
> *fears has not been made perfect in love.*
> —1 JOHN 4:18

A missionary couple brought Annie, a Nigerian girl, to live with them. The couple gradually accumulated enough money to send her to the United States to have a corrective spinal operation she so much needed in order to stand up straight.

Many of us have been bent double by the troubles of our past. Even though our condition is confining and painful, the thought of allowing the Great Physician to do the much needed surgery in our lives is still frightening. We are frightened by letting go of the status quo, as painful as it is. But this verse tells us how to become willing to allow God to straighten our bent-over lives into beautiful, strong ones. We simply rest in knowing how much the Lord Jesus loves us, and that the changes he desires for us will bring joy and peace and fulfillment to our lives. By resting in his wise love we receive the willingness we need for the surgery ahead and the assurance of positive results.

Dear God, when I go through the pains of life, may I always use you as my physician.

For God has not given us a spirit of fear, but of power and of love and of a sound mind.
—2 TIM. 1:7

In the 1960s people became aware of the masks we use as survival mechanisms. Catch phrases like "Be real" and "Tell it like it is" became part of the rallying cry of the hippie movement. And though that youth culture contained many unfavorable elements, this plea for openness and honesty deserves lasting emphasis. For many of us, however, the thought of facing another person and speaking honestly of hurts, regrets, bitterness, or hard feelings is frightening.

Perhaps these thoughts and feelings were similar for a young, sensitive pastor named Timothy. He was like a son to the apostle Paul. Paul reminds Timothy that instead of being fearful, he should release the three wonderful gifts which were his in the Lord. He had the strength of God to help him do what was right, the love of God to help him desire what was right, and the wisdom of God to help him know how to accomplish what was right.

As we consider what God is asking of us, this verse can be a great encouragement. Because of the Holy Spirit's power in our lives we are able to do what is right by forgiving and asking to be forgiven. In short, we have everything we need to take this important step toward a new openness with others and a deeper walk with God.

———

Lord, my desire is to take off the superficial masks I have been wearing so I can be honest and open with my fellowman.

> *Though I speak with the tongues of men and of angels, but have not love, I have become as sounding brass or a clanging cymbal. . . . And though I bestow all my goods to feed the poor, and though I give my body to be burned, but have not love, it profits me nothing.*
>
> —1 COR. 13:1, 3

The society we live in has a favorite message—if we are talented enough, intelligent enough, and believe in ourselves enough, then we can have whatever we want. We will be somebody important.

In the first two verses of 1 Corinthians 13, Paul completely dismantles this philosophy by telling the worldly-wise Corinthians that no matter how talented, smart, and determined we are, if we don't have real love—God's kind of love for others (and ourselves)—*we are nothing*. Then in verse 3 we find that Paul addressed the issue of codependency long before twentieth-century psychiatrists had given it a name. He zeros in on a personality which sacrifices itself completely and unsparingly for others and yet acts without love.

As we work to replace the bad feelings we've had about others and ourselves with feelings of true love and compassion, this powerful chapter can speak to us and move us toward the willing heart God wants us to have.

I realize, God, that my usefulness on this earth hinges on loving others your way. Thank you for the perfect example of love that was demonstrated by your son, Jesus.

*Judge not, and you shall not be judged. Condemn
not, and you shall not be condemned. Forgive, and
you will be forgiven. Give, and it will be given to
you: good measure, pressed down, shaken together,
and running over will be put into your bosom. For
with the same measure that you use, it will be
measured back to you.* —LUKE 6:37–38

A motivating and marvelous principle of the Christian life is that God takes great pleasure in meeting us more than halfway. As we become willing to make amends to others, and release them and ourselves from the bitterness we have carried, the Lord Jesus is there, eager to reward and encourage even our feeble attempts. When we ask the Lord to help us let go of judgment and condemnation, we will soon be aware of remarkable changes taking place within us. The Holy Spirit will begin a wonderful healing work in our lives. As we give our forgiveness and amends to others, the Lord will give back to us. When the late R. G. LeTourneau spoke of this wonderful verse, he liked to remind people that, yes, God gives in return to our giving, but God always uses a bigger shovel!

He was speaking of material wealth, but the principle remains the same. We can never outgive God. Each step of obedience and faith that we take will bring a bounty of spiritual blessings.

I thank you, Lord, that your shovel is a lot bigger than mine. May I be known as one who gives rather than one who takes away from others.

Behold, My Servant whom I have chosen, My
Beloved in whom My soul is well pleased; I will put
My Spirit upon Him, and He will declare justice to
the Gentiles. He will not quarrel nor cry out, nor
will anyone hear His voice in the streets. A bruised
reed He will not break, and smoking flax He will
not quench, till He sends forth justice to victory.
And in His name Gentiles will trust.

—MATT. 12:18–21

What a beautiful picture of the Lord Jesus' gentleness and power are these verses quoted from Isaiah. Jesus, the Beloved Servant and Son, was God in the flesh. His actions and life while he was on earth show us clearly God's character and concerns.

He was so compassionate toward the downtrodden and sinners that Isaiah describes him as careful not to break a battered reed. He would not extinguish a wick struggling to stay lit. But that gentleness was underscored by his great and awesome power. The very Savior who could speak kind and encouraging words to a woman caught in adultery could as easily raise the dead, drive out demons, and control the very forces of nature.

The power that resurrected Jesus from the dead to be our everliving Lord is the same power that he offers us to alter the course of our lives. It is ours when we become willing to reach out and accept his offer of love, forgiveness, and strength.

Lord Jesus, thank you for strength and power to overcome and heal hurts. You are all I need. Amen.

"Take heed to yourselves. If your brother sins against you, rebuke him; and if he repents, forgive him. And if he sins against you seven times in a day, and seven times in a day returns to you, saying, 'I repent,' you shall forgive him." And the apostles said to the Lord, "Increase our faith." So the Lord said, "If you have faith as a mustard seed, you can say to this mulberry tree, 'Be pulled up by the roots and be planted in the sea,' and it would obey you."

—LUKE 17:3–6

Jesus, the Great Physician, knew how dangerous the festering resentment of an unforgiving spirit is. To be sure, it is dangerous to the one against whom it is directed. But even more so, it is dangerous to the poor soul who continues to clutch the putrid baggage of resentment to his breast. This is why Jesus said, "Take heed to *yourselves*." Care about *yourself* enough to forgive your brother.

Many of us have scarred and troubled childhoods filled with disappointment and hurt. Letting go of that pain seems all but impossible to us. It must have seemed so to the disciples as well, because after Jesus' instruction concerning forgiveness, the first words out of their mouths were "Lord, increase our faith." But Jesus declares that just a little desire and faith can make an incredible difference.

Lord Jesus, I find myself unable to release my grip on these bags of resentment I have carried about for years. By your Holy Spirit's power, help me to release them and give to you all my hurts. Help me to truly forgive others as you have forgiven me.

> *I cried out to You, O LORD:*
> *I said, "You are my refuge,*
> *My portion in the land of the living.*
> *Attend to my cry,*
> *For I am brought very low;*
> *Deliver me from my persecutors,*
> *For they are stronger than I.*
> *Bring my soul out of prison,*
> *That I may praise Your name;*
> *The righteous shall surround me,*
> *For You shall deal bountifully with me."*
>
> —PS. 142:5–7

David was surrounded by his enemies. They were about to destroy him. He had taken refuge in a cave, but he knew the cave could not save him—the enemy was too strong. David looks to the Lord for safety and deliverance. He acknowledges that God alone can bring his "soul out of prison." When we struggle with addictive behaviors, we feel as if our soul is in prison. The chaos and confusion in our lives make us prisoners of guilt, fear, frustration, and pain. Our sanity is threatened by the inner forces controlling us.

David knew the cure for such a situation. David shifts his focus from his strong enemies to his stronger Lord. He rejoices in his true refuge and reveals his complete trust and faith in the Lord by declaring confidently, "You shall deal bountifully with me."

Dear Father, help me remember that even though the enemy of codependency is strong, you are infinitely stronger. You are my refuge and strength.

For He will deliver the needy when he cries,
The poor also, and him who has no helper.
He will spare the poor and needy,
And will save the souls of the needy.
> —PS. 72:12–13

There are four key words in these verses to help us understand how God wants us to respond to him.

First, we must see ourselves as *needy*. As long as we continue to pretend or assume that we are strong and able in ourselves, we cannot take even the first step toward physical, emotional, or spiritual healing. Deliverances will only come for those who acknowledge that they are *needy*.

Second, we will finally begin to see that deliverance *when* we cry to God. We may feel great frustration and anguish of soul, but God is waiting for us to actually cry out to him from the depths of our being.

Third, we won't be able to bring ourselves to this point of crying unto God until we become *poor* in spirit. When Jesus said, "Blessed are the poor in spirit for they shall see God" the word *poor* means *humble*. As long as we are too proud to admit our failures and powerlessness we cannot begin to see God work in our lives. When we begin to see the reality of our condition, we may naturally look to friends or relatives to help us escape. But when we come to grips with the fact that God alone is our source of healing, we are ready for true liberation.

Lord Jesus, I have been in bondage for so long. I am not able to release myself. Your power alone is sufficient to deliver me and give me true liberation.

> *And many who had believed came confessing and*
> *telling their deeds.*
> —ACTS 19:18

Almost as soon as a child can talk we discover that this precious bundle of energy and joy can also lie. My younger child is a born risk-taker. Because of this personality trait, we as parents found ourselves having to discipline him quite often. Sometimes it seemed it might be easier on all of us just to believe the little lie he had told to avoid discipline. And yet we all learned that once the truth was admitted, even if discipline had to follow, my little son felt cleansed and happy soon after.

This same principle held true for the believers at Ephesus; and it does in our own lives as well. When we come humbly confessing our sins and shortcomings to the Lord and others, we will be amazed at the cleansing and release that the Holy Spirit will give us. Even though it may seem easier to continue to deny or excuse our behavior, we will discover that the relief and cleansing of confession will bring new strength and power to our lives.

Dear Father, I admit my shortcomings and sins to You. Give me the humility to confess to others those things I need to. Thank you for the wonderful cleansing and release that confession brings.

> *O Lord, open my lips,*
> *And my mouth shall show forth Your praise.*
> *For You do not desire sacrifice, or else I*
> *   would give it;*
> *You do not delight in burnt offering.*
> *The sacrifices of God are a broken spirit,*
> *A broken and a contrite heart—*
> *These, O God, You will not despise.*
>
> —PS. 51:15–17

One important reason that David stayed in such close fellowship with God throughout his life was his willingness to be humble before God and others. Humility is an attitude that God has been building in us throughout our recovery program.

David uses the words "a broken and contrite heart" to describe what God values in a person. God finds this far more beautiful and useful than any religious rituals or acts of piety.

The words "broken and contrite" connote humility and commitment to changing an unacceptable attitude or behavior. In the same way that David asked God to help him to "open his lips" and bring praise to God, we should depend on God to bring a new power and grace to our lives as we seek to correct past wrongs and achieve healthy ways of relating to the people around us.

And as we determine to admit our faults and make proper amends for each situation, our words and actions will "sing aloud of the Lord's righteousness."

Lord, please whittle away at me until I am shaped into the personalized mold you have for me.

> *Blessed are the peacemakers, for they shall be*
> *called sons of God.*
> —MATT. 5:9

My dad used to tell me, "There are two ways of doing things—the easy way and the right way."

Most people do want peace in their lives, but many will never know the complete peace available to them because they aren't willing to be a true peacemaker. We may want to just put the past behind us or at least sweep it under the rug and get on with our lives. That is the easy way, the world's way of doing things. But we are the children of God. And one of the main ways that people will know we are the children of God is by seeing that we are peacemakers.

A true peacemaker stands out in a crowd. His attitude is so different from the world's that people are bound to notice.

We can have the courage and wisdom we need to be a true peacemaker because of Jesus' love working in us and through us. With our hearts full of God's love and peace, we can extend forgiveness and make appropriate amends where we need to. Then our lives will have a harmony and beauty which never seemed possible before, and the difference will make others very aware that we are "the children of God."

In my pursuit for peace, Lord, I pray for discernment and wisdom that only you can give.

> *But the mercy of the LORD is from everlasting*
>   *to everlasting*
> *On those who fear Him,*
> *And His righteousness to children's children,*
> *To such as keep His covenant,*
> *And to those who remember His*
>   *commandments to do them.*
>   —PS. 103:17–18

David had learned a precious truth. God's mercy is for those who *fear* Him. To fear God, however, does not mean to be frightened; instead it means to be *careful* to honor, obey and serve with humility.

Each day we must admit our shortcomings to God and ask him for strength to overcome our problems. As we are careful to maintain this honest and humble frame of mind, God responds to us with his priceless gift of mercy. He doesn't deal with us "according to our iniquities." Instead he pities us as a father pities his own child and remembers that we are fragile and weak.

And since God is merciful and gracious to us, we should be that way toward ourselves as well. No, we should never ignore or excuse our character defects. But we must remember not to condemn ourselves either. Each day is a chance for growing. If we fall, the Lord Jesus is there to pick us up, forgive us, and set us on the right track again. "His mercy is from everlasting to everlasting *on those who fear Him.*"

Lord, the more I immerse my mind in your Word, the more I understand and appreciate your mercy.

> *Watch and pray, lest you enter into temptation. The spirit truly is ready, but the flesh is weak.*
> —MARK 14:38

No matter how many years we've known Jesus as Savior and Lord, no matter how strong we are in our Christian walk, Jesus' words of warning to Peter, James, and John apply to us as well. Within us will always lie the capacity to manipulate, to become angry, to pity ourselves, or to become fearful and return to old patterns of behavior.

It is significant that in Mark 14:37 Jesus addresses Peter as Simon, which was his name before he became a disciple. Perhaps Jesus was trying to help Peter see how close he was to falling back into his old life-style. Soon after, Peter denied Christ.

When Jesus tells the disciples to "watch," he is exhorting them to be alert to the spiritual dangers around them. And by telling them to pray, he is reminding them to continually acknowledge their dependence upon God rather than themselves. Jesus knew their "spirits" (their inner desires and intentions) were willing and eager to follow him. But he also knew how easily they could be overwhelmed and defeated.

How we need to take Jesus' words to heart today, to daily watch—evaluating and staying alert to the spiritual dangers around us. How necessary to stay humble in prayer—acknowledging our dependence upon his strength and wisdom each day.

Lord, may I heed your admonition and never take for granted my spiritual standing with you. Grant me the insight needed to be aware of the spiritual dangers that surround me.

*For I say, through the grace given to me, to
everyone who is among you, not to think of himself
more highly than he ought to think, but to think
soberly, as God has dealt to each one a measure
of faith.*
—ROM. 12:3

Pride is a confusing word to many people because we
use it to mean so many different things. We may talk
about *civic pride* and by that mean a proper respect
and love for our community. Or we use the word *pride*
to mean arrogant conceit and self-love.

When Paul wrote, *"Don't* think of yourself more
highly than you ought to," he meant, "Don't get too
cocky. Don't think you've got all the answers." When
we've had success in turning our lives around, we may
start to believe we have accomplished all that we have
on our own. Paul warns against that attitude.

On the other hand, neither should we become hypercritical or overjudgmental when we make mistakes
or slip back into past patterns of behavior. Paul wants
us "to think soberly" which simply means to have
sound thinking about ourselves. Our daily and weekly
inventory is exactly what we need to keep us "thinking soberly." Have we had success in breaking old patterns? We should praise God and continue to
acknowledge our need of his help. Have we failed in
our attempt to handle a problem? We can admit our
error and ask God's help to correct the situation.

*I realize, Lord, that a balanced view of self is essential for a healthy,
productive life. May I never lose sight of this fact.*

> *Therefore we must give the more earnest heed to*
> *the things we have heard, lest we drift away. For if*
> *the word spoken through angels proved steadfast,*
> *and every transgression and disobedience received*
> *a just reward, how shall we escape if we neglect so*
> *great a salvation?*
> —HEB. 2:1-3

The children were enjoying the sunshine of a warm summer day. They had rowed carefully to the side of the lake farthest away from the power plant restricted area. They swam and played in the water quite a while before climbing into the boat, resting, and enjoying the gentle breeze. But their enjoyment turned to fear and dismay. The current had inch by inch carried them deep into forbidden territory. Fortunately rescued by a stern but caring patrolman, they learned a valuable lesson: "Give heed, lest you drift away."

This is a lesson we will all do well to remind ourselves of daily. Anyone can be enjoying the sunshine and gentle breezes of new assurance and progress in life so much that he or she may drift quite unknowingly to the brink of disaster.

The key word in the passage read today is *neglect*. Sometimes we may feel we have progressed to the point where the program is not really so important to us any more. And we can neglect it. This is dangerously like drifting toward the sinister power plant of our old character defects. By daily analyzing and monitoring our spiritual progress, we will be sure to give earnest heed, not neglecting our Great Salvation.

Dear Lord, help me not to drift away from you.

And I thank Christ Jesus our Lord who has enabled me, because He counted me faithful, putting me into the ministry, although I was formerly a blasphemer, a persecutor, and an insolent man; but I obtained mercy because I did it ignorantly in unbelief. And the grace of our Lord was exceedingly abundant, with faith and love which are in Christ Jesus. This is a faithful saying and worthy of all acceptance, that Christ Jesus came into the world to save sinners, of whom I am chief. However, for this reason I obtained mercy, that in me first Jesus Christ might show all longsuffering, as a pattern to those who are going to believe on Him for everlasting life. —1 TIM. 1:12–16

The apostle Paul never tried to hide his past. It wasn't that he was proud of the things he had done before Jesus changed his life. But in sharing his former life as a "blasphemer and a persecutor and a violent oppressor," Paul was able to more clearly show others just how merciful and gracious and patient God was.

Paul's attitude is a good one for each of us to emulate. God wants to use our triumphs over our past to glorify himself. Far too many people are struggling through life because they believe they aren't good enough for God to love or save. Sharing what we have learned—that "Christ Jesus came into the world to save sinners"—may be the key that opens the door of God's love to a struggling friend.

Help me, Lord, to learn from the negatives I have encountered in life. May I not allow these "tapes" to be repeated.

She opens her mouth with wisdom,
And on her tongue is the law of
*   kindness.*
She watches over the ways of her
*   household,*
And does not eat the bread of idleness.
Her children rise up and call her blessed.
    —PROV. 31:26–28

One of the greatest joys, and yet challenges, of being a wife and mother is in knowing the incredible influence our life has on our family. That influence is felt in three important ways—our words, our actions, and our attitudes. We can, daily with God's help, be the embodiment of this ideal given to us in Proverbs 31.

Our words can be filled with the wisdom and kindness because we are daily meditating on God's Word and seeking him in prayer. Just as Jesus told the disciples that "out of the abundance of the heart the mouth speaks" so we will discover that His love and wisdom will be evident in our words to our family.

Our actions can bring honor to the Lord and security to those close to us. Day by day we can have both the inclination and the ability to do what needs to be done to keep our household functioning smoothly.

But the most important influence on our family will be our attitude. This is because attitudes are caught, not taught.

Lord, help me to demonstrate wisdom and kindness to those I meet today. May I never forget the fact that how I act talks as loud as what I say.

So God created man in His own image; in the image of God He created him; male and female He created them.

—GEN. 1:27

Understanding who you are is one of the key concepts in overcoming codependent relationships. When you can accept yourself and like yourself based on a biblical understanding of being created in God's image, you reduce the need to develop unhealthy relationships with other people.

Because we are created in God's image, we do not have the ability within ourselves to meet all of our needs. Part of our need is to have a personal relationship with Jesus Christ. In accepting Christ as the person who died for our sins, we can come into a personal relationship with God and have an eternal life with him in heaven. As we develop this personal relationship with Jesus Christ, we can understand our needs and that they can be met through him. His grace and his sufficiency is enough. We do not have to have those needs met through other people.

As we turn our lives and our wills over to him, we can begin breaking away from unhealthy patterns of dependency and look to God to help us restore healthy human relationships. We must not rely on others solely to define who we are. We must look at who we are based on the fact that we've been created in God's image; we need to define ourselves within his definition of who we are.

Lord, I can only be healthy when I see myself according to your Word. Give me your viewpoint of my image.

As the Father loved Me, I also have loved you; abide in My love.
                                                    —JOHN 15:9

Many times the foundation for unhealthy codependent relationships comes from not feeling loved. Many people who do not understand this longing to be loved and accepted develop unhealthy patterns of relating, attempting to attain that love from those around them. When the continual efforts to obtain this love from others is not fulfilled, a person experiences frustration, anger, and loneliness.

In order to obtain a healthy sense of who we are, we must first understand that we are loved and accepted by Jesus Christ. Jesus loves us with the same amount of love as his father loved him. He encourages us to remain in that love. By remaining in Christ's love, we can find the strength and the hope to continue in the daily pain and trials of life. Through that hope that we have in the love of Christ, we can learn to develop healthy boundaries and relational patterns with those around us.

May I realize that Christ's love for me frees me to develop healthy patterns of relating to others.

For You have formed my inward parts;
You have covered me in my mother's womb.
I will praise You,
For I am fearfully and wonderfully made;
Marvelous are Your works;
And that my soul knows very well.

—PS. 139:13–14

Who we are is not based on how our family treated us. In dysfunctional families we often develop a view of who we are based on how we perceived we were treated and viewed by that family. This sets up an unhealthy way to look at ourselves.

This verse reminds us that we were specially and uniquely created by God himself. The psalmist David proclaims that we are fearfully and wonderfully made and that God's works are wonderful. If we understand this, we can work toward a balanced view of who we are, based on the reality of what Scripture tells us.

As we accept that we are made by a God who loves us, we can begin to establish healthy ways of relating to those around us.

How special I am to you, O God. Strengthen me in establishing healthy relationships with others.

> *Trust in the Lord with all your heart,*
> *And lean not on your own understanding;*
> *In all your ways acknowledge Him,*
> *And He shall direct your paths.*
> —PROV. 3:5–6

Often as you struggle through codependency issues you will experience confusion, fear, anxiety, and uncertainty. Trust is hard, yet trust is required of us.

This verse does not mean that everything is going to work out perfectly. At times God will give you understanding and help in accepting the situation as it is. Sometimes all we have to rely on is trust in the Lord. If we try to lean on our own understanding, the situation becomes worse. Sometimes it takes faith to say, "God, I don't understand it. I don't like what is happening. But I do want to trust in you and not lean on my own understanding."

_____

God, in acknowledging you, my understanding doesn't have to make sense.

And He said, "Do not lay your hand on the lad, or do anything to him; for now I know that you fear God, since you have not withheld your son, your only son from Me."

—GEN. 22:12

Abraham was faced with giving up the very thing that he loved and wanted the most—his son Isaac. Sometimes as we deal with codependent issues, we feel so attached to our significant other. Through our healing process God tests us, as he tested Abraham, to see what is more important.

Is it God, or is it our relationship with our significant other that has priority in our life? Sometimes God calls us to test that relationship, that thing that we are dependent on and lay it on the altar. Are we willing to give it up? Do we trust God to be everything for us? Letting go of our addiction hurts. Yet, as we see in this test of Abraham, that as we give up those things, God will bless us. God doesn't want us to have unhealthy relationships.

God, you want what's best for me, even if it means painfully removing something that I hold dear. May I be willing to trust.

> *Be anxious for nothing, but in everything by prayer*
> *and supplication, with thanksgiving, let your*
> *requests be made known to God; and the peace of*
> *God, which surpasses all understanding, will guard*
> *your hearts and minds through Christ Jesus.*
> —PHIL. 4:6–7

So often people struggling with codependent issues become panicky and desperate. Only God can give them a sense of peace, of calmness, so important as you deal with these issues. The struggle to separate significant relationships is painful. Restoring your own life and rebuilding your relationships provokes a lot of opportunity for anxiety. Giving up that addiction to that person is going to be hard. If you trust God, then your hopes for recovery are far greater.

God, your peace can transcend all anxiety in my recovery process.

Turn Yourself to me, and have mercy on me,
For I am desolate and afflicted.
The troubles of my heart have enlarged;
Oh, bring me out of my distresses!
—PS. 25:16–17

As the psalmist David discovered the reality of pain in his life, he turned to God and shared his loneliness and affliction. We too cry out because we feel lonely, we feel afflicted, our heart's troubles have been multiplied. We ask God to free us from the anguish, but nothing in this world can completely and appropriately deaden the pain of needing a Savior.

We look to other people to take away the pain or the loneliness that can only be taken away by relationship with Christ. If you haven't experienced a personal relationship with Jesus Christ, I encourage you to consider your heart. Having your needs met through Christ is important in identifying why you have developed such unhealthy codependent relationships. Relationship with God, crying out to him, is important to understanding the loneliness and anguish in your heart.

God, you are the only relief for the pain in my empty God-shaped vacuum.

> *Now therefore, thus says the LORD of hosts:*
> *"Consider your ways! You have sown much, and*
> *bring in little; You eat, but do not have enough;*
> *You drink, but you are not filled with drink; You*
> *clothe yourselves, but no one is warm; and he who*
> *earns wages, Earns wages to put into a bag with*
> *holes. . . . You looked for much, but indeed it came*
> *to little; and when you brought it home, I blew it*
> *away. Why?" says the LORD of hosts. "Because of*
> *My house that is in ruins, while every one of you*
> *runs to his own house."*
> —HAG. 1:5–6, 9

A codependent person is consumed with meeting his or her own needs. That person may not appear to be self-indulgent. In fact, his or her thoughts are usually centered around the needs and concerns of others in his or her world. Still, it is indulgent to look to people to meet the needs that only God can fill.

When we do this, we not only deny ourselves healthy relationships, but we deny God proper respect and dependence. When we act in codependent ways, we are making people our God and worshiping them.

In order to develop and sustain healthy relationships, we must give up our obsessions to meet our needs in our own ways. We must look to God to direct us. He is that power greater than ourselves who can restore our sanity. All our efforts will be in vain if we don't trust God first to meet our needs.

If I focus on you, O God, I am free to love others in healthy ways.

There is a way which seems right to a man,
But its end is the way of death.

—PROV. 14:12

We like to think we know what is right in our relationships. However, often we are blinded by an unhealthy dependence that motivates our style of relating. We need to recognize that there is a power greater than ourselves that can restore us to sanity and that on our own we are unable to do this.

Ultimately, we destroy ourselves in following our foolish paths to what we feel is a "right" relationship. God alone is the author of relationship, and he alone can show us how to live.

Our own wisdom has driven us to codependent relationships and has lead to self-destructive behaviors. God knows we need relationships. He also knows how we can get off track in our relationships in unhealthy ways. This is why we need his wisdom and not our own.

God, your way can lead me to fulfilling relationships.

A man of great wrath will suffer punishment;
For if you deliver him, you will have to do it again.
—PROV. 19:19

We codependents often find ourselves rescuing others from their pain, fears, and inadequacy. When we remove what could be a logical consequence of their actions, inevitably we set ourselves up to rescue again and again. We develop what is called an enabling role, enabling people to continue in wrong patterns. This is wrong. We need to admit to God, to ourselves, and to the other person the exact nature of our wrong. Keeping another person functional in order to feel secure ourselves is wrong. It is wrong to rescue people, in unhealthy ways, from the natural and logical consequences of their actions.

Lord, help me to see that rescuing is often not a one-time event, but develops into a pattern of enabling that person to avoid the consequences of his actions.

Through wisdom a house is built,
And by understanding it is
*   established;*
By knowledge the rooms are filled
With all precious and pleasant riches.
        —PROV. 24:3–4

Building healthy relationships takes wisdom and understanding. Healthy relationships develop between individuals who have healthy self-esteem. Healthy self-esteem comes from understanding who we are in God's eyes.

Still, relationships just don't happen. We don't naturally know how to create and sustain healthy relationships. Relationships must be developed and require work. The basic elements of trust, love, mutual respect, communication, giving and receiving—all in appropriate ways are characteristics of healthy relationships. We can learn much about each of these essential characteristics by studying how God relates to us and how he relates to Jesus. He epitomizes healthy relationships.

God, your wisdom and understanding should be my pattern in developing healthy relationships.

The LORD is near to those who have a broken heart,
And saves such as have a contrite spirit.

—PS. 34:18

As we are dealing with the pain our codependency has caused and as we admit our unhealthy addictions, we can find comfort in this psalm. God really is close to us.

During our struggle to face the pain of not being able to have our needs met in unhealthy ways, we are not alone. We can rest assured that the Lord is close to us. When we break off unhealthy relationships, we will feel extraordinary pain and brokenheartedness. When the unhealthy addiction or relationship is no longer an option, we can find comfort and strength in the Lord.

God, you are truly there for me in the midst of my worst pain.

Lord, all my desire is before You;
And my sighing is not hidden from You. . . .
My loved ones and my friends stand aloof from
    my plague,
And my kinsmen stand afar off.

—PS. 38:9, 11

We hit bottom. We reach a point where all we have left is to place ourselves before God. He sees us fully. Our friends avoid us and ignore our pain. They run because they are uncomfortable around us. They are not sure how to help. They also want to avoid facing any pain in their own life.

As you are going through recovery, you will feel lonely and rejected at times. You will have a deep longing for a relationship, but no one is there. At these times your heart is laid wide open to God. As C. S. Lewis once said, "God whispers to us in our joy and shouts to us in our pain."

May I take advantage of the pain in my life to discover what lessons you have for me.

God is our refuge and strength,
A very present help in trouble.
Therefore we will not fear.
—PS. 46:1–2

I love rapelling down mountains (as long as they aren't too high). It's fun to bounce freely down a long mountain secure within two ropes. The hardest part, though, is jumping off the cliff. Even though I know my guides have secured my ropes, I still harbor concern as I stand at the edge.

We often feel the same way while working through the recovery process. Sometimes we find ourselves in periods of trouble, loneliness, and desperation. These stir up worry and fear inside us. Our first thought is to rely on our old codependent ways to get rid of these feelings. It is in these times that we need to rely on God.

When I am rappelling, I don't really want to stand at the edge of that cliff for the rest of my life. Neither do you want to live the rest of your life in your codependency. As I relied on the ropes to hold me; in recovery we must rely on God to hold us.

God really is a refuge. As we try to break that unhealthy pattern God's strength will see us through. We must recognize that there is someone to run to, someone who isn't part of our unhealthy codependency routine. He is there for us, and we need not fear.

_____

God, your strength is a necessary element in working through the recovery process.

Have mercy upon me, O God,
According to Your lovingkindness;
According to the multitude of Your tender mercies,
Blot out my transgressions.
Wash me thoroughly from my iniquity,
And cleanse me from my sin.
For I acknowledge my transgressions,
And my sin is ever before me.   —PS. 51:1–3

An important aspect of recovery is admitting to God that we are unable to deal with our addictions or the wrongs we have committed against others. We've been running from ourselves. We don't want to see how bad off we really are nor how much we have hurt others. We believe that if we just don't admit it, it won't be true. That kind of thinking won't get us anywhere. Let's be honest.

The wonder of this step is God's response to us. God's love is unfailing. He can and will blot out our transgressions, wash away our iniquities, and cleanse us from our sin. Real healing takes place through the confession of our soul.

Admitting to ourselves, to God, and to others that we have failed has a powerfully cleansing effect. God wants us to be humble and ask him to remove our sins and our transgressions. This humility frees him to work in and through our lives.

God, your unfailing love invites me to be honest about my short-comings.

> *Create in me a clean heart, O God,*
> *And renew a steadfast spirit within me.*
> *Do not cast me away from Your presence,*
> *And do not take Your Holy Spirit from me.*
> *Restore to me the joy of Your salvation,*
> *And uphold me with Your generous Spirit.*
> *Then, I will teach transgressors Your ways,*
> *And sinners shall be converted to You.*
> —PS. 51:10–13

What makes a good teacher? A good teacher must have previous knowledge of the topic. In this verse David is a good teacher because he has personally responded to the topic he will teach others. In your life, it is important for you to share what you have been learning with others.

Taking what we have learned and sharing it with others is an important aspect of recovery. Healing must be done first in our own lives before we can teach others. But we can share what we have learned so far with those God brings into our lives. However, with our pattern of codependent behavior we need to be careful not to be premature and, as a result, end up back in addictive, unhealthy relationships. We need to remind ourselves not to venture out until we are at a stable point in our own lives, or we can go back down the road to unhealthiness.

Steps taken toward helping others must come after I take personal steps to help myself.

*And He said to me, "My grace is sufficient for you,
for My strength is made perfect in weakness."
Therefore most gladly I will rather boast in my
infirmities, that the power of Christ may rest
upon me.*
                                                    —2 COR. 12:9

When athletes begin to train for major events, they must first admit their weakness. Though they may appear on television and proclaim their strength and their abilities to overcome the opponent, privately they address their own weaknesses. Then, they choose a training method that will strengthen their weaknesses. If they had not addressed their weaknesses, they would be still weak when they faced their opponent.

Weakness is not all bad. In fact, weakness often brings us to the point of recognizing our unhealthy behavior. It was probably at a place of weakness that we admitted we had a problem and began the recovery process. When we admit our weaknesses, God's power can restore us to sanity. Without the first step of humbling ourselves and admitting our need for help, growth and progress cannot take place.

Humbling myself to a point of admitting my weakness is a first step in allowing you, God, to make the necessary changes in my life.

> *What is man that you are mindful of him,*
> *And the son of man, that You visit him?*
> *For You have made him a little lower than the angels,*
> *And You have crowned him with glory and honor.*
> —PS. 8:4–5

We live in a society that glorifies its stars. Athletes, politicians, actors, receive numerous gestures of praise from fans. These include applause, letters, special gifts. Have you ever wished that you could change places with one of them to receive the glory and praise? You are glorified too, and not just by people, but by the very God of the universe.

We are crowned with glory and honor by the very God who created us. Imagine all the fanfare and pageantry that the greatest human might receive and this does not even compare to the reality of being glorified by God.

We need to affirm our value. Seeing our worth to God is an important aspect of breaking codependency. As we begin to feel good about ourselves based on who we are to God, we don't need others to tell us we are valuable.

I want to live a life free of unhealthy codependent relationships. Show me that I can, Lord.

Confess your trespasses to one another, and pray for one another, that you may be healed. The effective fervent prayer of a righteous man avails much.

—JAMES 5:16

Many people carry around an invisible bag of guilt. It tortures them every day. It is full of hundreds of issues that the person feels guilty about. The carrier doesn't know what else to do about them, so they stay right there behind him weighing him down.

It is hard to recognize our wrongs. It is hard to see that our unhealthy dependence on another human being for self-esteem is wrong, along with the many other issues stuffed inside our bag. In recovery, we must open up this bag and display the issues before ourselves, others, and God.

This openness to God, ourselves, and others is a necessary aspect of our reconciliation with God. By confessing we realize the sovereignty of God. We see that he is in control and that our trust and faith needs to rest in God. We realize that he has devised a way for us to resolve our guilt.

Let me discover that confession is a cleansing action which restores a right relationship with you.

> *For I am persuaded that neither death nor life, nor*
> *angels nor principalities nor powers, nor things*
> *present nor things to come, nor height nor depth,*
> *nor any other created thing, shall be able to*
> *separate us from the love of God which is in Christ*
> *Jesus our Lord.*
> —ROM. 8:38–39

As we look at self-esteem issues in working through unhealthy dependency with others, we need to understand and accept God's love. People who grow up in unhealthy homes where they aren't loved or shown love develop a warped view of who they are. They develop a sense that they are unimportant, that they don't count, or that they are no good.

If we stop and evaluate who we are in light of God's love for us, we can develop a healthy sense of self-worth. God's love can heal the wounds created by not being loved in the ways we needed. As a result of believing in God's love, chances that we will use people in unhealthy ways are reduced. We will avoid developing painful codependent relationships.

We have lived in fear and desperation of not having love. Here love is promised with no chance of loosing it.

———————

Understanding the depth of God's love for me protects me from developing unhealthy relationships.

For as he thinks in his heart, so is he.
"Eat and drink!" he says to you,
But his heart is not with you.
　　　　　　　　　　—PROV. 23:7

As we go through the recovery process we must take an inventory. We need to look at who we really are and what our faults are. Growing up in a dysfunctional home, a person can develop beliefs about himself which are inaccurate. Still these beliefs play a major role in affecting who we are and how we relate to the world. If I believe I am inadequate and insecure and in need of someone else's approval in order to feel good, I'm going to open myself to develop unhealthy relationships with others.

As I develop an understanding of what is inside of me in my thinking and who I am, I can understand more of why I act the way I do. And as I begin to change that thinking, then I begin to change who I am. And if I begin to believe that, I am healthy. When I realize that, I'm acceptable and I do not need others' acceptance and approval in order to be okay. Then I can break free of the chains that bind me to unhealthy codependent relationships.

Wrong beliefs about who I am can affect my relating to others in healthy ways. Proper understanding of who I am leads to healthy ways of relating to others.

> *And do not be conformed to this world, but be transformed by the renewing of your mind, that you may prove what is that good and acceptable and perfect will of God.*
> —ROM. 12:2

Have you ever been in a carnival or fair and entered the House of Mirrors? When you look into any one of the mirrors you see a distorted vision of yourself looking back. Though they resemble you in many ways, they are distorted versions of yourself.

This happens throughout life by the messages we receive about ourselves. We begin to believe we are not lovable. This verse tells us how to get away from those distorted beliefs. It is easy to leave the House of Mirrors and look into a normal mirror and see what you really look like. It is harder to change our beliefs about ourselves.

This verse tells us to be transformed by renewing of our minds. We are renewed as we understand God, as we understand who we are in Christ Jesus, and that our worth and our sense of who we are is not based on what we do. When our worth is based on God's love for us, we can break free of those chains that bind us to unhealthy relationships. We are no longer bound to those people whose acceptance we once needed. We are free to love and to give, not for their acceptance, but because we already are accepted. What a freeing experience this can be!

Transforming my mind from the false beliefs gives me a strength and power to move into people's lives in healthy ways.

Therefore do not worry, saying, "What shall we eat?" or "What shall we drink?" or "What shall we wear?" For after all these things the Gentiles seek. For your heavenly Father knows that you need all these things. But seek first the kingdom of God and His righteousness, and all these things shall be added to you. Therefore do not worry about tomorrow, for tomorrow will worry about its own things. Sufficient for the day is its own trouble.
—MATT. 6:31–34

So many of us don't really know what to do about worry. In our American system someone found a way to capitalize on this problem. Do you remember when the worry rock hit the scene? It was a commercial success. Did it really help? For some it may have just because it diverted their attention, or made them laugh at their worrying. For others it probably made their fingers raw and did nothing for the fears and worry inside.

Codependents struggle with worries about things that cannot change. Instead of attempting to change them, we should trust in God because he knows our needs. If we seek him first, all the things that concern us will be worked out.

God is our antidote for worry. When we can learn that he is on our side, that he really cares about the things that concern us, we won't worry. God is our ultimate worry rock. With him, we have no need to worry.

I really don't need to worry, God, because you are greater than any of my problems. Help me remember this today.

> *This is a faithful saying and worthy of all*
> *acceptance, that Christ Jesus came into the world*
> *to save sinners, of whom I am chief. However, for*
> *this reason I obtained mercy, that in me first Jesus*
> *Christ might show all longsuffering, as a pattern*
> *to those who are going to believe on Him for*
> *everlasting life. Now to the King eternal, immortal,*
> *invisible, to God who alone is wise, be honor and*
> *glory forever and ever. Amen.*
>
> —1 TIM. 1:15–17

In these verses we see Paul confessing the inventory of his life. He states the fact that he had been the worst of sinners. But at the same time Paul recognizes Jesus' display of patience and love for him. He gives glory to God because of this awareness.

Recovery includes taking inventory. This means that we have to admit things about ourselves we do not like. But we must become brutally honest if we are going to heal. Paul is an example of what happens if we will do this. He was able to confess who he really was. This brought him to a place of greater joy as he realized that God loved him even with all his faults.

God, accept me even in my worst condition.

Now faith is the substance of things hoped for, the evidence of things not seen. —HEB. 11:1

A parachutist has faith. He has faith in a tiny string that hangs off the side of his backpack. When he jumps from an airplane he has faith that when he pulls that string, a huge parachute will open and guide him safely to the ground.

So often in the midst of pain and even recovery we are unable to see the overall picture. We feel uncertain about the advice we have been given. We are unsure that letting go of that unhealthy dependence really is the right thing to do. We are scared and confused, and fearful for our very existence.

It takes faith to recover. We cannot always see what is going to happen. But as we put our faith in God and as we work to deal with our unhealthy relationships, we can break the addictive cycle. We can learn what it is to have healthy relationships with those around us.

Faith is essential to the recovery process, Lord. Without it I will never let go and let you take control of my life.

> *Honor your father and your mother, that your days*
> *may be long upon the land which the LORD your*
> *God is giving you.*
> — EX. 20:12

Many codependents, having grown up in dysfunctional families harbour anger, bitterness, and resentment toward parents for their inability to love completely. Some people may have suffered physical, emotional, or even sexual abuse from their parents, and the anger, resentment, and bitterness is logical in these circumstances.

However, this verse commands that we honor our fathers and mothers and this commandment is one with a promise. God promises us long, healthy, enjoyable life on the earth when we honor our parents.

The first step in truly honoring parents is to face the rage and bitterness in our hearts toward them. Then we move to forgiving them and to deciding how we can best honor them. For some, parents might be dead, or unwilling to work on the strained relationship. The path toward honoring parents will be different for different people, but needs to be addressed in our recovery process.

Lord, help me resolve bitterness and anger toward my parents as an essential part to the recovery process.

*You will keep him in perfect
   peace,
Whose mind is stayed on You,
   because he trusts in You.
Trust in the Lord forever,
For in YAH, the LORD, Jehovah
   is everlasting strength.*
                    —ISA. 26:3–4

One day Jesus took his twelve disciples out on a boat. He was tired and fell asleep. Suddenly a storm raged tossing the little boat and threatening shipwreck. During this time Jesus didn't stir, so the disciples woke him in fear. Jesus simply told the wind and the waves to stop and in an instant they were perfectly still. Jesus purposely went out on the boat that day to demonstrate that he can bring peace during the storm. This was an important lesson for them to learn as their future included many storms.

Our path to recovery is not without storms. But, in spite of the storms we can have peace. God is our peace. He alone is everlasting; he will always be with us. If we put our trust and our dependency in humans, they can leave or die or abandon us. God will not do any of these to us. He will be with us forever, even when we may abandon him. God can bring you peace.

I will trust in you, the everlasting rock, to be my peace.

> *Therefore whoever hears these sayings of Mine, and does them, I will liken him to a wise man who built his house on the rock: And the rain descended, the floods came, and the winds blew and beat on that house; and it did not fall, for it was founded on the rock. Now everyone who hears these sayings of Mine, and does not do them, will be like a foolish man who built his house on the sand: And the rain descended, the floods came, and the winds blew and beat on that house; and it fell. And great was its fall.*
>
> —MATT. 7:24–27

The great California earthquake during the 1989 World Series is a vivid reminder of the need for a firm foundation. Many of those who lost homes had hoped they were built on firm foundations.

The basis for a healthy self-esteem depends upon the foundation. If we build our foundation on God, the solid rock, when times of stress and storm come, we will not be destroyed. But if our foundation is built on wrong things, like the man who built his house on the sand, the rains will come and the house will fall.

So often we base our foundation on what other people think of us. Codependency is needing someone else's approval in order to accept who we are. This is an illustration of building our house on sand. Building our house on the rock means allowing God to be our foundation. Stress, difficulties, other problems in life cannot take away our value and worth.

Building my life on the solid foundation of Christ gives me the power I need to overcome the storms of life.

Blessed is the man who trusts in the LORD, and whose hope is the LORD.
                                    —JER. 17:7

A sure way to develop unhealthy relationships is to trust in other people's reactions to us for a sense of who we are. As codependents, we establish trust in other human beings to define ourselves. If we look to others to give us that definition, we will constantly need to be working for their love and acceptance.

We have learned to trust in other people, now we need to learn to trust in God. If we trust in him, we won't be let down. We are blessed if we trust in the Lord.

We need to trust God for many things in the recovery process. We need to trust him for a sense of our self-esteem. We need to trust that he will see us through any pain our issues might cause. We need to trust that he will show us how to stop any pain we have created for others. Recovery is a process of trust. We will always have a problem with trust if we are trusting in the wrong person.

―――――――――――

I trust in you for a sense of acceptance; I will not depend upon another's approval.

> *Then He said to His disciples, "The harvest truly is*
> *plentiful, but the laborers are few. Therefore pray*
> *the Lord of the harvest to send out laborers into His*
> *harvest."*
> —MATT. 9:37–38

When you find a product that works for you, do you keep it a secret? Do you share your good news with your friends who might need the product? Sometimes you are met with disinterest, but many times it is well received.

People need to know about Jesus. People need to know about recovery. We need to share what we have learned with others. Share that Christ can be the missing link in their healing and that they can find hope through the recovery process. We need to share how building a foundation with Jesus Christ has enhanced our recovery. When you have gained an understanding and have worked through painful issues and have grown, sharing with others further enhances your own growth. It also helps other people get out of bondage and on the road to recovery.

When I share about a personal recovery process, I provide hope for those who are hurting.

> *Immediately Jesus made His disciples get into the boat and go before Him to the other side, while He sent the multitudes away. And when He had sent the multitudes away, He went up on a mountain by Himself to pray. And when evening had come, He was alone there.*
>
> —MATT. 14:22–23

Christ was able to set appropriate boundaries for his physical, mental, emotional, and spiritual health. He had been busy ministering to the multitudes words and favors of healing. He sent the disciples and the multitudes away and then he went up alone on the mountain to pray.

We need to get alone to pray for strength and renewal. Setting these healthy boundaries for ourselves enables us to live a more productive and healthy life. Christ could have ministered and healed people twenty-four hours a day and still not met all the needs. His purpose wasn't to meet physical needs perfectly on earth. His purpose was to give eternal spiritual healing which comes from accepting him as Savior. We need to realize our limitations. We cannot meet every person's needs. If we did, perhaps people wouldn't realize their need for a Savior.

We all have a need to have a time for refreshment. Part of the refreshment is being alone and getting away from others.

Time alone is essential to evaluate our relationships with others.

> *Therefore, if anyone is in Christ, he is a new*
> *creation; old things have passed away; behold,*
> *all things have become new.* —2 COR. 5:17

Caterpillars to butterflies; it is a remarkable process. A furry little worm becomes a beautiful butterfly. It can soar in places that a worm could never go. This is what happens to us when we become new through the process of recovery.

We need to be ready to have God remove all the defects of our character. This is done by asking Christ to come into our lives, acknowledging his death on the cross for our sins, and asking him to make us a new creature.

If we accept Christ then we can become a new creature. The old things about us have passed away and all things are new. This is the step that is missing for many people as they struggle to overcome dependency issues. They have never accepted Christ and become, as the Bible talks about, a new creature. As a new creature we have the resources needed in overcoming unhealthy relationships.

———————

Christ can be the new start I need to overcome unhealthy dependencies.

*And whenever you stand praying, if you have
anything against anyone, forgive him, that your
Father in heaven may also forgive your trespasses.*
                                    —MARK 11:25

One of the key elements in working through significant underlying issues which tie into our developing
unhealthy relationships is the issue of forgiveness.
Many times people experienced abuse in the homes
they grew up in. Many times they experienced cruelty
beyond belief.

In order to live a healthy life, we must be willing to
forgive those who have hurt us just as God has forgiven
us. The abuse and damage from the past will continue
to plague us in the future unless we relinquish its reign
over us. This involves being willing to relinquish certain rights.

Choose not to demand my rights for the hurt that I
have suffered. Step outside the world of logic and into a
world of mercy. To give up our rights is a sacrifice
which frees us of the damage that hatred and bitterness can do to our lives. It seems illogical, but its healing powers are amazing.

Forgiveness is a key element in resolving underlying hurts.

The Pathway to Recovery for Codependency

At the Minirth-Meier Clinic, our approach to recovery focuses on addressing an individual's hunger for love, his or her life history, and the codependent traits which need to be reprogrammed. The following devotionals use the ten-stage treatment program (as presented in the book *Love Is a Choice*) as their focus. The seven devotionals for each stage of recovery should not imply that a person should be able to work through these stages in ten weeks.

Growth and recovery from codependency is different for each individual. For some the stages will take years to completely work through. A stage could take either months or minutes to work through, depending on the individual. The stages do provide a step-by-step process for changing behavior patterns.

Sometimes the healing process which codependents experience can be likened to a roller coaster ride. When a person becomes ready to start the recovery process, usually he isn't at the top of the roller coaster (free of pain), but at a point fairly far down.

As recovery progresses, things don't suddenly get better. The first five stages of recovery go deeper into pain. But this steep drop provides the impetus for the uphill healing. There will be other drops and hills in the future, but none as tough as the initial "plunge."

Where can I go from Your spirit?
Or where can I flee from Your presence?
If I ascend into heaven, You are there;
If I make my bed in hell, behold, You are there.
If I take the wings of the morning,
And dwell in the uttermost parts of the sea,
Even there Your hand shall lead me,
And Your right hand shall hold me.

—PS. 139:7–10

You've been invited on a journey. The journey will take you to a place you've never been before. Others have described it to you as the most worthwhile adventure they have ever taken. But no one has pictures or brochures so you can see for yourself before you go. You've also been warned that the adventure requires endurance. Though the journey is freeing, it takes courage and determination to complete it and reach the inner peace waiting on the other side.

The journey is the pathway to recovery from codependency. The first stage of this journey requires the most courage of all—the courage to relive and acknowledge the pain from the past. But you will not be alone in your pain. God is right along side of you, weeping for you, hoping for you, loving you, no matter what you think of him.

God will not let you go alone. Though you foolishly believe that he might abandon you too, you are wrong. There's nowhere to go from his presence.

God, help me to believe that my past can be restored, that there's healing for those secret wounds.

> *Brethren, I do not count myself to have*
> *apprehended; but one thing I do, forgetting those*
> *things which are behind and reaching forward to*
> *those things which are ahead.* —PHIL. 3:13

I'm so tired of hearing about codependency and dysfunctional families. If I let myself, I could come up with a lot worse childhood stories than they show on TV." Those are the words of Janice. She began forgetting, conceivably as early as age two, the beatings, the tantrums, the horror that was a daily experience for her.

In reality Janice did not forget those scenes. They haunted her adult behavior. She was a workaholic married to an alcoholic. She was trying to rescue her family of origin by creating chaos in her own family.

Forgetting means erasing the pain from the memories. It involves recognizing the severity of the damage. Too many people, like Janice, want to erect new walls around an old crumbled structure. They appear to have forgotten on the outside, but inside they are a crumbled mess.

To forget, you must acknowledge the pain from the past and identify the ways your past has taught you lies about yourself—"You're not good enough, you're not worth anything, you will never amount to much." God says, "You are loved, you are wanted, you are special." There's only bondage in Janice's kind of forgetting. Hers isn't forgetting; it's repressing. Forget and reach, there is a better way to live.

God is always within reach of my heart.

> *So when they continued asking Him, He raised*
> *Himself up and said to them, "He who is without*
> *sin among you, let him throw a stone at her first."*
> —JOHN 8:7

The Pharisees had caught a woman in the very act of adultery. They dragged her half-clothed into the presence of Jesus. They hoped to trap Jesus, to find a way to accuse him. They made one mistake—underestimating both the acceptance and the condemnation of Jesus.

As you come into God's presence—caught in the very acts of your many sins, wounded by the sins that others committed against you—recognize that nothing you are going to face about yourself is new or shocking to God. He is fully aware of all that you have been through. It won't be a surprise to him. If you come to him in humility, He will look at you eye to eye, fully aware of all that you have done, and all that has been done to you to cause your pain. And, he will fully accept you, in Jesus Christ.

If you won't come to him, if you choose to hide from your sins and those committed against you, you will be just like the Pharisees. You will be trying to run from yourself by looking at other people. Your quest for happiness and contentment can never be found in running. It comes from finally being found out by one who is safe and accepting.

God, help me to realize that rest doesn't come from running. I can have your rest, when I face my sin and my pain.

*Yea, though I walk through the valley of
    the shadow of death,
I will fear no evil;
For You are with me;
Your rod and Your staff, they comfort me.*
                                        —PS. 23:4

There will be days when death seems more appealing than handling the pain of life. King David, the writer of these words, was well acquainted with personal pain. The words he wrote reveal his secret strength for coping with life—to adopt a larger vision.

It's easy when you are in the depth of your pain to look all around and only see fear and anguish. When David saw his life this way, he also remembered that he was not alone. Even when he was at the absolute bottom—the shadow of death—he was accompanied by a wonderful companion. He did not need to fear the evil all around, because God was with him. When David realized this, he was comforted.

God is with you too. You may feel that you are surrounded by death and evil. You are not alone. God will help you get through the pain and the hell. His presence is a reality. He wants to guide you out of your painful past. Take courage as you enter the valley of the shadow of death. For this stage of exploration and discovery is certain to make you feel that you step on treacherous ground. You must walk through it to get to the peace and rest that awaits you in this life.

God, I am walking through the valley of the shadow of death. I believe that you are with me. You will not abandon me.

> *For we must all appear before the judgment seat of Christ, that each one may receive the things done in his body, according to what he has done, whether good or bad.* —2 COR. 5:10

Most read this verse in fear. They tremble at the terrible thought of looking at all they have done in their lives for good or bad. Subconsciously, they really don't want to think about it.

A major reason that people won't naturally, or easily, fulfill this stage of exploration and discovery is the strong rejection they have experienced. Few have ever had the experience of being exposed and still being accepted.

In Christ, we are exposed. At the judgment seat we will be consciously exposed. God knows all the good and the bad we have done. The judgment seat isn't designed to drag some new confessions out of us. It is to show us what God already knows about us. And at that judgment seat, those who have believed in Christ will be accepted completely for the good and bad. Those who do not believe will not. This seems rather unreasonable in our human logic. But his Word says that he will accept any who accept his provision for the bad in their lives.

Exposure with acceptance is available for you in Christ. It is the only way you can begin to break away from your codependent patterns.

God, I'm frightened to look at myself, but you see me fully. Help me to face myself. Help me heal my pain.

*And they heard the sound of the LORD God walking
in the garden in the cool of the day, and Adam and
his wife hid themselves from the presence of the
LORD God among the trees of the garden.*
—GEN. 3:8

Just like Adam and Eve everyone wrongly believes
that it is best to hide from guilt and shame. You have
been in hiding for many years. You might have become such a good hider that you are able to hide from
yourself. But if you want to get out of your destructive
codependent cycle, you must come out of hiding.

It wasn't in hiding that Adam and Eve found restoration. It was in exposure that they were restored. That
exposure brought pain, as they were cursed and
thrown out of the garden. But it ended in restoration as
God made his plan to welcome them back. This plan
included the provision of Christ. Before he sent them
away from the garden, he made clothes for them as a
picture of the restoration that was to come.

Don't hide from yourself. Face the pain of exposure
for the hope of restoration. You can be restored from
the life of pain and sadness that you live in now. There
is hope for you. But you must deal with the things that
keep you set on living this destructive way. Looking
at the pain won't be easy. Remember, resolving these
issues will bring restoration. Also, remember that exposure before God in Christ will always end in
restoration.

_____

*God, help me come out of hiding. Help me to feel your strength to
truly face my pain.*

> *And you shall know the truth, and the truth shall make you free.*
> —JOHN 8:32

Jesus told this to his disciples. The truth he was referring to was the truth of God's plan for them. He told them that if they understood the truth, that God sent him as their Savior to be a once-for-all blood sacrifice for their sin, then they could be free.

That is the truth you must face to experience freedom spiritually. Only then can you truly break away from your bondage to sin.

Freedom does come from knowing the truth. Facing the truth about yourself in the reality of God's love will also set you free. You will be set free from the patterns of unhealthy behaviors. As you come to know the truth about yourself, you will see how these unhealthy behavior patterns began in your life. When you know the truth of God's love and acceptance, you will begin to make the changes in your life that will result in your freedom from your bondage and addiction to codependent relationships.

———————

God, let me know your truth so that I can experience the freedom that you promise. Help me see the truth about myself that traps me in my self-destructive behavior patterns so that I can be set free.

And the LORD God said, "It is not good that man should be alone; I will make him a helper comparable to him."
—GEN. 2:18

God created a wonderful garden, full of precious metals, flowing rivers, fresh fruit, exotic plants, beautiful animals and a perfect man. Everything God had created was good. He said so himself. But he found one thing that was not good. It was not good for man to be alone.

Adam didn't feel alone. He was fulfilled in his perfect abode and his perfect relationship with God. Still, God knew. So, he showed Adam his need by assigning him the task of naming the animals. It was after this that Adam first realized that he did not have one like himself to relate to. This is when God created a woman.

Human relationships were created and designed by God to meet legitimate needs that other things could not meet. Relationships are essential in human life.

Because of sin, these relationships have become perverted. Relationships have a tremendous potential for good and evil.

You have been impacted by relationships that are destructive, but God wants us to have good, strong, healthy relationships. The only way to move toward healthy relationships is to survey and understand the power that your relationships have in your life.

It's not God's plan for me to be lonely.

> *A man who has friends must himself be friendly,*
> *but there is a friend who sticks closer than a brother.*
> —PROV. 18:24

As you look at your relationships, have you noticed unhealthy patterns? Relationships are essential in this life, but sometimes we need to learn how to develop and maintain healthy ones.

You need friends. In order to have the right kind of friends, you need to learn how to be "friendly" in a healthy way. It is unhealthy if all your relationships hinge on your being a doormat or your being the center of attention. Good, healthy friendships involve mutual caring and mutual respect.

David was a wonderful friend to King Saul's son Jonathan. Jonathan and David took a vow of loyalty to each other and one another's children. Jonathan helped David escape from his father's rage. Jonathan not only risked his own life, as Saul could have gotten mad enough to kill Jonathan, he also risked his right to the throne. David was so heartsick when Jonathan was killed in battle that he took Jonathan's family in his home and treated them as his own family.

This is the kind of friendship you need in your life. You must stop setting yourself up as the center of all relationships or hiding your real self. You must stop turning to food, alcohol, drugs, sex, as your best friend. You must stop letting everyone walk all over you, just so you won't make someone mad.

A true friend likes me no matter what.

A friend loves at all times,
And a brother is born for adversity.
—PROV. 17:17

Who is your best friend? Who has touched you most deeply for good? Are you satisfied with the depth of your relationships? Where do you need to develop better friendships? What keeps you from having the type of friends that you need?

Fair weather friends, as they are called, are many; the kind that are with you during the hard times are truly godsent. What kind of friend are you? Are you a fair weather friend, or do you stay by your friends during the storms of life? Have you been using the idea that you must stand by your friend as an excuse to let them abuse you? There is a need for balance in friendships and relationships.

Do you have the kind of friends you need? If not, start praying for God to send you someone to befriend in a healthy way. Remember friendships are reciprocal. You give and they give.

Who do you turn to when you are sad and lonely? God is there; he is your twenty-four-hour friend. Ask him when you need his friendship. Ask him when you need a human friend. Be open and willing to develop new relationships that are healthy. Be ready and willing to be there for your friend when he or she needs you.

Value your friendships; you will need them someday.

> *You shall love your neighbor as yourself.*
> —MATT. 22:39

How do you love in relationships if you don't love yourself? You will never develop healthy mutual relationships if you don't learn to love and accept yourself. Your accepting others will always be for the wrong reasons. You will use them to make yourself look better. You will deny yourself because you can't stand to displease them. You will never have intimacy if you aren't a whole person yourself.

How do you begin to love yourself? Face the facts that you aren't perfect and you don't have to be perfect. Forget the messages that have been pounded in your head that you are no good and rejectable. Realize that God accepts you just the way you are. His friendship with you doesn't depend on the way you look or on anything you do. It simply and fully depends on your realizing your unacceptability apart from Christ and basking in his love for you. His love went to the point of dying, so that if you will only believe, you can have eternal life.

If God accepts you (and he knows all about you, even more than you can consciously conceive), why can't you accept yourself? When you learn to accept yourself, you will instantly be the kind of friend that others really need. You can offer them true acceptance. You will know when to stand by them and when to confront them. You will know how to truly love.

The secret to true friendship is to truly love myself.

Two are better than one,
Because they have a good reward for their
* labor.*
For if they fall, one will lift up his companion.
But woe to him who is alone when he falls,
For he has no one to help him up.
                                —ECCL. 4:9–10

You can't get away from it—God clearly wants you to have friendships as you walk through this life. Yes, many of your relationships in the past have resulted in abuse and pain. Still, there is a God-created void in you that needs friends. Yes, you need to discover how you set yourself up in negative relationships, or you need to face why you don't get involved with anyone. But, you still need to develop friendships.

Because relationships are so important in this life, you must acknowledge how they helped you develop. Relationships have been significant in influencing your good and bad characteristics. Stage two of breaking the codependency cycle involves surveying those relationships. It may involve breaking patterns of relations with some of those people, but it never involves giving up on relationships. You may have a long way to go and a lot to relearn about relationships. You may have no idea what healthy relationships are all about. But realize you have developed unhealthy patterns out of legitimate needs in your life. You need relationships, so ask God to show you how to develop healthy patterns of relationship where two are better than one.

God, help me understand what healthy friendships are all about.

> *See that no one renders evil for evil to anyone, but*
> *always pursue what is good both for yourselves*
> *and for all.*
> —1 THESS. 5:15

As you survey your relationships, you are bound to face repressed anger from the past. Man's cruelty to man is an astonishing reality. Don't get caught in the trap of trying to avenge the wrongs you remember from these relationships. This will only lead you into a different kind of bondage.

Rather, face your rage privately, in your support group, and with your counselor. Cry out to God from your pain. Recognize fully the power that relationships have had in your life, both for good and for evil. But don't give up on relationships altogether.

God wants you to live at peace. God wants you to be in healthy relationships. He doesn't want you to be bitter and withered. He wants you to get to the place that you can forgive those who have wronged you. He wants you to forgive, so that you can have peace now and in future relationships.

Peace in relationships seems like such a farce. But you tell me to work toward this, God. I must throw myself at your feet for this one, God. I do not have the ability on my own.

If it is possible, as much as depends on you, live
peaceably with all men.   —ROM. 12:18

You do not completely control your ability to be at peace with all men. God's advice for healthy living is this—do your part to live at peace. Don't make your goal to force others to live at peace with you. Learn to live at peace with yourself and others.

This may seem a slight difference, but it is an important one. God wants you to be able to be restored with all the people who have wronged you. But he also knows that all the people who have wronged you won't face their sin and change their ways. Therefore, you cannot necessarily have peace with all men. Yet he wants you to have peace with all men in your heart.

He wants this for your own good. Those people who have wronged you can rob you of personal peace. Maybe what they did was long in the past. Still, it can affect you and your relationships. This is why God wants you to be at peace in your relationships, so you can have peace in your own soul.

God, there are people in my past I can't forgive without your strength. There are people I don't have the strength to ask forgiveness from. Show me what depends on me to live at peace with others. Help me see where it is not my responsibility. Help me accept this and live in peace.

*I speak in human terms because of the weakness of
your flesh. For just as you presented your members
as slaves of . . . lawlessness, so now present your
members as slaves of righteousness for holiness.*
—ROM. 6:19

You may feel powerless over your addictive behavior.
Your behavior has become such habit after years or
months that, though you try to stop, it never happens.

You must realize that stopping this addictive behavior is impossible without God. You must pray daily,
even constantly, for a power greater than your own to
overcome the addiction and its compulsive power. Ar-
range your life to avoid old habits and patterns. Recognize the urge to fall back to old patterns when facing
stress.

You didn't become addicted overnight. Breaking an
addiction doesn't happen overnight. It happens over
nights, hours, even moments of small choices not to
partake of your old ways.

Just as you slowly yielded yourself to those old addictions, now begin yielding yourself to a new way of
living. Don't expect not to feel compelled by your old
behavior. But don't ignore the first tug. Recognize it
and ask God to help you not give in. Deal with your
feelings directly and make a choice not to numb them
by your addictive behavior. After times of faithfully doing this, you will find that you have changed your behavior. You have begun yielding yourself to God.

God, help me yield to your way.

I can do all things through Christ who strengthens me.
—PHIL. 4:13

If you are ever going to overcome your addictive behavior, you will have to admit that you cannot overcome your addiction alone. You can overcome it only with God's strength. You must face the fact that you alone are powerless to overcome your problem. Then, take courage in the fact that God can give you the strength you lack.

Paul found this to be true on his own pathway in life. He did not have the strength to face the burdens of this life; still he faced them because he relied not on himself alone, but on God. You too do not have the strength in yourself. This is why you have developed your addiction. But your addiction has let you down. It deceived you into thinking that it would help you cope. Now you have more to cope with than you had before you started your addictive behavior. Not so with God. He will help you overcome your addiction. It is his strength that will make the difference in your life both for your addictions and your sad feelings.

Recognizing your own powerlessness may seem weak. But it will probably be the strongest thing you ever do. It will give you the strength from above if you look to God. You need more than yourself to overcome, and God is the answer to your need.

God, help me to rely on your strength and realize my strength is not enough.

I find then a law, that evil is present with me, the one who wills to do good. —ROM. 7:21

Just as Newton discovered the law of gravity, you must discover the law of evil. When you set out to do good, evil is right there with you. You will be tempted daily, even momently to give into your old patterns of behavior. It is one-step-at-a-time process.

Don't ignore the unhealthy thoughts that tell you, "Just this once," "You really need it," or "You really blew it. There is no hope for you." Recognize those thoughts and change them. Deal with the pain underneath the addiction and choose your healthy plan for coping.

It is a daily struggle, but not a struggle without great rewards. There is addiction-free life out there for you. A life where you can grow into the person you can and want to be.

Remember you are not alone as you resist the law of evil. God will be there with you, helping you discover the good that is within you.

The pathway away from your addiction will not be easy, but it will be worthwhile. Give your healthy thoughts room to grow, and they will lead you to a new life. Don't let the evil or bad thoughts win today.

Good and evil will struggle within me today; which will win?

The LORD will give strength to His people;
The LORD will bless His people with peace.
—PS. 29:11

Some people read this verse and think "I'm sure he does for others, but not for me." God promised his strength to all those who call upon him. His is a strength we all need to cope in this world. He knows this and that is why he freely offers his strength for anyone who believes.

If you feel as if you don't have God's strength, ask yourself, "Do I believe?" Do you believe that he loves you and accepts you in Christ? Do you believe that he has power and strength? Do you believe that he wants desperately to give you his strength?

After you believe, then begin to call upon him daily, even momently for his strength. Recognize the times when your own strength is fading. Call out to him and ask for his power. Ask, even before you are at a point of need. Face the reality that you cannot overcome this alone.

The key to accepting God's strength is accepting your own powerlessness. Give God praise for the ways he strengthens you. Recognize the times you have partaken of his strength. Observe the strength of God. Make the reality of God's strength replace your weakness.

God, you are mighty and your name is full of power. Help me partake of your strength, for I have none of my own.

A wise man is strong.
Yes, a man of knowledge increases strength.
—PROV. 24:5

Wisdom and knowledge will help you overcome your addiction.

You must know yourself and your weakness. You must know how to change your world to avoid falling. You must learn how your soul hungers for relationship. Recognize how you have gotten off track trying to fulfill your hunger in illegitimate ways. Learn legitimate ways for filling your hungry soul. Knowledge is recognizing that what comes natural is not necessarily right. Education is essential to changing your behavior.

Develop wisdom. You need the wisdom to recognize the emptiness that your wrong behavior will lead you to. Become wise about the paths ahead and that danger may be disguised as an easy way out. The easy way could be only a way to deeper pain.

Fighting an addiction means not following innate desires. Healthy behavior is not natural behavior, but rather learned behavior. Accept that you are in a learning process, and commit to educating yourself and increasing in wisdom and knowledge. There you will find the strength to overcome your addiction.

It's not natural to live the right way. No one comes by healthy behavior without wisdom and knowledge.

For we do not want you to be ignorant, brethren, of our trouble which came to us in Asia: that we were burdened beyond measure, above strength, so that we despaired even of life. Yes, we had the sentence of death in ourselves, that we should not trust in ourselves but in God who raises the dead.

—2 COR. 1:8–9

You will reach points of despair as you work to conquer your addiction. Paul and his fellow travelers knew that kind of despair. Their goal to preach the gospel around the world was good, just as your goal is to break the cycle of destructive addictions.

The goal is good, but sometimes when it is difficult to achieve or you have blown it, you might feel as Paul and his friends did, like giving up. Do not give up on your goal. Keep pressing on. When you reach a block in the road, keep going.

At those times of despair you need to turn to God. Realize, like Paul and his friends, that you do not have the strength, but God does.

God, help me fight despair as I fight for recovery. Remind me that you are with me helping me not give in to my temptation. I need to realize that with you there is no need for despair.

> *I beseech you therefore, brethren, by the mercies of God, that you present your bodies a living sacrifice, holy, acceptable to God, which is your reasonable service. And do not be conformed to this world, but be transformed by the renewing of your mind, that you may prove what is that good and acceptable and perfect will of God.*
>
> —ROM. 12:1–2

God desires that you live your life in peace and contentment, transformed from your addictions. A transformation is taking place in your life from a person overpowered by the world to a person empowered by the Word of God. This transformation takes place as you confront the lies you believe with the truth of God's Word.

The first lie you must confront is that your addictive behavior will heal your pain. Your addictions have become so compulsive because of the degree of your pain. Yes, your behavior has created a diversion to a certain degree, but it has been the source of more pain in your life. Your addiction has become self-defeating.

The truth is that you can be healed from your pain. God will provide the healing. Each time you are tempted today to give in to your addictive behavior, acknowledge to yourself that your addiction won't heal you. Look to God to give you a new way of living and facing life.

———————

God, I'm trying to be transformed. Give me your strength, because I'm powerless without you.

Therefore a man shall leave his father and mother and be joined to his wife, and they shall become one flesh.

—GEN. 2:24

These words meant for married couples are essential to a healthy marriage. They are also helpful for all adult children. Developing into a healthy adult and creating a new family system is the goal of family life. Codependent persons have no idea what a healthy family life is all about; therefore, they do not recognize that they have not left their dysfunctional family.

You may find yourself a thousand miles away from your parents, or your parents may be deceased; but you still may not have left them emotionally. You probably carry their dysfunctional patterns in your own life and may be blind to the ways your parents still have power over you.

You must leave your old family systems and begin new healthy patterns of relating. Be willing to discover the pain and dysfunctional patterns you learned in your family of origin. Face how you continue to live by them today. Recognize how important it is for you to discontinue those patterns in order to live a healthy life.

God, it's easy to know when you have left your family to begin a new one or live on your own. But how do I recognize the ways I have not left my mother and father? How am I hanging on to them? And how is that hanging on destroying my life? Help me see where I need to change.

> *Blessed be the God and Father of our Lord Jesus*
> *Christ, the Father of mercies and God of all*
> *comfort, who comforts us in all our tribulation,*
> *that we may be able to comfort those who are in*
> *any trouble, with the comfort with which we*
> *ourselves are comforted by God.*
>
> —2 COR. 1:3–4

Leaving home and saying good-bye in a healthy way means that we must grieve over our loss. All losses must be grieved before they can be resolved. God wants to comfort you in your time of loss.

Patty had worked in counseling for a year and a half resolving the emotional incest that occurred between herself and her father. It was interesting that it was his idea for her to seek counseling, and he paid for it though he was out of the country. Because he was out of the country, she had not seen him at all while she was in counseling. When he came for a brief visit, Patty was overwhelmed in facing the ways her father had failed her and helped make her an emotional cripple, not willing to commit to any other man.

Her counselor was not with her at the moment of seeing her father again. But God was there to comfort her and see her through the visit with the appropriate outward graces. Even more, God helped her to genuinely grieve her legitimate loss. She began to open her heart that night even more to genuine relationships.

Isn't it comforting to know that we have an ever-present Comforter who can get us through our grief?

All I must do is look to you, you will get me through this pain.

> *For God commanded, saying, "Honor your father*
> *and your mother"; and, "He who curses father or*
> *mother, let him be put to death."*
>
> —MATT. 15:4

Saying good-bye and leaving home does not equal cursing your father and mother. In fact, ultimately it involves forgiving your father and mother. Cursing and blaming parents is not healthy. If you spend your life focusing on how your parents have wronged you, then your only hope would be for them to change. For most codependents, their parents are too sick to ever be able to make things right.

The reason for recognizing the damage parents have done in your life and leaving and saying good-bye isn't for the purpose of cursing them. Face the damage and the pain that has occurred in your life as a result of parenting. Then, forgive. You may still have to set up boundaries with them if they continue to hinder you from living your life for God. But don't get in the habit of blaming or cursing your parents. Naturally you may do this when you first acknowledge your pain in stage one. But move to forgiveness. Developing healthy patterns in your life does not depend on your parents and the decisions they make for their lives. It depends on you and your response to God and the comfort that he offers you.

Father, help me to forgive the crimes against me by my family as you have forgiven the crimes I have committed against you.

> *And everyone who has left houses or brothers or*
> *sisters or father or mother or wife or children*
> *or lands, for My name's sake, shall receive a*
> *hundredfold, and inherit everlasting life.*
> —MATT. 19:29

It is frightening to leave behind the people you hold dear. Sometimes, however, to follow a path of healthy living and to grow more into the person God wants you to be, you must. Take that difficult step. But it is not a step you take in vain. You are promised life as a result of following hard after God.

Today, you are working on leaving and saying good-bye to your old ways of relating. The ways that have brought you to despair are the same ways that feel most comfortable to you. You have intense pain trying to let go of your family. But if you don't, you will never be the person God wants you to be.

He promises that if you leave them, he will supply your every need. You must put him first. He desires your best even more than your family. You can trust him, even if it comes to a point of saying good-bye to parents and friends.

God, I'm frightened to say good-bye. Leaving doesn't come easy. You know what is best. I will trust you to lead me. Let me see what you want for my life.

He who loves father or mother more than Me is not worthy of Me. And he who loves son or daughter more than Me is not worthy of Me.

—MATT. 10:37

Family relationships hold a powerful position in your life. Parents have a significant impact on their children for good or for evil. The phrase "blood is thicker than water" is very true. The same people you belittle, ignore, take for granted are the people you will stand up for if they are under siege.

The power that family bonds hold in your life must come second to your relationship with God. This is not because God doesn't want you to have fulfilling relationships. He wants you to experience wholeness in those relationships, and you can only know this when you put him first and his ways ahead of family members.

God must come first in regard to family. God doesn't say that you should not love mother, father, sister, brother. He says that you should not love them more than him. When he is first, all other relationships come into perspective. You must believe that God loves you and puts you first. He knows what you need and desires for you to live a life that brings honor to him and peace to your soul. Don't fall into the trap of putting your family above God.

Help me understand how to love and forgive my family. Help me come to see their proper place in my life. I will begin by putting you first as your Word instructs.

But Ruth said
"Entreat me not to leave you,
Or to turn back from following after you;
For wherever you go, I will go;
And wherever you lodge, I will lodge;
Your people shall be my people,
And your God, my God."

—RUTH 1:16

Ruth made the same courageous journey you are making. She stepped out boldly and forcefully, even though her mother-in-law Naomi did not give her very much encouragement. Ruth was leaving everything familiar to her to go with a depressed woman to a land far away. She left her parents and family, a culture and traditions.

She left because she had tasted a relationship with God and wanted to try God's way of living. Her own culture was plagued by promiscuity, child sacrifices, and cult worship. Even in Naomi, Ruth saw something hopeful that there was a God out there to love her. She said good-bye because of her belief that God's way was better than the ways she had known all her life.

You have been asked to say good-bye and leave home. This leaving involves determination and commitment. Even when the familiar is destructive, to leave what you know is difficult. In saying good-bye, you will venture into areas unknown. Your faith is that God does have a plan and direction for you.

God, I'm so afraid to leave my familiar territory. It has been all that I have known. Thank you for walking by my side.

*Finally, brethren, farewell. Become complete. Be of
good comfort, be of one mind, live in peace; and
the God of love and peace will be with you.*
—2 COR. 13:11

Paul loved all the people he had met and ministered to
in Corinth. They were very special to him. He was willing to say good-bye because he knew that a part of his
mission included leaving the people he held so dear.
Each church he helped create held a very special place
in his heart. If left to his own plan, perhaps he would
have just stayed on in one of those places and enjoyed
the fellowship.

But Paul believed God and listened to his plan. He
knew leaving was necessary to experience fully all
that God had planned for him. Leaving took the same
kind of courage you must have. But, to get on with the
plan God has for your life, you must say good-bye.

*God, I must leave. The act of saying good-bye will be sad. Still, I know
that your plan is awaiting and exciting. I want to go where you lead
me. I will trust that you will take care of the people I leave behind.*

> *The Lord is near to those who have a broken heart,*
> *And saves such as have a contrite spirit.*
>
> —PS. 34:18

God knows that you are broken and hurting in your grief. He knows what tomorrow will hold for you and he wants to see you through. Where does he plant himself when he knows his dear ones are grieving? Right there as close as he can possibly be.

He holds his arms around you. He envelops you with his love. He encompasses you with his closeness. As you pour out your soul, as you empty your heart, he never leaves you, but grieves with you.

As you grieve your loss, imagine him right there beside you. Let his closeness become a reality for you. Take courage to get through your pain, knowing that you will never be alone. Use that mental picture of him holding you in your grief during your day. When you feel hurt or alone, recall the image of God holding you close. God is faithful far beyond any degree of human faithfulness you could muster. He will stick beside you even when you try to leave him in your grief. He is always close, but still closer to those who are grieving. He knows you need his extra closeness. Staying aware of this will help you through the hard times.

Help me see you close, dear Lord, just as you say you are. Help me feel your hugs, dear Lord, and know you are never far.

To everything there is a season,
A time for every purpose under heaven. . . .
A time to weep, And a time to laugh;
A time to mourn, And a time to dance.
—ECCL. 3:1, 4

Grief brings healing to the soul. Most often people want to avoid grief, a deeply painful emotion. But to deny or run from grief only creates more pain. Actually, grief will heal the pain in your life.

The good part of grief is knowing that it will pass. Grieving passes through stages of denial, anger, and weeping to genuine resolution. It doesn't last forever. In fact, if you will let yourself grieve, the scars from the past will be healed. You will be free of your pain sooner if you face the sorrow that grief brings.

There will be a time to laugh. And yes, you will dance again. The whole world doesn't fall apart when you give yourself time to grieve. For most, the world gets brighter and clearer after resolving grief.

Grief has a purpose in your life. It was God-designed to bring you to a place of peace. This is your time to grieve. Will you release its healing powers in your heart?

---

*Grief won't **last** forever. Lord, may I weep now so I can laugh again?*

> *Jesus wept.*
> —JOHN 11:35

It's known as the shortest verse in the Scriptures. Jesus' sorrow stands out among the hundreds of mourners all about. Jesus was present at the funeral of Lazarus whom he knew he would soon raise from the dead. Friends and family of Lazarus wept in despair, as Jesus quietly entered the scene. Lazarus' sisters poignantly looked in Jesus' eyes and said, "If only you had come sooner."

Many believe that Jesus wept at the crowd's unbelief on this dreary occasion. Others observe his weeping as the genuine sorrow of this sad hour. He knew what was about to happen. He knew that he would momentarily raise Lazarus from the dead as a sign of his deity. Still, an overwhelming sadness overcame his soul and he broke down and wept with the others.

The picture of death brings grieving, even when the outcome may be known. Jesus knew that Lazarus wasn't dead for long. Still, He grieved. He didn't lose anything for his tears, only greater joy when Lazarus did live again. You too, will not lose but gain by your weeping and grieving. You have experienced genuine losses. Don't use rationalization, or depersonalization, to distance you from your pain. Face them as genuine losses and do the next natural step—grieve.

Grieve completely and fully and you will experience deeper joy and peace.

He is despised and rejected by men,
A man of sorrows and acquainted with grief.
—ISA. 53:3

Jesus himself is personally acquainted with grief. He understands what you are going through, but he is acquainted with the other side of grief as well. He knows the peace that only God can give in a time of sorrow.

Agony, pain, sorrow, despair—no matter how desperate you feel, God knows your pain. He not only knows what it is to grieve, he also knows intimately what your loss is. He knows that you will reach a time of peace in your soul, find an inner strength from grieving. You will realize that you can live on in spite of your loss. You will discover that grieving a loss acknowledges the severity of your pain, and the reality that you can go on with your life.

Jesus experienced more sorrow and grief than any human could possibly bear. Because he kept his perspective during the grief, he was able to finish the course he set out to finish. He died for the sins of all humans. If you allow grief to do its work in you, you will be empowered to do what God has designed for your life.

———————

God, help me to believe that when my soul is overwhelmed with grief, you know how to get me through.

> *Then he said to them, "My soul is exceedingly sorrowful, even to death. Stay here and watch with Me."*
> —MATT. 26:38

Jesus was abandoned by his best friends when in the midst of his deepest grief. Abandonment and grief are very heavy loads to bear. They almost did Christ in. He prayed in the garden if there be any other way, let this cup pass from him. Still, though abandoned by the very men he came to save, our Savior followed through with God's plan.

Some may abandon you in your grief. People in your world may not understand. Some will not care enough to help, and some will not know how to help and may avoid you altogether. But God will always stay near. You will not be abandoned in the ways Jesus was. He died to make sure that wouldn't happen to another human soul.

Your grief may be overwhelming. It may be the most difficult stage thus far in your journey. You are not alone. You will not be abandoned. God will stay by your side. He will see you through. He will help you find the strength to bear up under this pressure. You will see a brighter tomorrow.

Thank you for being strong enough to work through your grief, Lord. Help me allow my grief to take me to the place of peace.

"Be angry, and do not sin": do not let the sun go down on your wrath.
                                        —EPH. 4:26

An essential element of grieving is facing your anger. You will be angry with different situations and with different people, even those you always clung to. Perhaps you will see that the "right" parent had his or her faults also. If you truly grieve, you will become truly angry. Resolving anger is a part of resolving your grief.

Don't be afraid of your anger. Don't be afraid to experience it while you are grieving. Don't get confused when you find yourself angry when you think you should be sad. Anger is a secondary emotion. Deeper than your anger, you will find your genuine sadness. But you must deal with your anger to resolve your sadness.

When God says do not sin in your anger, don't be foolish and self-destructive in your anger. Face your anger fully without harming yourself or other people. Write letters, hit pillows, scream into oceans. Don't use your anger as an opportunity to sin. Use it as an opportunity to face all that is inside of you and let God lead you as to what you should do with it.

God, you don't want me to sin in my anger, but you do want me to face and acknowledge my anger. In your perfect timing help me see fully all that I am angry about. Help me not to sin as I face anger your way.

> *So when He had looked around at them with*
> *anger, being grieved by the hardness of their hearts,*
> *He said to the man, "Stretch out your hand." And*
> *he stretched it out, and his hand was restored as*
> *whole as the other.*
> —MARK 3:5

Jesus is our example of true grieving. Here the very religious leaders of God's chosen people rejected his own Son when he stood in their presence. You can imagine that this was reason for Jesus to grieve. Those who had studied God's Word the most could not see that the Jesus who stood before them was the very long-awaited Messiah.

It grieved Jesus to be accused by the people who should know better. Part of his grief included anger at them. Still, deeper than the anger, he grieved. Just like you, Jesus was angry. Just like you, Jesus was sad. He is an example of healthy grieving in that he grieved each relationship as He experienced it.

You are probably grieving over past relationships. Your anger and sorrow may include people who have long since moved out of your life. Hopefully, one day you will be like Jesus in that you can grieve for the people and situations as they happen. Follow his example for your life, and you will experience a deeper peace than your soul has ever known.

Make me like Jesus. Help me understand the importance of grieving over painful relationships.

I will praise You,
For I am fearfully and wonderfully made; . . .
My soul knows very well.
                                    —PS. 139:14

Not many men or women believe this. Most people despise themselves. Whether it be their noses, their weight, their intellect, somehow they always come up flawed. They feel inferior and constantly compare themselves with others.

David could look at himself and realize that he was a wonderful creation. Certainly he was flawed, but he was able to see beyond the flaws. He saw that somehow those flaws must have a purpose in God's plan. The physical characteristics that are unchangeable help you keep yourself in perspective. If you accept them, you will gain the same freedom as David.

Can you look in the mirror and celebrate like David that you are fearfully and wonderfully made? Can you call yourself wonderful? There is certainly reason to. You bear the image of God. All humans are created in his image. Our unique likeness to him makes us fearfully and wonderfully made.

———————

Help me see the wonder in your creation of me. Help me learn to celebrate my own special qualities whether the world sees them as flaws or worthy characteristics.

> *For God so loved the world that He gave His only begotten Son, that whoever believes in Him should not perish but have everlasting life.*
>
> —JOHN 3:16

Does God really love you? If so, how does he show it? How can you really know if you are loved by God? Does God love you uniquely, or does he just lump you in with everyone else?

Most codependents are walking around the world with the core belief that they are unlovable. They have spent most of their lives trying to replace the love they never got and always coming up empty. Every failed relationship engraves the words from their past "I am not lovable" deeper in their heart.

The truth is that, yes, you are loved. You are loved deeply and uniquely. You are loved so much that Christ himself died for you just so he could be with you. If you were the only person to ever respond to the gospel, Jesus still would have come and died to bring you home. You are not unlovable.

There may have been people in your past who were unable to love you. You may act in ways that make you difficult to love. But there is one fact you can never escape—you are loved purely and completely by your Savior. And this means that the perception that you are unlovable is false.

I am loved.

All that the Father gives Me will come to Me, and the one who comes to Me I will by no means cast out.

—JOHN 6:37

The statement, "I am bad" rings through the heads of many codependents. Life becomes an endless search for a way to validate yourself. That core belief that "I am bad" undergirds almost all behaviors and thoughts. The fear that you will someday be found out as "bad" keeps you on a cycle of performance and fear.

You carry the fear that you will be discovered and cast away. If you belong to him through Christ, God says that he will never cast you away. Isn't that a wonderful thought! He will never deny anyone who belongs to him no matter how bad or good they are.

The reality is that we are all bad to a certain degree. But our badness or goodness does not affect our security with God. The only issues that affect our standing with him are if we believe that we are sinners and accept Jesus Christ's death as the payment for our sin. Believe and be accepted. In Christ, we can never be bad enough to be cast away. Though we may be bad, we are accepted.

Lord, I believe in you. I know I am accepted by you no matter how bad or good I act.

> *Do not be wise in your own eyes;*
> *Fear the LORD and depart from evil.*
> —PROV. 3:7

So many of the perceptions people have of themselves are wrong. If they rely on their own wisdom they will come up very short of what God really wants for them.

You need to learn how to escape your own wisdom, because it isn't wisdom after all. It is more likely lies that have been pounded into your head by years of abuse. You must learn to leave your own wisdom and begin to rely on God's wisdom.

This is essential concerning the perceptions you hold about yourself. Naturally, your perceptions will be far from the worth, dignity, and value that God has of you. But how do you rely on his wisdom? First, identify the unconscious, negative beliefs about yourself that drive your behavior. Then replace them with the truth and wisdom of God. Discover your dignity in the midst of your depravity.

Lord, help me escape my own wisdom and grow wise in you.

For we dare not class ourselves or compare
ourselves with those who commend themselves.
But they, measuring themselves by themselves,
and comparing themselves among themselves,
are not wise. —2 COR. 10:12

Comparing yourself to others results in wrong perceptions about yourself. You believe that you must be what someone else is to define yourself as successful. There are two problems with this.

First, your perceptions of others and their success may be inaccurate. You are looking at them from the outside. Many may see you and think you are a very self-assured person. Would they be right? You may be missing the reality of the condition of the person on the inside. If you really walked in their shoes, you might find that they are very much like you.

The second problem that arises from comparing yourself with others is that you are unique. God did not create us as carbon copies of each other. What a boring world this would be if he did. You have your own unique characteristics and gifts, and the discovery of these gifts is a maturing experience. Growing to accept yourself and validate yourself is freeing. In doing this you become truly wise.

God, help me to see myself the way you do. Keep me looking up to you and not around to others. I don't need the approval of others to validate myself. You have given me your words to guide me.

*So God created man in His own image; in the
image of God He created him; male and female
He created them.*
—GEN. 1:27

Every person who has ever been born bears the
image of God. As worthless as you may have felt in
your life, you cannot escape value and worth because
you possess the image of God.

Bearing the image of God puts your life and existence in a whole new category. If you are a Christian,
you not only bear the image of God, but you also have
the Holy Spirit living in you—you carry the spirit of
God.

With this knowledge, can you look at your Creator
and tell him that there is nothing valuable about you?
Can you escape the value he has placed on you? Where
can you go from the image? The image remains with
you, no matter how you look on the outside.

You reflect God himself. In this you have an inescap-
able worth and dignity.

---

*Help me realize my value. Help me be aware that I do have your
image in me.*

> *I said, "You are gods,*
> *And all of you are children of the Most High.*
> *But you shall die like men,*
> *And fall like one of the princes."*
>
> —PS. 82:6–7

You are created in the image of God. You are the child of the Most High. But, will you, like the Pharisees live like mere men and die in your ignorance? Won't you face the dignity that flows through your bones because you reflect God's image?

Your depravity often blinds you to the dignity that God has placed on you. You will die in your ignorance too, without a proper perspective of yourself. This is not to say that you should count yourself equal to God. This was Satan's awful mistake. But you should see how in your fallen human form, you still reflect the character of God. It is that character of God that drives you to do the good that you have done in your life.

You have the image of God in you. How you treat that image will determine many of the paths you take in life. Will you acknowledge that you have great worth and dignity? Or will you ignore the image of God in you—that you are worth redeeming—and die in your destructive view of yourself?

God, it is your image in me that helps me do any good in my life.

> *I press toward the goal for the prize of the upward*
> *call of God in Christ Jesus.*
> — PHIL. 3:14

Living out the work that God has begun in you is the focus for your day. Recognizing old patterns and developing new ones is the next stage of your journey away from codependency. One way to keep yourself on the right path is to recognize the prize awaiting you.

The prize is the high calling, the dignity that God wants to bring to you. This dignity is something that you have and doesn't depend on how other people treat you. This prize is freely given by God to you. His intimate and personal calling gives direction and hope for the future. Where your future once looked dreary and dead, now you can enter life and have energy to face each day enthusiastically.

Your journey toward healthy living plateaus at this stage. It's a plateau of confidence in a new way of living. You will experience relief from allowing the old behaviors to stay in your past. You will reach a time of comfort with your new behaviors and thinking. You are trying out the new system you have learned. It's a race with a prize, and the prize is one of the best available to mankind—peace of heart.

God, I'm running to receive your prize. It is a privilege and high calling to even be in this race of healthy living. Thank you for the invitation and the strength to run this race. With you by my side, I know I can get through.

Therefore we are buried with Him through baptism into death, that just as Christ was raised from the dead by the glory of the Father, even so we also should walk in newness of life. —ROM. 6:4

Brand new babies delight almost everyone who looks upon them. People stop and smile as they pass a newborn on the street. New life stirs something in most of us. You are a new life. You are experiencing something new in your life. Many whom you pass on the street will have no idea what has been happening inside of you. Still the newness is recognizable to you and should be celebrated.

Newness is a cause for celebration. It is also a cause for fear and uncertainty. You have ventured out on a new way of living. You are not sure that you can leave the past behind. Can you really experience life without carrying around the guilt and shame? Can you enjoy life apart from belittling your every move? Yes, you can.

Acknowledge your fear and uncertainty as you celebrate your new life. When you do venture in your new behavior, recognize your awesome steps. Celebrate the fact that you were able to be assertive with your boss and not revert to your old way of relating. Do something new today and give yourself credit. Be proud of your healthy choices.

———

Father, thank you for making me new. Help me recognize that the strength comes from you and be proud that I made the choices.

> *Then I will give them one heart, and I will put a*
> *new spirit within them, and take the stony heart*
> *out of their flesh, and give them a heart of flesh,*
> *that they may walk in My statutes and keep My*
> *judgments and do them; and they shall be My*
> *people, and I will be their God.*
> —EZEK. 11:19–20

God is the Author of newness. He knows how desperately we all need a new start, and he doesn't give up on us when we blow it. Today is a new day, an opportunity to shine and grow in him. He will give you the newness when you choose to trust in him.

God doesn't say that he will give newness as long as you obey him perfectly. He knows this is impossible. He says he will give you newness if you purpose to walk in his statutes today. What has God shown you to change today? Are you willing to do it? If you do it for God, he will take away your stony, hard heart and give you newness and life.

We must have faith enough to tell him we will obey him; he will do the rest. Press forward today to live your life anew. Trust God to change your heart, to calm your fears, and to give you the newness he promises.

God, make me new. Help me act in my new ways. Take away my heart of stone and replace it with a heart of flesh that lives and breathes and finds joy on this earth.

Through the LORD's mercies, we are not consumed,
Because his compassions fail not.
They are new every morning;
Great is Your faithfulness.

—LAM. 3:22–23

Your new way of living won't come naturally. Your instinctive behaviors have led you to codependency; your healthy behaviors are learned. Now you are living in a new way.

These new behaviors won't come overnight. Time and decision making leads to more healthy patterns. God's mercy begins each morning, and his mercy surrounds you as you grow in your new way. You do not have to do it perfectly or all at once. What really matters is that you do it. Change your behaviors in small ways at first. Accept the abundance of God's mercy that he sends your way while you change.

Don't slide into your old patterns of thinking; don't give up. What matters to God is that you are trying; he will give the mercy to take care of the rest.

God, it is your mercy that motivates me to go on today. It is only your mercy that has brought me here. Remind me of your love and mercy today because sometimes I am so merciless on myself.

*Therefore, if anyone is in Christ, he is a new
creation; old things have passed away; behold,
all things have become new.* —2 COR. 5:17

Salvation in Christ brings newness in life. Christ described this newness to Nicodemus as being "born again." When you accept Christ as your personal Savior you are reborn spiritually.

When you resolve the pain from your past that has created your codependent behavior, you are reborn psychologically. The old patterns are still with you; the old belief systems permeate your thinking; yet you have tasted of life in a different way. You have seen the source of these unhealthy patterns. You now know why you do the things you do. Just the insight you have gained makes you new.

Now you must allow that insight to grow into your behaviors and relationships. This is more difficult, but it is the next step in your journey toward healthy living. Now that you have seen yourself, will you go back to your old ways? Or will you enter into the new ways that God has planned for you?

---

*God, you have made me new in Christ. Help me live out my newness,
and not give in to my old ways of thinking.*

And David said to Gad, "I am in great distress. Please let us fall into the hand of the LORD, for His mercies are great; but do not let me fall into the hand of man."

—2 SAM. 24:14

These are the words of a man who was very much like you. He found himself following his own way to deal with pain and finding that way bankrupt. The futility of his behavior had convicted him. He was wrong, and he was ready to change. The man was King David, and his sin was to number the people, something God told him not to do.

One way that David may be different from you is that he knew God. His experience of God motivated the words he spoke. He desired to be found out by God. He would rather be exposed before God than any man. As you grow to know and experience God more fully, you can have this same reality, this same motivation to live your life in a new way.

Just like David, you have seen yourself and the ways you have sinned and been wrong. Now, you are trying to change the way you were living. Remember like David did that God is a merciful God. He will be merciful to you as you put your new beliefs and behaviors into practice. You will find that God is more merciful to you than you are to yourself.

You are a merciful God. Thank you, Lord, I need your mercy. Thank you for giving me the opportunity to live my life in a new way. Help me grow into the person you want me to be.

> *As newborn babes, desire the pure milk of the*
> *word, that you may grow thereby, if indeed you*
> *have tasted that the Lord is gracious.*
>
> —1 PETER 2:2–3

Imagine yourself as the person you want to be. What would you be like if you made all the changes in your life you know you should? Imagine what it would be like to be perfectly content being you.

It would be wonderful if you could make all those changes with the blinking of your eye. But it is not possible that way. You will become like a newborn babe. A newborn babe cannot get up and walk, feed himself, or get a job. The simplest tasks are complex to him. That's how you are emotionally. You are learning a new way of living; you won't go out and conquer all your relationships in one day.

Your changes will seem small at first, but don't let that discourage you. Celebrate those efforts to relate in the new way, just as you would the first time your infant rolled over. Each step should be celebrated. With time and effort you will be soaring emotionally. Remember, however, that you start as a newborn babe.

God, help me not expect too much from myself today. Help me acknowledge the new and good efforts I make toward healthy living. Help me see your graciousness that allows me to enjoy these new experiences.

A father of the fatherless, a defender of widows,
Is God in His holy habitation. —PS. 68:5

God promises orphans that he will be their parent. Children desperately need parents, for they are totally dependent emotionally, financially, and physically. Your parents were not perfect, probably not even in one of these three areas. However, God promises that he will make up for this if we depend on him.

He is your parent if you have accepted Christ as your Savior. As your Father, he wants to have that intimate place in your heart that longs for a strong, protective, wise provider. Will you let him reveal himself to you in these ways? Will you allow him to show himself as your Father? Will you accept his wisdom and discipline? Will you yield yourself to his fatherly love?

If you will, you will gain energy and direction on your journey. You will forgive your earthy parents for their failures. You will learn to live with some of the relational emptiness caused by others' inability to respond rightly. You will be led into good and healthy relationships.

Father God, I am willing to give you the chance to be my perfect parent.

> *But when the fullness of the time had come, God
> sent forth His Son, born of a woman, born under
> the law, to redeem those who were under the law,
> that we might receive the adoption as sons.*
>
> —GAL. 4:4–5

If you believe and accept God's Son as your redemption from your unworthiness, then you have been adopted by God. And as an adopted child, you are an heir with Christ. Can you imagine what a wonderful privilege you have been offered? Not something you earn, no way to be good enough, no way to be worthy—you receive this privileged position.

You who accept Christ are *chosen* children of God. He adopted you after he knew you. He knew that you would be unworthy and sinful, but he did not turn you away. He still wanted you. So he made a way for you to be adopted. All you must do to become adopted is to accept that Christ was your payment.

Your earthly parents may have rejected, neglected, abandoned, or abused you. Your heavenly Father wants to accept, help, heal, and love you. The healing begins when you realize that you are his child. You will be whole and ready to face whatever your day brings. Because, no matter what, you know whose child you are. You know that there is Someone who is always on your side.

Father, my father, help me remember whose I am. Help me walk each step today fully aware of the fact that I belong to you, that I have been adopted at the highest price anyone could ever pay.

*And because you are sons, God has sent forth the
Spirit of His Son into your hearts, crying out,
"Abba, Father!" Therefore you are no longer
a slave but a son, and if a son, then an heir
of God through Christ.*
                                        —GAL. 4:6–7

God does not see you as a servant, but a son. He
doesn't want to be seen by you as a Master, but a
Father. He wants to hear you cry to him, "Abba,
Father," which means Daddy. He wants you to realize
that no matter how your earthly father treated you, he
is your perfect Father. He will be the loving, kind, consistent, disciplining Helper that you need.

He wants you to feel safe in his love. You need to be
assured that there is Someone bigger than you who
will guard you and keep you. There is a Father who
seeks your best in every situation in life. He is that
Father, and you are his child. Imagine your earthly parents as you wished they would be. Imagine them
always reacting in ways that were best for you. Think
of them disciplining you for your good. Think of them
telling you how much you were loved and cherished.
This is what you have in God. He is your Father.

*Father, Abba Father. Loving, merciful Father. Disciplining, wise,
accepting—these describe you, Father. Help me see you in my day.
Help me rely on you as a child does a dad.*

> *For the Father Himself loves you, because you have loved Me, and have believed that I came forth from God.*
> —JOHN 16:27

The Father himself loves you. He doesn't send a second-class angel or any other being to fill the need in your life. He does it himself. He himself loves you.

He also wants to be recognized as Father in your life. Jesus could have used any number of Greek or Hebrew names to refer to God. However, you will find over and over that Jesus referred to him as Father. It seems rather important that you conceive of God as your Father. He is powerful, all-knowing, supernatural—still he is as personal and loving as a father should be.

Jesus always looked to him as his Father. He believed that his plans were best. He did not rebel against them, although at times they brought pain into his life. He knew that his Father could see how things would turn out. He knew that his Father loved him, no matter what his circumstances in life were.

God, you tell me that you personally love me. This is a thought too wonderful for me. Help me remember this during my day. I'm loved and cared for personally by the God of the universe.

For whom the Lord loves He chastens,
And scourges every son whom He receives.
                    —HEB. 12:6

God is the loving, kind father you need to picture. He is also a wise father. He knows that you are determined to go your own way, one that will only lead to disaster and destruction. As your Father, he does not stand idly by and watch you die in despair.

God is a Father who disciplines all those whom he calls his own. He sends events and circumstances in your life to help you develop into a healthy, mature Christian. He is gentle and kind, but he is not a doormat. He is not puny and fearful. He doesn't love you because he needs you. His love is pure. His love always does what is best for you even when you don't agree that it can be best.

May I remember, O Lord, when I am being disciplined by you, that it is really because you love me.

> *But you know this proven character, that as a son*
> *with his father he served with me in the gospel.*
> —PHIL. 2:22

Family bonds are not limited to bloodlines. Paul and Timothy are an example of that. Paul saw Timothy as a son and loved him as a son. They were spiritually father and son. Christian relationships can grow into these types of relationships. When they do, they provide a catalyst for strength and growth.

Don't look for Christian brothers or sisters to change the reality of your past. Look to them to stimulate growth in the future. Always remember that they are human and they will fail you. But keep in mind that they can help you grow and develop as a Christian.

Churches can provide family relationships. You can develop friends who will stick by you closer than some of your blood relatives. Be careful not to slip into your codependent patterns with your Christian friends. But do reach out. Meet their needs and allow them to meet your needs. Family was designed and created by God. Today's families are far from the design God intended, but still they are important. The church can be another family environment.

God, help me find the friends and relationships you want me to have. Help me not get caught up in my old codependent relationships again.

When Jesus therefore saw His mother, and the disciple whom He loved standing by, He said to His mother, "Woman, behold your son!" Then He said to the disciple, "Behold your mother!" And from that hour that disciple took her to his own home.
—JOHN 19:26–27

As Jesus was dying on the cross to pay the price for all the sins of the world, his mind focused for a moment on the needs of just two people. His physical body battered and broken, his heart bleeding with emotional pain—Jesus thoughtfully considered his earthly mother. He knew her need for relationship, for someone physically present to depend on like a son. Jesus assigned that task to one of his disciples.

The disciple took that task and completed it from that moment on. Christians can do likewise for one another. You can look to older Christians as spiritual parents to guide you in your walk toward healthy living and intimacy with God. You can be like a child to an elderly person who needs your help. You could stop by an older person's home and visit with them weekly.

The stage of reparenting can be complemented by developing healthy family relationships in your life. Identify when you are beginning to slip back into your old patterns. Don't allow codependency to ruin your new relationships.

God, show me who is my mother and father, sister and brother. Help me reach out to others. Help me accept Christian family relationships. Keep me from getting into old, unhealthy patterns.

> *Let each of you look out not only for his own*
> *interests, but also for the interests of others.*
> —PHIL. 2:4

As a person in recovery, you may have lost sight of the needs of others. Don't fall into the trap of self-centeredness. Facing yourself fully and painfully realizing the ways you have gotten off track in relationships has been essential to your growth. Don't, however, stay so focused on yourself that you do not see the legitimate needs of others in your life.

In your path of recovery, you will find that balance is the key to healthy living. Don't just look to your own interests; look also to the interests and needs of others. Hopefully, you have gained insight into how people have influenced your own life for good or bad. Now, you can try to have positive influences in the lives of people you know. Your spouse, children, and friends have needs that could be acknowledged by you in healthy ways.

Keep my life in balance. Help me avoid focusing so intently on myself that others blur in the background.

And be kind to one another, tenderhearted,
forgiving one another, just as God in Christ
also forgave you. —EPH. 4:32

Kindness and codependence are not synonymous. You may not know how to fulfill this Scripture in your relationships, but kindness and forgiveness are definitely qualities that God wants for your life. The alternatives are bitterness and selfishness. Developing the character of bitterness and selfishness has not been what your recovery was all about.

You are learning a new kindness and a new forgiveness. You will need to forgive some people in your life but keep boundaries with them. Many people could abuse your kindness, and you need to be careful not to use your kindness to develop codependent relationships with others. But don't stop reaching out and caring for people.

Ask God to lead you to true kindness. Do your acts of kindness to glorify him, not to cover up your pain. Take steps to build up others. Many find that when they reach out to others for God's glory, they feel more blessed for the kind deed they did. This can be your experience too as you grow into healthy relationships.

May my habit be to reach out in kindness toward others.

> *Bear one another's burdens, and so fulfill the law*
> *of Christ.*
> —GAL. 6:2

Who has helped you bear your burdens? Was there a special friend who reached out to you in your time of need? Have you thanked them?

Do you know how to bear others' burdens without getting caught once again in the trap of codependency? Ask God to help you so you can become the person he desires for you to be. You will miss out on a great deal of pleasure in this life if you do not learn how to truly help others.

Bearing another's burden does not mean solving his or her problem. It does not mean feeling responsible for the problem; it does mean sympathizing with the pain. Recognize what you can and cannot do for this person and accept the reality of your limits. Pray for them and let them know you are thinking about them and are concerned with what they are experiencing.

Your journey toward healthy living does involve reaching out to help others. Are you ready to grow in this way? If so, you will gain wonderful blessings, not the bondage of codependency.

In what I do for others, Lord, you bless me in return.

For this is the message that you heard from the beginning, that we should love one another.
—1 JOHN 3:11

Giving up on love and relationships is not an option for you if you want all that God has for you in this life. God has told us this message from the beginning; we should love one another. How good are you at loving?

You've experienced many feelings in your recovery. You have acknowledged to yourself more pain and shame than you ever thought you could bear to see. You saw it, and you are still alive. In fact, you are more than alive—you are loved. The motivation for you to reach out and love others is the reality that you have been loved by the greatest of all lovers who could ever exist—God.

When you realize this all-consuming fact, that you are loved, you have a different perspective for loving others. You don't love them because you need them or because you are nothing. You love because God motivates you to do so. You are already accepted completely in Christ. Now you reach out truly for the purpose of exposing others to God's great love through your life.

_____

God, help me love others the way you have loved me. Help me make a difference through my mark of love in their lives as you have in mine.

> *And above all things have fervent love for one*
> *another, for "love will cover a multitude of sins."*
> —1 PETER 4:8

Finding ways to develop your ability to love will enhance your life tremendously. What you thought was love led you to the greatest pain and betrayal in your life. Even so, don't give up on love.

God says to love fervently. The whole issue of love is not just a brief command in Scripture. It is the very character of God. Thus, those who know him and are close to him will reflect that same character in their lives.

Where have you stopped loving? Where are you experiencing pain in your life? Where are you unhappy and lost? Would loving in those situations help? Do you need eyes of love to see the situation in a different light?

Do you know someone who cares about you? Of course God does care for you. He knows you need to give and receive love to journey further into maturity. Do you need someone to love? Do you need someone to love you? Ask God to supply your need for love. He is the one who says it is important in your life. Ask him to lead you along the paths of true Christian love.

God, you want me to seek love fervently in my life. I'm frightened. I need your help. Guide me to true love. Help me experience your kind of love today.

*Therefore if you bring your gift to the altar, and
there remember that your brother has something
against you, leave your gift there before the altar,
and go your way. First be reconciled to your
brother, and then come and offer your gift.*
—MATT. 5:23–24

You probably have already started making some difficult changes in your relationships.

God puts a great deal of emphasis on relationships,
and he cares very much about the state of your relationships. Relating to him fully and growing in him is
impossible if you ignore your human relationships. Relationship with God is not an escape from your human
relationships. Relationship with God enhances your
human relationships.

He holds you accountable for your relationships.
You need to depend on him to show you when and if
you need to make a relationship right. He is worshiped
more deeply by you when you show and express his
character of love in your relationships.

Figuring out relationships is a difficult process. You
have relied on your counselor to guide you, for many
beliefs you held about yourself kept you blind to what
you really needed to do. Rely on God to show you how
to relate the way he desires for you.

*God, show me where I need to make things right in relationships.
Give me the willingness to do your will.*

Brethren, if a man is overtaken in any trespass, you who are spiritual restore such a one in a spirit of gentleness, considering yourself lest you also be tempted.
—GAL. 6:1

How much do you care about your brother? Do you care enough to risk confronting him if he is consistently living in destructive ways?

To confront a brother every day is not healthy nor necessary. Yet, would you confront someone if God laid him on your heart? Would you risk what he would think of you?

Before you answer that too eagerly, would you do it with meekness and humility? Could you see that you yourself, but for the grace of God, could be doing the same or similar sin for which you confront him.

Think about it. You are growing into the person God wants you to be. Is there a need for you to humbly confront individual(s) that you know?

God, I don't want to hold anything back. Lead me in my relationships. I want to be accountable to you.

*Therefore, since Christ has suffered for us in the
flesh, arm yourselves also with the same mind, for
he who has suffered in the flesh has ceased from
sin, that he no longer should live the rest of his
time in the flesh for the lusts of men, but for the
will of God.*
—1 PETER 4:1–2

In Christ you can leave your past behind. As you have learned, it is impossible to leave your codependency without his power.

Don't expect too much of yourself. Learned behaviors take time and effort to practice in your daily experience. Reward yourself for small accomplishments during the day. Pat yourself on the back when you find yourself being assertive where you would have otherwise been a doormat or overly aggressive.

Have the mind of Christ when he came to earth to do his Father's will. A human body was foreign to him. It did not always feel right to do the things he knew his Father wanted him to do. So, how did he do it? He focused on the wisdom of God, not on his daily situations and how uncomfortable they were.

This is true of your daily walk too. You will be doing things that are foreign and uncomfortable. Don't focus on how hard or insignificant each new behavior is; instead focus on how important it is to do this small task to reach your bigger goal—freedom from codependence.

*Help me do what you did, God. Help me focus on the larger goal and
see that the little steps are the only way to reach that goal.*

Call upon Me in the day of trouble;
I will deliver you, and you shall glorify Me.
—PS. 50:15

Any good maintenance program will include calling on God for strength to carry it out. This is not a sign of weakness, but of strength. For it is when you are weak that he can be strong.

When you get in trouble, let the first step be prayer. You will need supernatural power to overcome. God wants to deliver you, he promises to deliver you, and you bring glory to God each time you overcome.

You are so special to God that when you call to him in your trouble he will come to your side and see you through the right choices. You must trust him more than your old behavior patterns. Even though those patterns are self-destructive, they create a diversion for you. When you call upon God, you have to face the reality of your pain and see your trouble fully to experience his deliverance. New and sometimes difficult, yes—but once you have tried it and found him faithful, he will replace your unhealthy behavior patterns.

Call out to God in your trouble today. Remember, don't berate yourself that you can't overcome without him. You were designed that way. You need God.

Before I start my day, I ask for your deliverance. Deliver me from my trouble and help me grow in dependence on you.

Create in me a clean heart, O God,
And renew a steadfast spirit within me.
—PS. 51:10

As you face today remember that what happened yesterday doesn't make victory today impossible. Ask God to create the clean heart you need. Be willing to confess your sins. Accept his cleansing and the fresh start he wants to give you.

We all need fresh starts. You can have a fresh start today if you pray the same prayer of David in Psalm 51:10. David prayed this prayer after the biggest of his many sins—adultery, murder, and cover-up. As unworthy as he must have felt, he knew God would be faithful to create him anew.

You may feel unworthy. Perhaps the past few days have not been as victorious over your old behavior patterns as you wanted them to be. Maybe you didn't meet goals you had set for yourself. God hasn't stopped reaching out to you. He wants to help you.

Look to him today. Ask him to create a new spirit in you. Ask him to clean you. Start your day fresh and new in Christ.

Forgive me for my sins. Thank you for changing me so far. Help me see where I can change today.

> *A man who isolates himself seeks his own desire;*
> *He rages against all wise judgment.*
>
> —PROV. 18:1

Perhaps you have felt like a fool most of your life. You believed there was nothing worthwhile or good in you; otherwise people wouldn't treat you as they have. Hopefully, through your recovery, you have found these beliefs to be lies.

Now you are ready to face the world with a new way of perceiving and accepting reality. As you do this, you will indeed become truly wise. You will be wiser for forgiving those it makes no sense to forgive. You will be wiser for understanding that you are not responsible for other people's lives. You will focus on what God desires for you to do for yourself and others and leave their response to him and them.

You are beginning to understand wisdom. How do you like it so far? How do you like living your life according to God's plan? It hasn't been easy, has it? Tomorrow may have more difficult tasks than you met so far. But with each experience you go through with God as your help, you will become wiser and more able to face the future.

God, give me your wisdom. Sometimes the tasks I've had to do were difficult and unnatural. But, I've seen them free me. Help me trust your wisdom as I live my life today.

For I know the thoughts that I think toward you, says the LORD, thoughts of peace and not of evil, to give you a future and a hope. —JER. 29:11

Can you imagine God sitting and thinking of specific plans and hopes for your life? This is exactly what he tells you he is doing. He has so many hopes and good thoughts for you. He wants peace to replace the evil in your life. He wants your future to be bright.

Ask him to show you what those thoughts include. Let him guide you in your future choices. Let him inspire you to live your life in healthy ways.

What could it be that God is thinking for you? Imagine what those thoughts for peace may be. See yourself living on this earth at peace with yourself and God. Can you imagine peace amidst storms and evil in this world? God can.

God wants you to recover from codependence. He wants you to find peace and satisfaction. He has only good thoughts and plans for you.

God, show me some of thoughts and plans you have been thinking for me. Help me see what you may want me to do to accomplish those thoughts.

> *Trust in the LORD with all your heart,*
> *And lean not on your own*
> *understanding;*
> *In all your ways acknowledge Him,*
> *And He shall direct your paths.*
> —PROV. 3:5–6

You have made a plan to maintain your healthy behaviors. Commit that plan to God. Ask him to bring glory to himself through your life. Ask him to bless your plan and show you ways to change it or develop it. Ask him for the strength to carry out your plan.

Acknowledge that the plan you have made is impossible without God's help. Ask him daily to help you with your plan.

Learn to trust God. At times you will doubt that he really is on your side and lighting your path. At times your path seems dark and lonely. Trust that he is with you and turn your perspective to find out how and why.

Even when my path seems dark, I believe that there is light.

And let us not grow weary while doing good, for in due season we shall reap if we do not lose heart.
—GAL. 6:9

Have you gotten weary yet? You will. It is all a part of growth. Don't feel like a failure because you get tired. It's hard work to change all the thoughts and behaviors that come most naturally to you.

Don't feel selfish and small because you desire a reward for your changes. I once had a patient who felt disappointed when she came in for her monthly check-ups after hospitalization and shared the positive choices she made. Although I always encouraged her and praised her for her efforts, she felt inside that it wasn't enough. She confessed that it took so much effort that she thought a parade, similar to the ones given for war heroes with all the confetti and fanfare, would do the job.

You desire a reward for your labor. You are promised one. Your hard work and determination are not in vain. You will reap your reward—peace and contentment in life, ways to deal with your pain when you have neither peace or contentment, and also a reward in heaven if you accept Christ as your Savior.

God, I'm weary. I want a reward. You know all of this and have it planned in due season. Thank you.

Hope for Recovering Codependents

Without hope, true recovery from codependency is impossible. Your unhealthy behavior pattern did not develop suddenly; your whole life has probably been spent trying to be good enough, to do enough, to have enough. *Hope* is a word you rarely used unless in some vague, wish-for-the-moon sense.

But now you are on the road to recovery. It's harder than you thought it was, but it's also more exciting. For the first time you can envision a future that is different from the past. You can use the word *hope*, not as synonymous with *cope*, but rather defined as *victory*.

*For whatever things were written before were
written for our learning, that we through the
patience and comfort of the Scriptures might have
hope. Now may the God of patience and comfort
grant you to be like-minded toward one another,
according to Christ Jesus.*
　　　　　　　　　　　　—ROM. 15:4–5

Have you ever noticed that some people are able to walk through the darkest valleys with a song on their lips and victory in their hearts? Is it just personality that makes some travelers crumble under the load, while others appear stronger for having carried it? Where does their courage come from? Romans 15:4–5 tell us that God's Word is the storehouse where the treasures of perseverance, encouragement, and hope are kept. We can make as many withdrawals as we want, and there will always be more available. This is because an infinite God is the supplier of these precious commodities. Perservance, encouragement, and hope are in short supply in our bankrupt world. But God has supplied all that we need each day that we live in the precious pages of his Word.

Thank you, Lord, for the encouragement you give me through your Word. It is a comfort to know you are always willing and ready to guide me through life's difficult moments.

Now may the God of hope fill you with all joy and peace in believing, that you may abound in hope by the power of the Holy Spirit. —ROM. 15:13

If anyone's circumstances could have been an excuse for negative thinking, it was Paul's. Beatings, shipwreck, deprivation, and plots to kill him were commonplace in his life. Yet Paul's letters virtually ring with the joy and hope he had in Jesus Christ. Hope is one of the most important ingredients to a meaningful life. And the precious message of Romans 15:13 is that our loving Father is the source of our hope, not the circumstances of our lives. We don't need a certain job or a particular person or any material possession to bring us the joy and peace and hope that our hearts crave. It is all there in *abundance,* as we yield our lives totally to the power of the Holy Spirit.

Dear Lord, keep me from clutching too tightly to my heart the things of this world. Let my hands and heart stay open to receive the priceless blessings of your joy and peace and hope.

*For your obedience has become known to all.
Therefore I am glad on your behalf; but I want you
to be wise in what is good, and simple concerning
evil. And the God of peace will crush Satan under
your feet shortly. The grace of our Lord Jesus Christ
be with you. Amen.*   —ROM. 16:19–20

When we begin to truly recover from codependency,
the changes in our personality will be obvious to all.
Our obedience to the principles of God's Word will give
new power and strength to our lives and bring joy to
the hearts of other believers. We may begin to believe
that because we have overcome our past, the future
will be easy and carefree. We may even begin to take
our new life for granted, thinking we can put ourselves
into any situation and come out unscathed. Here is
where we need to be careful. The Lord wants us to be
looking daily to him through prayer and Bible study so
that we can continue to be "wise in what is good." He
also wants us to realize our vulnerability and stay as
far away as possible from things which might ensnare
us.

When we conscientiously practice these things, we
are assured that God's peace will be ours in great measure and that victory over Satan's schemes to defeat us
is assured.

----

*Lord, in a world that teaches we can only "cope" with our problems,
you give us hope for victory and peace. Thank you.*

Therefore, behold, I will allure her,
Will bring her into the wilderness,
And speak comfort to her.
I will give her her vineyards from there,
And the Valley of Achor as a door of hope;
She shall sing there,
As in the days of her youth,
As in the day when she came up from the
land of Egypt. —HOS. 2:14–15

Israel's history was full of ups and downs. In one of the down times, the prophet Hosea called the people to repentance and told them God still cared and would someday restore them to himself.

Many of us have known very difficult times as well. Some of us have experienced being brought into a type of wilderness so that we would finally be able to hear his voice. This verse assures us that out of that wilderness will come *good* fruit. God also declares that out of the Valley of Achor (which means trouble) God will give his people a door of hope. God does not take pleasure in the suffering of his people. Sometimes, however, he has to use suffering to teach us valuable lessons. Once we have learned those lessons by heart, our valley of trouble actually becomes a doorway of hope.

Lord, I trust you. I know you do not allow anything to come my way except that it is for my ultimate good. As a result, I rest in this hope.

> Though the fig tree may not blossom,
> Nor fruit be on the vines;
> Though the labor of the olive may fail,
> And the fields yield no food;
> Though the flock be cut off from the fold,
> And there be no herd in the stalls—
> Yet I will rejoice in the LORD
> I will joy in the God of my salvation.
> The LORD God is my strength;
> He will make my feet like deer's feet
> And He will make me walk on my high hills.
> —HAB. 3:17–19

Because our creation is fallen, no life or time is immune to struggle and heartache. But deciding how we will respond to these inevitable troubles determines our ultimate success or failure.

The prophet Habakkuk lived in an age when the future of his country looked very bleak indeed. There was corruption within and the threat of conquest without. Habakkuk struggled with what he saw happening around him. But instead of throwing up his hands in defeat, he ends his book of prophecy on a note of crystal-clear triumph.

Even if drought and war destroyed every vestige of material and societal security, Habakkuk declared his determination to *exult* in salvation. You see, this prophet knew that no matter how hard the struggle was, God would give him strength.

Dear Lord, thank you that you are my confidence in the midst of trouble. Your provision for me is always perfect and complete.

*Hold fast the pattern of sound words which you
have heard from me, in faith and love which are
in Christ Jesus.*
—2 TIM. 1:13

One of the greatest causes of hope for any believer is that God is faithful. This precious truth stands out in bold relief next to a world where faithfulness has gone out of style. Are you tired of marriage or a mate? Just say good-bye. Have you been offended by someone at church? Find a new one. Such shallow and simplistic thinking abounds in our society and is little by little dismantling it.

But what joy and peace and hope belongs to the child of God who knows his Father is always faithful. God never gives up on us, never turns his back on his beloved, blood-bought children. In fact, even when we are so fearful or depressed or disobedient that our faith seems to be gone, God is still there, saying, "You belong to me—I will always be a Father to you, loving you, disciplining you, comforting you, guiding you." Why? Because when the almighty God of the universe looks at you and me, he sees us as so completely locked into himself that to deny us would be to deny himself.

*Dear Father, thank you for your faithfulness. Help me to respond to
your faithfulness by being more faithful to you.*

> *. . . that by two immutable things, in which it is impossible for God to lie, we might have strong consolation, who have fled for refuge to lay hold of the hope set before us. This hope we have as an anchor of the soul, both sure and steadfast, and which enters the Presence behind the veil, where the forerunner has entered for us, even Jesus, having become High Priest forever according to the order of Melchizedek.*
>
> —HEB. 6:18–20

When my children were small, anything that overwhelmed them caused an immediate and consistent reaction. They would run to me, grab me around the leg, and hang on for dear life. From this "safe" vantage point, they could gaze at whatever troubled them with confidence.

God gives us much the same picture in these verses in Hebrews. Each of us have fears and struggles in life. These are useful if they cause us to flee for refuge to Jesus. The words "entered within the veil" draw forth the picture of the Jewish high priest entering behind the temple veil into the Holy of Holies. Our hope and security in Jesus is steadfast because that hope takes us into God's very presence. Here we are safe. We don't have to be tossed about by waves of unhappy memories or present circumstances or future fears. When we abide in his presence, our hope and confidence are sure.

Dear Father, I want to constantly abide in your presence so that my life will reflect your strength and peace.

No temptation has overtaken you except such as is common to man; but God is faithful, who will not allow you to be tempted beyond what you are able, but with the temptation will also make the way of escape, that you may be able to bear it.

—1 COR. 10:13

Habits form the foundation of everyday life. We all have certain eating habits, work habits, and sleep habits. These things tend to give our lives stability, unless they are habits which are bad for us in one way or another. Breaking a bad habit and replacing it with a new one can be a tedious and frustrating experience. Sometimes we feel as if the old bad habit has us by the neck, choking our aspirations and desires for a better life in the Lord. The apostle Paul uses the word *seize* or *overtake* to describe the constant temptation of a bad habit. Yes, he declares, we all have temptation. But how encouraging that Paul doesn't stop at this forlorn pronouncement. Instead, he declares the secret of victory.

First, all trusting must be completely in God who is faithful, instead of in our own frail ability to overcome. Second, *knowing* that God will *never* allow us to be pushed beyond what we can bear strengthens and steadies us. Third, taking the way of escape which God has promised to provide (instead of the way of indulgence) makes us able to endure the temptation. If we make these steps a habit in our daily lives, victory now and good hope for the future are within our grasp.

Dear Lord, thank you for the way of escape from temptation.

> *Unless the LORD builds the house,*
> *They labor in vain who build it;*
> *Unless the LORD guards the city,*
> *The watchman stays awake in*
> *vain.*
> *It is vain for you to rise up early,*
> *To sit up late,*
> *To eat the bread of sorrows;*
> *For so He gives His beloved sleep.*
> —PS. 127:1–2

Many of us were brought up to believe that hard work was the measure of a person, and that if anyone wanted something badly enough and worked hard enough, he would be a success. Children were taught not only to say, but believe, "I am the master of my fate, I am the captain of my soul."

But we who have followed this formula know that these things are hollow at best—and indeed could be considered treacherous lies.

In contrast, this passage from Psalms declares eternal truth to us. First, we must continually acknowledge our utter dependence upon God for any success we hope to have in our lives. But the most wonderful message in these verses is that not only is our God in control, but he also takes special joy in giving good gifts to us who are his beloved. As we meditate daily on his Word and speak to him in prayer, we will discover that this sovereign, powerful God is a loving Father who delights to see us resting in him, looking to him for direction, and rejoicing in his marvelous gifts.

God, thank you for loving me and desiring your best for my life.

I have become all things to all men, that I might by all means save some. Now this I do for the gospel's sake, that I may be partaker of it with you. Do you not know that those who run in a race all run, but one receives the prize? Run in such a way that you may obtain it. And everyone who competes for the prize is temperate in all things. Now they do it to obtain a perishable crown, but we for an imperishable crown.

—1 COR. 9:22–25

One of the seeming paradoxes of Christianity is that believers are free people who are servants. Since we have been freed from sin and self, this very freedom has allowed us to become the servants of Christ. Because we belong to Christ, we are free from other people's control and power over our lives. Now we can freely choose to do whatever it takes to share the message of God's love and regeneration with them.

The last part of this passage could be summed up in one word—*vigilance*. No one ever gets to the point where there is no longer a need for spiritual self-discipline. Later in this chapter Paul compares this need to competing in the athletic events of racing and boxing. He is reminding us that the "opponents" are always near, trying to trip us up or catch us off guard.

How important it is for each of us to be viligant in our relationship with God, continually using the tools he has given us to keep our lives in the center of his will, covered with the peace and serenity of his grace.

I pray for vigilance, Lord. May I not slip again into dysfunctional, codependent relationships.

> *Jesus answered and said to her, "Whoever drinks of this water will thirst again, but whoever drinks of the water that I shall give him will never thirst. But the water that I shall give him will become in him a fountain of water springing up into everlasting life."*
>
> —JOHN 4:13–14

For most of us, life has been a thirsty experience. We have thirsted for love, security, self-worth, and peace. Many of us tried to quench that thirst through control, addictions, and other inappropriate behaviors. But now at last we have come to know the one who can satisfy the deepest thirst of every human spirit. We have put our trust in Jesus Christ who gives to us, as he did the woman at the well, a fountain of water springing up into everlasting life. When some people think of everlasting life, they think of life after death in heaven with the Lord. But this is only part of what everlasting life means; eternal life begins the moment we accept Christ as Savior.

So how do we as believers participate in the joy and peace of everlasting life right now? We do this by getting to know our precious Lord better each day.

It is significant that the Lord connects water with the Word of God. Just as water is physically essential for quenching our thirst and cleansing our bodies, so the Word of God performs the same functions for our spiritual lives. Not only does it cleanse our souls, but it also quenches the deep thirst of our spirit as we listen to his voice and respond.

Thank you for giving me your Word to quench my thirst.

You are my hiding place;
You shall preserve me from trouble;
You shall surround me with songs
of deliverance.
I will instruct you and teach you in
the way you should go.
—PS. 32:7–8

The times of our confusion, struggle, and guilt are ending. A new day of grace has dawned upon our lives. In the strength of the Lord we will lose our fears and entrust to him every memory, every action, every attitude.

David continually acknowledged his total confidence in God, who became to him a hiding place and surrounded him with "songs of deliverance." And just as God delivered David from his foes, the Lord will deliver us from our shortcomings and old behavior patterns. When God sees us humble and trusting before him, he will bring about changes in our lives to repair the damage of our past and restore us to wholeness.

As we reflect on this passage, it is comforting to know that God takes a special, personal interest in each one who belongs to him. We are not just a number or statistic to him; his relationship to us is supremely important to him. And because it is, we can have the faith to humble ourselves before him and allow him to transform our lives into beautiful examples of his serenity and love.

Thank you, Lord, for being my hiding place when I need it and for directing my pathway through this life.

This I say, therefore, and testify in the Lord, that you should no longer walk as the rest of the Gentiles walk, in the futility of their mind, having their understanding darkened, being alienated from the life of God, because of the ignorance that is in them, because of the hardening of their heart; who, being past feeling, have given themselves over to licentiousness, to work all uncleanness with greediness. But you have not so learned Christ, if indeed you have heard Him and have been taught by Him, as the truth is in Jesus: that you put off, concerning your former conduct, the old man which grows corrupt according to the deceitful lusts, and be renewed in the spirit of your mind.

—EPH. 4:17–23

Letting go of old habits is easier said than done. Each of us must come to the point where we are truly committed to making that break with our past.

That struggle reminds me of Linus and his blanket in *Peanuts*. Sometimes, Linus will fling the tattered, dirty blanket behind him, determined never again to pick it up. Yet, in a moment of weakness he runs for the comfort it seems to offer.

Paul encouraged the Ephesians to determine once and for all with God's help to throw away that dirty, dark blanket of sin and to desire to be completely "renewed in the spirit of your mind." That renewal can take place only when we have become totally willing and ready for God to work radically in our lives.

Lord, I realize that my codependent relationships stem from a habit I have chosen to adopt in order to cover up my weaknesses. And with your help I now choose to throw away that dirty blanket.

Remove from me the way of lying,
And grant me Your law graciously.
I have chosen the way of truth;
Your judgments I have laid before me.
I cling to Your testimonies;
O LORD, do not put me to shame! . . .
Teach me, O LORD, the way of Your statutes,
And I shall keep it to the end.
Give me understanding,
And I shall keep Your law;
Indeed, I shall observe it with my whole
heart.
　　　　　　　　　　　　　　　　—PS. 119:29–34

Psalm 119 is called the wisdom psalm. As we work through our problems, accept our weaknesses, and look to God for strength, we will sow the seeds of true wisdom in our own lives and reap a harvest of peace and joy. The psalmist is grieved over his shortcomings and longs for God to change him. He continually acknowledges his need for God to be in control of his life.

Instead of trying to correct things himself, he simply turns in total readiness to God. God alone can teach, give understanding, make him walk, and incline his heart. In other words, the psalmist desires to let God do all and anything that needs to be done in his life. And even though the psalmist is still aware of the problems in his life, his real focus is on God and the power of his Word. When we can focus so completely on God's power, we will find strength—and ultimately victory.

Lord, I know I am not strong. But my trust and focus is not in myself. You are wise and strong. As I yield my thoughts and actions to your control, I know I will reap a wonderful harvest of peace and joy.

He who dwells in the secret place of the Most High
Shall abide under the shadow of the Almighty.
I will say of the LORD,
"He is my refuge and my fortress;
My God, in Him I will trust."

—PS. 91:1–2

When we choose to trust Jesus as our Savior and to turn our will and life over to Him, we are given entrance to a most marvelous place. Through the Holy Spirit who indwells us, we are lifted into "the secret place" where blessings and untold treasure abound. We are given access to the very mind of God. Here, the love and protection of our precious Lord can continually enfold and support us. The problem comes when we use our "secret place" more like a motel than a permanent home. We may want "just a little talk with Jesus" to make it right. But the psalmist uses the words *dwell* and *abide* for good reason. We can't know the peace and security and help of God unless we are habitually in his Word and in communion with him through prayer. As we begin to do this, we will be delivered from the snare of our old habits and the pestilence of troublesome attitudes.

The truth of his Word will shield our minds from fear and doubt. And knowing how completely we can trust him will give us confidence and hope for the future.

Lord Jesus, I long for the peace and joy that come from dwelling in your presence. Thank you that you desire to give me these things as much as I desire to have them.

For he has not despised nor abhorred the affliction
of the afflicted;
Nor has He hidden His face from Him;
But when He cried to Him, He heard.

—PS. 22:24

During the process of recovery, sometimes we still end up feeling "afflicted." I find it really comforting to know that God doesn't disregard us or consider us worthless (hide his face from us), even if we tend to put ourselves in that category! He won't withdraw from us or ignore us.

The truth is that God still loves us and wants us to come to him in our neediness. He hears our prayers when we genuinely ask for his help and comfort. More than that, he desires to walk with us through our distress. He will give us the strength and power to progress beyond the pain in our present circumstances. Only he will never disappoint us.

Father, thank you that you don't scorn me when I'm having trouble getting through the mess in my life. Thank you for listening to me and being my true friend. Help me to remember that you want to give me the strength to continue seeking real health and wholeness in you.

> *He will not be afraid of evil tidings;*
> *His heart is steadfast, trusting in the LORD.*
> *His heart is established;*
> *He will not be afraid.*
>
> —PS. 112:7–8

As recovering codependents we find it very easy to get upset over bad news. It's tempting to focus on a difficult situation especially if it's happening to someone else, and not deal with our own personal issues. Because of this tendency, one of our biggest problems is a lack of stability. We need a steadfast heart, one that trusts in God and does not fear, and to be able to sit back and allow God to handle problem situations that we do not have the ability to control.

Because he is unchanging, we can find our stability in him. His love for us doesn't vary, not even when our performance doesn't match up to our expectations. No matter what kind of "bad news" comes our way, we can single-mindedly trust in the Lord. Isn't it great to know that in Jesus Christ we can really be secure? No wonder we don't have to be afraid.

Father, thank you for your Word that reminds us who you are and how we can be emotionally healthy by trusting you. Help us to turn the "bad news" in our lives over to you, to work out the circumstances through your love and power.

For thus says the High and Lofty One
Who inhabits eternity, whose name is Holy:
"I dwell in the high and holy place,
With him who has a contrite and humble spirit,
To revive the spirit of the humble,
And to revive the heart of the contrite ones."

—ISA. 57:15

Many African traditional religions contain stories of a high, creator god who became disgusted with human beings for some reason and has ignored them ever since, living in his lofty heaven. All too often, perfectionistic, codependent people in our society also have the same view of God. But this verse states that God *is* concerned with his creatures.

Many struggle with maintaining confidence and hope in God in their daily lives, and this verse can bring great comfort to those needing renewal from God in this area. He promises to revive us if we are humble and repentant. The fact that the holy God would occupy himself with people is tremendous reassurance. God requires of us only that we be humble before him, honestly searching ourselves and repenting of our wrongs. Then through Jesus' death, he promises to forgive and restore us, to give back our confidence and hope.

Thank you, Father, that your love and care reach down to us, even though you are exalted and holy. Thank you that you have made a Way for us to know you, to find our confidence and hope restored through Jesus Christ.

> *And He said to me, "My grace is sufficient for you,*
> *for My strength is made perfect in weakness."*
> *Therefore most gladly I will rather boast in my*
> *infirmities, that the power of Christ may rest*
> *upon me.* —2 COR. 12:9

What does it mean to boast in our infirmities? Sometimes it's easy to read this and not realize that Paul is saying he is happy with, even proud of his weaknesses. How could anyone ever be proud of being weak? How could anyone be happy that he was not able to handle the circumstances of his life? Especially as codependents, we usually tend to try to hide any problems or weaknesses we might have. We don't want to admit even to God that we are vulnerable in certain areas.

But that's exactly what the apostle Paul is saying— he is glad that he is weak! Why? Precisely because it is at that point—when we can admit our weakness—that God can take over in our lives. He covers us with his grace; he protects us with his power. He works to heal us where we are. Even if he chooses not to change our circumstances, his omnipotence will be revealed through our lives as we allow him the freedom to empower us in our weakness. But he will only help us as we are willing to confess our sins and weaknesses and turn ourselves over to him.

Thank you, Lord, that your power is available to me. Help me to be willing to admit my weakness, both to you and to appropriate other people, so that your power may be at work in me.

You number my wanderings,
Put my tears into your bottle.
Are they not in your book?
—PS. 56:8–9

God knows all about my pain. He knows how troubled I am (my wanderings); he has kept a record of my tears. This verse refers to the ancient Middle Eastern practice in which mourners would catch their tears in a bottle (or water skin) and place them at the tomb of their loved ones, thus showing how deep their grief really was. But even without our continuing the same custom, God knows the depths of the pain we have been through. It's all written in his Book—he feels our pain along with us.

And what's more, he's on our side! When we come to him with our problems and resulting pain, he will deliver us. Our "enemies"—both human and circumstantial, both personal and exterior to our person—will be turned back, defeated. Any true victory, such as our recovery from codependency, depends on our crying out to God for his intervention in our lives. We can't defeat our enemies through our own efforts, and God doesn't ask us to. He will work on our behalf. He is for us—that knowledge alone can be healing.

Thank you, Lord, that you know me intimately. My tears can never be hidden from you. Help me to defeat my "enemies" through your strength and power. Thank you that I can count on you to be for me.

> *No eye pitied you . . . to have compassion on you;*
> *but you were thrown out into the open field . . . on*
> *the day you were born. And when I passed by you*
> *and saw you struggling in your own blood, I said to*
> *you . . . "Live!" . . . I made you thrive like a plant*
> *in the field; and you grew, matured, and became*
> *very beautiful. . . . you were naked and bare. When*
> *I passed by you again and looked upon you, indeed*
> *your time was the time of love; so I spread My wing*
> *over you and covered your nakedness. Yes, I swore*
> *an oath to you and entered into a covenant with*
> *you, and you became Mine.* —EZEK. 16:5–8

This passage is very graphic, describing specific Jewish ritual practices that were not performed for the infant, here a figurative picture of Jerusalem. Many of us, as recovering codependents, struggle with abandonment issues. It is very comforting for us to know that God will never abandon us, and that he says to us, "Live!" wanting us to live an abundant life (John 10:10).

He looks at us and finds us lovable and lovely. His love covers our shame and the utter nakedness of our efforts to control our world. He gives us the acceptance and security we are looking for. He covenants with us to be our merciful Lord. The very best part of all is that we become his; we belong.

Lord, I'm so glad to be yours. I'm thankful that I can trust you never to abandon me.

> *Therefore let no one glory in men. For all things*
> *are yours . . . the world or life or death, or things*
> *present or things to come—all are yours. And you*
> *are Christ's, and Christ is God's.*
> —1 COR. 3:21–23

What happens when we start to boast (glory) in men and what they can do? As codependents, if we are glorying in others, putting them on pedestals, we easily become addicted to them. We become people-pleasers instead of God-worshipers, or we become so concerned with the other's needs and emotions that we try to take over God's role in that person's life.

In opposition to this attitude of glorying in men, Paul reminds us that in Christ we possess all things—this world, life and death, the present and the future. Because we belong to Christ we have all of his resources available to us. We don't need any of the things, people, or events we so often become addicted to. Above and beyond all of this, in Christ Jesus we are also united with God. Now, that's something we can really glory in!

Dear Lord, help me not to boast about other people or myself. Help me to remember that through my union with you I possess all things. Thank you for the glory that exists inherently in Jesus Christ.

> *Now our Lord Jesus Christ Himself, and our God
> and Father, who has loved us and has given us
> everlasting consolation and good hope by grace,
> comfort your hearts and establish you in every
> good word and work.*   —2 THESS. 2:16–17

Two things stand out to me in Paul's prayer for the Thessalonians. The first is that we are loved by God. Even after a time in recovery, we may still find it difficult to remember this, sometimes even to believe that God could love us. I'm not perfect—how could he love me? But the Scriptures tell us over and over again, and not just here, that he does. It's awesome to know that the God of the universe loves me!

The second thing is that this God who loves me is able and wants to encourage (another way to say console or comfort) me and strengthen me. Paul's prayer mentions both good deeds and good works. As we accept the inner strength and encouragement that the Lord gives, he will empower us to speak and act in a way that is in accord with his will. And his consolation is everlasting, eternal. It doesn't just happen when we are performing well, but it is available to us all the time. God will produce lasting results in our lives that lead to our complete recovery, that will be evidenced in our words and deeds.

Thank you, Lord, that you're my Father who truly loves me. Thank you for the everlasting encouragement and comfort you give through your grace in my life.

Show me Your ways, O LORD;
Teach me Your paths.
Lead me in Your truth and teach me,
For You are the God of my salvation;
On You I wait all the day.
    —PS. 25:4–5

What do we know about the ways of the Lord? All the ways of the Lord are loving and faithful. He is benevolent and full of mercy. To whom does the Lord teach his paths? Those who reverence and obey him will learn his path for them and will know his truth. Giving reverence to the Lord—standing in awe of his omnipotence (controlling power) and holiness (absolute goodness)—results in the knowledge of God's truth and his ways. It is incredible that God would let human beings in on such magnificence, that we can be party to his love and faithfulness! But he *is* our God, and our hope is in him. We can wait on him, knowing that his ways are only good and that he will teach us about himself. He is the God of our salvation. When we know his truth and his ways and practice them, we are finally on the path to recovery.

Lord, it's fantastic that you provide all we need for emotional and spiritual health and wholeness. Help me to humble myself before you and seek to know you and your truth intimately. Thank you for your love and faithfulness.

> *Therefore do not cast away your confidence, which*
> *has great reward. For you have need of endurance,*
> *so that after you have done the will of God, you*
> *may receive the promise.* —HEB. 10:35–36

It's pretty easy to throw away our confidence in God and his will for our lives when adverse circumstances or difficult relationships with others come about. We may find ourselves rebelling and forgetting that holding tight to our confidence in the Lord brings a rich reward. It's not easy to have patience, to let God work things out in his own time. We want to fix things, right now!

Another way to translate *patience* in this verse is *perseverance*. What does it mean to a recovering codependent to persevere in doing the will of God? Only God working in another person or through some set of circumstances can effect a cure. Only he is in control. That's why we can really have confidence in him. Patience and perseverance in doing the will of God means letting go, allowing him to work in your own life; to do his will through you, letting *him* decide what is best for others. Our receiving what he has promised doesn't depend on whether we have fixed everyone and everything that came across our path. According to this passage, it depends on keeping our confidence in him, being patient, so that we can do the will of God.

Lord, it's so hard to allow you to work in my problem situations, to trust that you can and will handle everything for good. Give me the patience to wait for you to act. Thank you for these verses that remind me how you want me to live, so that you can work in my life.

*Therefore humble yourselves under the mighty
hand of God, that He may exalt you in due time,
casting all your care on Him, for He cares for you.*
—1 PETER 5:6–7

I like to think of the Serenity Prayer as a corollary of
this passage. In order to be able to honestly pray the
Serenity Prayer, we need to have humbled ourselves
under God's omnipotent hand. In practical terms this
means to confess our need of his intervention in our
lives, to submit to his healing hand, even though the
situations he leads us through may be painful. Only in
this way can we have the "serenity to accept the things
we cannot change," because we know that his help
will come at just the right time.

The word translated *care* in this verse might be better translated *anxiety*. In this case it denotes self-
centered, counterproductive worry—the kind codependents are especially good at! Anxiety and prayer
are completely opposing forces, so incredible tranquil-
ity comes when we commit all our cares to God in
prayer. His care for us is beyond our understanding
and covers us completely.

*Lord, I'm really good at getting myself all worked up over some prob-
lem instead of turning it over to you. Lord, I want you to be in control
of my life. Help me to be truly humble before you, committing all my
worries to you. Thank you that you care for me perfectly.*

> *God is my strength and power,*
> *And he makes my way perfect.*
> *He makes my feet like the feet of deer,*
> *And sets me on my high places.*
> —2 SAM. 22:33–34

These verses are set in the middle of one of David's songs of deliverance. God had freed him from the tyranny of all his enemies, including Saul, and he was singing his thankfulness to God. He acknowledges God as the source of his strength and power. It can be very difficult to give credit to anyone else, even the Lord God. We would like to be able to say that we fixed it, that we are in control, that we have power in ourselves.

But the truth is that only God has true strength and power to give us through the working of the Holy Spirit in our lives. When we give up trying in our own strength and acknowledge God, requesting his deliverance, then he will make our ways perfect. He can give us stability and freedom in perfect balance so that our emotional and spiritual "feet" are like the feet of a deer. We will be able to climb the "mountains" in our life with joy and confidence in God. Rejoicing in the victory he gives us, we can get "high" in the best sense, without any fear of adverse consequences. His perfect way for us will continue to be the path of hope and healing.

Lord, remind me constantly that only you are sovereign, that only you can give true strength and power to overcome the negative experiences in my past and present. Thank you that your way is perfect.

Do not hide Your face from me;
Do not turn Your servant away in anger;
You have been my help;
Do not leave me nor forsake me,
O God of my salvation.
When my father and my mother forsake me,
Then the LORD will take care of me.
—PS. 27:9–10

Most codependents have experienced rejection and abandonment, especially from their parents. This has resulted in self-esteem problems, fear, and an inability to trust. We are afraid that if we allow ourselves to feel our own anger, we will lose control. We are afraid that if someone else is angry with us, they will reject us.

But God will never abandon us. He will not reject us in anger. Even when he doesn't approve of what we're doing, he still accepts us. Although our earthly parents didn't love us perfectly, God does. He will not forsake us. He has given us a new basis for self-esteem. He loves us so much that he went ahead with creating us even though he knew that we would sin, even though he knew it would cost him his only Son to bring us back into fellowship with him. We can know with certainty that he will never abandon us, that he will love us no matter what happens. We can always go to him for encouragement and strength.

Lord, help me to remember that you loved me enough to die for me. Help me to live as though I really know and believe it. Thank you that you will never reject or abandon me.

> *And the glory which You gave Me I have given*
> *them, . . . I in them, and You in Me . . . and that*
> *the world may know that You have sent Me, and*
> *have loved them as You have loved Me.*
> —JOHN 17:22–23

These two verses made a startling change in my perception of myself as a child of God. I'm not sure exactly where my misconceptions came from, but I certainly didn't believe that God the Father loved me as much as he loved Jesus. I mean Jesus was perfect; he always did what his Father wanted, even if he knew it would be painful. Here Jesus says that he has given us the same glory that God the Father gave to him. He states that he is in us, just as the Father is in him. He accepts as a matter of fact that we are loved by God just as much as he is.

But the thing that impresses me even more, that changed my whole conception of the purpose of God's work in my life, is that everyone I come in contact with will know that God the Father really did send Jesus into this world by the reflection of his love in all the circumstances and relationships in my life. Try substituting your name for all the *them*'s in this verse. I hope it will uplift you as much as it did me.

Father God, it is awe-inspiring and humbling to know that you love me as much as you love Jesus, your only begotten Son. I want you to work out your love in my life so that everyone will know that you sent Jesus as our Savior. Thank you.

*I call heaven and earth as witnesses today against
you, that I have set before you life and death,
blessing and cursing; therefore choose life, that
both you and your descendants may live; that you
may love the LORD your God, that you may obey
His voice and that you may cling to Him; for He is
your life and the length of your days.*

—DEUT. 30:19–20

How can we choose life and blessing instead of death
and cursing? It seems to me that admitting that we are
powerless, that we don't and can't control our world
ourselves, is the first step. The second is to cast ourselves on God, asking for his help to solve our problems.

The result of choosing life isn't just for ourselves, but
for our children, our descendants. Since we have become aware of the concept of generational sin, we can
really understand what is meant here. When a codependent person chooses life instead of death and
works on changing him- or herself with God's help,
then all of his or her family reap the benefits.

Notice the part about clinging to God. This implies
that it is not so much a once-and-for-all decision, but
that it is an ongoing process, a choice that we make
daily, to love the Lord God and obey his voice. He
really is our life!

*Thank you, God, that in you there is life. Help me to choose you and
obedience to your voice, that I and my children may live.*

> *Consider the work of God;*
> *For who can make straight what*
>   *He has made crooked?*
> *In the day of prosperity be joyful,*
> *But in the day of adversity consider:*
> *Surely God has appointed the one*
>   *as well as the other.*
> —ECCL. 7:13–14

God is sovereign, he controls both the "straight"—or good—and the "crooked"—what is seemingly bad—of our lives. It may be the "crooked" that he has created, or the "crooked" that we have caused for ourselves and that he has allowed for a purpose. We make mistakes; we create suffering for ourselves and others by disobeying God's instructions for life.

These verses don't espouse fatalism, but they remind us of who is really God. Human beings can't change anything that God has resolved or allowed. However, we don't have to be full of fear when all kinds of "crooked" circumstances exist in our lives. We know that he is a God of love who has promised us that every situation in the lives of those who love him will work out for good. No matter how big the mess in our lives, God has blessed it. His purposes in our lives will not be thwarted.

God, help me to trust you. Help me to consider all my problems as things you have allowed in my life. Help me to remember that you are my loving, heavenly Father and to be thankful for your working in my life.

Do not be wise in your own eyes;
Fear the LORD and depart from
*   evil.*
It will be health to your flesh
And strength to your bones.
           —PROV. 3:7–8

Codependents are sort of a paradoxical group of people. We struggle with low self-esteem, but we also think that we can figure out what is best for everyone else and that we know just how to fix them up. We seem to think that we're pretty wise, that we know a lot of answers. However, these verses warn us against this type of thinking. Only God is truly wise, and the best thing we can do is to honor and obey him. The strength to depart from evil, to refuse to do wrong, is a natural consequence of a healthy fear of God.

One of the wonderful results of obeying and honoring God is the good health that it brings. Here the reference is seemingly to good physical health, although the use of the word *strength* (or refreshment) could easily refer to good mental health. Another interesting consideration is that the word translated *health* in verse 8 can also mean *medicine*. In other words, it's just like good medicine for us to obey and honor the Lord. It will ease the pain we are going through and heal the wounds of the past. I find great comfort in this: Doing what God wants is also the very best way to continue our recovery.

Lord, so many times I decide that I can handle things and I don't look to you for wisdom. Make me truly wise as I honor and obey you. Thank you for the healing you are working in my life.

When I kept silent,
My bones grew old through my
groaning all the day long.
For day and night Your hand was
heavy upon me;
My vitality was turned into the drought
of summer.
I acknowledged my sin to You . . .
I said, "I will confess my transgressions
to the LORD."
And You forgave the iniquity of my sin.
—PS 32:3–5

Confessing our sins to God can be a very frightening prospect. After all, he is Lord of the universe. What might he do to someone who has broken his commands? So we continue to carry the burden. Our sins distress us even while we ignore or deny their existence. Even if we have experienced his forgiveness before, we allow our difficulty with trusting others, even God, to stand in the way of peace and fresh energy to work on our recovery.

When we confess our sins to God, we find that his love for us is unconditional. His forgiveness is complete and everlasting. We realize that he is not looking for ways to punish us, but that he wants to strengthen and guide us. With the guilt of our sins removed, we will find relief and peace.

Lord God, help me not to try to cover up my sins or deny my responsibility for them. Remind me of the forgiveness that is waiting for me with you. Thank you for your unconditional love that wants to restore me to health and wholeness.

Thus my heart was grieved,
And I was vexed in my mind.
I was so foolish and ignorant;
I was like a beast before You.
Nevertheless I am continually with You;
You hold me by my right hand.
You will guide me with Your counsel,
And afterward receive me to glory.
—PS. 73:21–24

When our thoughts are full of bitterness, we don't react in a healthy way. When our feelings are hurt, we tend to focus on ourselves and don't make progress in recovery. This verse likens someone experiencing these reactions to a dumb animal. Ouch! That hurts! Many really struggle with their feelings and reactions. Even when we "know" how to handle our negative thoughts, we don't always manage to keep on the road to recovery.

Even though we may fall to such ugly depths, God is still with us, and he will not let us go. His wisdom is available to counsel us. He gives us the strength of will to work through unhealthy thoughts and reactions. And that's not all! At the end of our lives here on earth, he will receive us into heaven with honor to be with him forever.

Lord God, thank you that you understand me even when I don't understand myself. Thank you that you are there to give me wisdom and strength when I can't handle things myself.

> *Remember my affliction and roaming, the*
> *wormwood and the gall. My soul still remembers*
> *and sinks within me. This I recall to my mind,*
> *therefore I have hope. Through the Lord's mercies*
> *we are not consumed, because his compassions fail*
> *not.*
> —LAM. 3:19–22

One of the most important parts of the recovery process is continuing to take moral inventory, keeping in touch with oneself on a daily basis. Here Jeremiah likens his past and present suffering to liver bile and the bitter plant known as wormwood. He remembers all that he has been through, the painful wandering of his soul.

But there is one thought that lifts his spirit and gives him hope. He knows that God is merciful and will not destroy him completely. He realizes that God's love is everlasting and unconditional. He is faithful to his promises to forgive and restore his child. He will lead us through the blackness of the past and into the sunlight of new life in him.

Thank you, Lord God, that you are faithful to yourself and therefore faithful to all that you have promised your children. Help me to remember your love and mercy so that I have the strength to face myself and my problems.

*For the weapons of our warfare are not carnal
but mighty in God for pulling down strongholds,
casting down arguments and every high thing that
exalts itself against the knowledge of God, bringing
every thought into captivity to the obedience of
Christ.*   —2 COR. 10:4–5

Our God will prepare us for warfare against the addictions and problems we face, but we have to allow him to. His weapons—meditation, prayer, his Word, the power of the Holy Spirit in our lives—are not weapons that are esteemed in the world around us. They are not weapons that appeal to our human pride; instead their use requires us to humbly submit ourselves to God.

When we are willing to accept his lordship in our lives, then the strongholds of our codependency can be pulled down. These weapons will demolish all of the faulty reasoning and the denial that continue to trouble us during our recovery process, that keep us from a fuller knowledge of God. As we strive to hold every thought obedient to Christ, then our redemption and wholeness will be the exciting result.

Thank you, Lord God, that the weapons you offer us are truly effective. Thank you that you have provided for our healing. May we become completely subject to your lordship in our lives.

Who among you fears the LORD?
Who obeys the voice of His Servant?
Who walks in darkness and has no light?
Let him trust in the name of the LORD
and rely on his God.　　—ISA. 50:10

It is very possible after we have really begun to walk with God and are gaining some victories, that the darkness will seem to fall again. The light at the end of the tunnel will be lost and our hope will be shaken. We're not always sure what the factors are that arise to create such a situation, but we can find our way out of the tunnel.

The way we began is the way we have to go on. Honoring and obeying the Lord as the only Power great enough to help us was our starting point in the recovery process. Realizing that he did want us to be his child and would never abandon us was next. We understood that God the Father and Jesus his Son really love us through meditating on what Jesus did for us on the cross. If we continue to trust in the Lord and rely on him, the darkness will eventually fail, and the light will return.

Lord, I want to continue to honor and obey you. When everything around me seems to be slipping back under the darkness, help me to trust you to keep me on the right path.

But now, thus says the LORD, who created you, O Jacob, and He who formed you, O Israel: "Fear not, for I have redeemed you; I have called you by your name; You are Mine. When you pass through the waters, I will be with you; and through the rivers, they shall not overflow you. When you walk through the fire, you shall not be burned, nor shall the flame scorch you."

—ISA. 43:1–2

God created you and me as surely as he created the first man or the nation of Israel. He commands us not to fear, for he has ransomed us. He has chosen us individually and we belong to him. It sometimes takes a long time before codependents believe this enough to be able to live as though it is true—we probably didn't doubt that there was a God, or even that he had sent Christ into the world to die on the cross to save sinners. But we couldn't believe that we were included in his wonderful plan. Why would God choose us to be his own? He was always there, but we may have allowed all the pain and sadness in our lives to keep us from seeing him.

Slowly and steadily as we searched to know him, he has revealed himself to us. He has walked with us through every difficult circumstance. Sometimes we succeed and sometimes we fail, sometimes we even forget that he is there, but he is always with us.

Thank you, Father, that you have called me by my name, that I am yours. Thank you that you have promised to be with me at all times and in all circumstances.

> *Let us draw near with a true heart in full assurance*
> *of faith, having our hearts sprinkled from an evil*
> *conscience and our bodies washed with pure water.*
> *Let us hold fast the confession of our hope without*
> *wavering, for He who promised is faithful.*
> —HEB. 10:22–23

A sure guarantee of our eventual recovery is maintaining a close relationship with God. Four conditions are listed in these verses for drawing near to God. All of them are characteristics that are very difficult for a codependent person to cultivate. The first is a sincere heart, really wanting to know him. (We often have a hard time being honest with ourselves or others.) The second is faith that wholly trusts Christ. (Trust in another person is a very uncodependent quality.) The third is freedom from guilt in his presence. (What is a codependent if not someone smothering in guilt?) The fourth is cleansing—being washed on the inside by the blood of Christ is like being washed on the outside by pure water. (It's hard to humble ourselves and accept Christ's cleansing.)

In spite of all these obstacles, the only way to continue in recovery is to cling to God, not giving up the struggle nor turning back. Our hope is in him and he will be faithful to his promise to us.

Thank you, Lord God, that you have made a way for us to draw near to you. Thank you that you have sent your Holy Spirit into our world and into our hearts to guide us to you. Help us to cling to you and to the hope you have given us.

But we have this treasure in earthen vessels, that the excellence of the power may be of God and not of us. We are hard pressed on every side, yet not crushed; we are perplexed, but not in despair; persecuted, but not forsaken; struck down, but not destroyed—always carrying about in the body the dying of the Lord Jesus, that the life of Jesus also may be manifested in our body.

—2 COR. 4:7-10

Just as the people of the New Testament times hid their wealth in clay pots, God clothed his majesty in a human body. He has allowed us to know him through Jesus Christ, whose life we possess in our flawed, earthly bodies. He has worked out his plan in this way to show that, in spite of our weakness, he is glorious and totally sufficient to meet our needs. In this way he will receive the praise of the whole universe.

Because he lives in us, we can face the many problems in our lives. We may be troubled, but he keeps us from being crushed. He will protect us from despair when we doubt; he will never abandon us to our enemies whether they are human or spiritual; he will not allow us to be destroyed. In this way the life of Jesus is revealed in us as our human frailty reveals his glory.

Lord God, I have a hard time accepting that I am human and frail, but I know that this is all in your plan. Thank you that you will never allow me to be destroyed and that you will never abandon me. I want all the glory to go to you.

The Lord is merciful and gracious,
Slow to anger, and abounding in mercy.
He will not always strive with us,
Nor will He keep His anger forever.
He has not dealt with us according to our sins,
Nor punished us according to our iniquities.
—PS. 103:8–10

God is always there when we need comfort and love. He is compassionate, not because he made us and knows all of our weaknesses, but because that is who he is. That doesn't mean that he lets us off the hook completely when we sin and slip back into old habit patterns. He "strives" with us, accusing and rebuking us, so we will realize when we have slipped off the path of recovery. But this passage says that he doesn't keep after us, nagging us to do what he wants. God is not codependent! He also doesn't hold onto his anger forever. He's not dysfunctional!

If he punished us as we deserved for our sins and those sinful patterns that were passed onto us by our parents, we would never even have the opportunity of beginning the process of recovery. His love for us is pure and unconditional. Instead of chastising us for our sins, he sent Jesus to show us what love really is and how love acts. Most importantly of all we now know *who* love is: God himself.

Lord God, I'm so thankful that you are merciful and compassionate, but I'm also thankful that you don't let me wander away from your path without disciplining me. Thank you for continuing to work with me and allowing me to know your abundant love for me.

For as the heavens are high above the earth,
So great is His mercy toward those who fear Him;
As far as the east is from the west,
So far has He removed our transgressions from
  us.
As a father pities his children,
So the Lord pities those who fear Him.

—PS. 103:11–13

This passage of Scripture has been familiar to many of us since we were children, but we still may not understand at all the depths of God's love for us, because we may not have really eperienced the pity or compassion of an earthly father.

One Sunday in church our pastor explained this verse in a way that helps us know what it means to be loved and have our sins completely forgiven. He asked us to think about traveling north on the earth; if we kept going we would eventually wind up going south after we traversed the North Pole, so north and south "touch" each other, so to speak. Then he asked us to think about traveling east or west. I was overwhelmed when I realized that one could keep going east around the earth forever and never "bump into" a point where he began going west. My sense of freedom from sin and guilt was absolutely tremendous. God loves me so much that he forgives me completely.

Thank you, Lord, that you extend your love and compassion to us in whatever state we are in. Thank you also for the unqualified forgiveness that is ours in Jesus Christ.

> *You have given a banner to those who fear You,*
> *That it may be displayed because of the truth.*
> *That Your beloved may be delivered.*
> *Save with Your right hand and hear me.*
> —PS. 60:4–5

In the ancient world, banners were used to lead troops into battle and as rallying points during a battle. These banners inspired the troops and gave them courage and confidence. As we honor and obey God as his children, we can know that he has given us an inspirational banner to continue the struggle against the dysfunction in our lives. He wants us to know and live the truth, to be victorious in our fight against codependency.

He is our Truth. His "right hand" is a figure of speech used to signify his power and strength, which he will use on our behalf to deliver us from our unhealthy behavior patterns. The term that is translated *beloved* here is a Hebrew expression of special endearment. As God's beloved child, you can count on him to listen to you and deliver you. However, this doesn't imply that we can sit back and he will make it all happen for us. He expects us to change what we can change. Then he will handle the rest.

Father, thank you for your special love for me. Thank you that you give me a "banner" to inspire me to keep working on my recovery. Thank you that your strong right hand will help me and deliver me.

*For since the beginning of the world
Men have not heard nor perceived by the ear,
Nor has the eye seen any God besides You,
Who acts for the one who waits for Him.*
—ISA. 64:4

Our God is unique. No matter what other spirits (gods) people have worshiped in the past or presently do worship, there is no god like our God. In this verse, the characteristic of God that sets him apart is the fact that he does such wonderful deeds for people who wait for him, who hope and trust in him.

Waiting on God—what does it mean for a recovering codependent? One of the things I equate "waiting on God" with is the first part of the Serenity Prayer that asks for peace and calmness to accept the things I cannot change. When I can't do anything to change the situation, I have to depend on God to make a difference. Only he can work in other people's lives to transform their behavior. The best thing I can do is to trust him to work in my life, to give me the strength to modify my thought patterns and reactions. He is the only power greater than myself that I can trust to always act in my behalf.

Lord, I thank you for being the kind of God that you are. Help me to wait for you to act, to trust that you will make changes for the best in my life. Thank you that you will not betray my trust.

> *For you have not received the spirit of bondage*
> *again to fear, but you have received the Spirit of*
> *adoption by whom we cry out, "Abba, Father." The*
> *Spirit Himself bears witness with our spirit that we*
> *are children of God.*   —ROM. 8:15–16

One of the codependent's biggest problems is fear. Although we might know that fear makes us a slave, we remain caught in a vicious cycle of fear—lack of trust—people-pleasing or caretaking—the inevitable failure of these tactics, and so back to fear again.

But here we find the only true antidote to fear. We who have turned to God through faith in Jesus Christ have been given the Holy Spirit to live in us. He testifies that we are truly children of God, with all the attending inheritance rights and privileges. The Spirit's witness in our hearts reveals the especially intimate relationship we have with God the Father; we call him *Abba,* the Aramaic equivalent of "daddy" or "papa." Once we comprehend the loving communion with God that is ours, the cycle of fear can be broken in our lives. Then we are free to enjoy God and other people without being afraid of what they will do to us.

Father God, I need to be reminded that I am your child everyday, and that you truly love me. Help me to apply the testimony of the Holy Spirit in all my experiences.

The LORD is righteous in all His ways,
Gracious in all His works.
The LORD is near to all who call upon
* Him,*
To all who call upon Him in truth.
He will fulfill the desire of those who fear
* Him;*
He also will hear their cry and save them.
—PS. 145:17–19

These verses in praise of God's character as it is revealed in his dealings with his children are incredibly reassuring. They do, however, put some stipulations on our interactions with God.

He promises to be near us when we call to him if we are sincere. Do I *really* want him near to me? Do I *really* want a close relationship with him? God demands integrity of us, and integrity is often difficult or threatening for the codependent. If I want him to meet my needs and fulfill my desires, he asks that I "fear" or honor and obey him. Not in a people-pleasing way—"I have to do what he wants, or I won't get what I need"—but to truly put him in first place in my life, desiring only to know his will and obey it. God doesn't demand perfection from us; he is more interested in our intentions and motives. Remember, he is loving and merciful, and he wants to be near us and meet our needs.

God, thank you that you are righteous and loving, and that you do want us to know you and know that you are near to us. Thank you that you know I am needy and that you have promised to meet my needs.

> . . . *work out your own salvation with fear and*
> *trembling; for it is God who works in you both*
> *to will and to do for His good pleasure.*
> —PHIL. 2:12–13

These verses are not a command to earn our salvation and healing by good works—a command that would make good sense to a performance-oriented codependent. They refer instead to demonstrating our salvation through spiritual growth. Improving our relationship with God is a daily ongoing process. The "fear" that Paul speaks of here does not mean that we need to be afraid that we won't be perfect enough to make it; rather he is speaking of a reverence for God that exhibits itself in determination to know God and do his will.

In verse 13 the other side of the coin is revealed, and we see things from God's point of view. He is the source of any power and strength we have to grow spiritually and become the whole, healthy persons he made us to be. His pleasure, or purpose, for us is to know him and glorify him. We can trust him to work in our lives to accomplish that.

Lord God, thank you that I don't have to be perfect in order to receive the grace of salvation through Christ. Help me to strive to know you better and to allow you to work healing in my life.

> *Through [Christ] also we have access by faith into
> this grace in which we stand, and rejoice in hope
> of the glory of God. . . . we also glory in
> tribulations, knowing that tribulation produces
> perseverance; and perseverance, character; and
> character, hope. Now hope does not disappoint,
> because the love of God has been poured out in
> our hearts by the Holy Spirit who was given to us.*
> —ROM. 5:2–5

Christ introduces us into the very presence of God through the faith we have in him. This is the grace we find only in God, the hope that we will live joyously with him in eternity. In addition, he will accomplish the purpose for which he created us: God will work in us for his glory while we are here on earth!

As a result of our hope in Christ, we can rejoice in our sufferings. Not morbidly because we are suffering, but because we know he is working through our pain and difficulties, and we will eventually be victorious. He is producing in us perseverance and the kind of character that he desires and that is best for us.

The most wonderful part of this passage is that God will never disappoint us! Our hope in him is based on his love and faithfulness that he revealed so clearly in Christ's death on the cross. He pours this love into our hearts.

Father, your love for me is overwhelming. Thank you that you work in my life in such patient, wise ways. Help me to submit myself to your purposes in my life.

> *Therefore He is also able to save to the uttermost*
> *those who come to God through Him, since He ever*
> *lives to make intercession for them.*
>
> —HEB. 7:25

Sometimes during the course of recovery, we can slip pretty low and come to the conclusion that it is impossible for God to save us. "I'm just too evil and worthless for God to handle," we say. But God reminds us of this verse. No matter how awful we are, or think we are, God can still save us through the work of Christ on the cross. He is the greatest power in the universe, the omnipotent God.

The word *uttermost* here includes the ideas of completeness and permanence. We don't have to worry that we may not be completely covered by the blood of Christ. We don't have to be afraid that he'll give up on us and let us go. Because he always lives, we will always have him as our representative before God. Since this verse promises that Christ will always be there for us, we can rest peacefully in his care, knowing that he is interceding on our behalf.

Lord Jesus, thank you for the completeness of the salvation you have provided on the cross. Thank you that you will eternally intercede for me. Help me to remember this verse and restore my confidence in you when I waver.

And [Jesus] looked around to see her who had done this thing. But the woman, fearing and trembling, knowing what had happened to her, came and fell down before Him and told Him the whole truth. And He said to her, "Daughter, your faith has made you well. Go in peace, and be healed of your affliction."

—MARK 5:32–34

The woman who had touched Jesus' robe had a very great faith. She was desperate for healing and she had finally found the only source of real health. Her situation was overwhelmingly difficult—not only had she suffered much physical agony, but her very existence must have been emotionally painful. According to Jewish law anyone having contact with her would be ritually unclean, so she was shunned by everyone. What a sense of rejection and abandonment she must have felt! But she did not put her circumstances between her and her faith in Christ. Instead she put her faith in Christ between herself and her situation. She reached out to touch Jesus' robe believing that she would be healed. But Jesus didn't let her get away without acknowledging his miracle in her life. He wants us also to declare to others his working in our lives, sharing his healing presence with them, that they may also find wholeness in him.

Father God, thank you for the miracle of healing you are doing in my life. Help me to keep my eyes fixed on you so I'm not distracted by my pain and problems.

And [Jesus] was withdrawn from them about a stone's throw, and He knelt down and prayed, saying, "Father, if it is Your will, remove this cup from Me; nevertheless not My will, but Yours, be done." Then an angel appeared to Him from heaven, strengthening Him. —LUKE 22:41–43

In these verses Jesus shows us what it means to completely turn ourselves over to God. Even as his Father's only Son, Jesus still had to yield his will completely to God. It wasn't easy for him either—he sweat great drops of blood in his struggle. He was abandoned by God because he was the bearer of all the sin of the universe, so we would never be abandoned by him. He was able to face his upcoming death, because he trusted the Father and wanted God's will more than his own.

And then an angel came to minister to Jesus and strengthen him. Even Jesus needed strengthening for the trials he had to face. We do not need to feel that we have to handle our problems all by ourselves. It is not shameful to admit weakness and receive help. No matter how far we progress in our recovery from codependency, we will need to turn our will over to God each day and ask for his strength to continue our journey toward wholeness.

Lord God, I want to know your will and do it, but I often find myself putting my priority in other places. Help me to turn myself over to you every day.

I cried out to the LORD because of my affliction,
And He answered me.
Out of the belly of Sheol I cried,
And You heard my voice. . . . When my soul
  fainted within me,
I remembered the LORD;
And my prayer went up to You
Into Your holy temple.
                              —JONAH 2:2, 7

Often the Lord uses events in our lives to teach us about himself. Jonah declared his confidence in God's faithfulness to rescue him, even though the problems he faced were caused by his own disobedience. When Jonah thought he was as good as dead, with his life ebbing away inside the great fish, he remembered his God. Jonah finally realized that God alone was powerful and that he could not resist God's will without suffering for it no matter how far he tried to run, or how well he thought he concealed his actions. He cried out to the Lord in the midst of his circumstances, and God heard him. But what a mess he got himself into before he was open to obeying God's will.

Sometimes I remind myself a lot of Jonah. I think I can run away from difficulties or hide my problems from God and others. The solution to my situation remains the same as the one Jonah finally found for himself. I must call on the Lord. He will hear me and help me when I yield to being controlled by his will. He is always loving and will answer my cries with mercy and concern for my best good.

Father God, I love you for your care and concern for me, even when I get myself into difficult situations by my own wrongdoing.

> "But let him who glories glory in this,
> That he understands and knows Me,
> That I am the LORD, exercising lovingkindness,
>   judgment, and righteousness in the earth.
> For in these I delight," says the Lord.
>   —JER. 9:24

One of the common coping mechanisms of people with low self-esteem is boasting. Young children especially seem to indulge in bragging to help themselves feel as if they are really a part of the group they identify with. By the time we're older we've usually internalized our parents' admonition to "Stop bragging. It isn't polite." We aren't so overt about our boasting.

Here the Word gives us something we can honestly boast about. Understanding and knowing God are the only things that really count. To know him as Lord, as the supreme Lord who redeems us is both comforting and exciting. Understanding that he is kind and just and righteous in his dealings with his creation not only gives us peace and confidence in him, it is one of the most worthwhile pieces of knowledge anyone can have.

_____

Thank you, Lord, that you delight in being kind and just and righteous. Thank you that you want me to know and understand you. Help me to seek you above all else.

Who Himself bore our sins in His own body on the tree, that we, having died to sins, might live for righteousness—by whose stripes you were healed. For you were like sheep going astray, but have now returned to the Shepherd and Overseer of your souls.
—1 PETER 2:24–25

One of the codependent's constant battles is to remember that in Jesus Christ we are dead to sin. He carried all the burden and punishment of our sins for us on the cross. We are no longer condemned to suffer for our past sins or for those sins of our parents that were passed on to us. He has healed us from everything in our lives that keeps us from wholeness in himself. We are new creations of God as his forgiven, redeemed children. We are free to live a new life, free to be an instrument for healing in other people's lives.

He is our gentle Shepherd who keeps us walking on the path to recovery. He provides all our needs and is our constant guide and companion. He never leaves us alone.

He is our Overseer who shows us how to develop new behavior patterns that will end the codependent addiction cycle in our lives. He is patient with us. He does not reject us when we fail, but he encourages us to keep on trying.

Thank you, Father God, for your salvation that has healed me and freed me for new life in you. Thank you for being my faithful Shepherd and patient Overseer. Help me to look to you alone for the help I need to live a life that is righteous before you.

> *Finally, brethren, whatever things are true,*
> *whatever things are noble, whatever things are*
> *just, whatever things are pure, whatever things*
> *are lovely, whatever things are of good report,*
> *if there is any virtue and if there is anything*
> *praiseworthy—meditate on these things. . . . Rejoice*
> *in the Lord always. Again I will say, rejoice!*
> —PHIL. 4:8, 4

Paul really understood the effects of one's thoughts on everyday life. Whatever I allow to occupy my mind begins eventually to influence my behavior. The thought messages I give myself control my reactions. What I think about myself determines to a great extent who I am. That's why it is so important to seek to understand God and to know and do his will. It is vital that we know who God is and that he loves us unconditionally.

I don't think these verses mean that we are to deny any negative thoughts or circumstances in our lives, but they do tell us not to dwell on them. When something is extremely painful for me, I have a hard time letting go of it and trusting God with it. These verses teach us how we can be successful at turning things over to God. Thinking of God, how incredibly wonderful he is and the beautiful things he is doing and wants to do in our lives can really help us to let go and let God. Learning to rejoice in him and his will is the key.

Lord God, I want to learn to praise you for who you are and not just for good things I can see happening in my life. Help me to rejoice in knowing you.

Because he has set his love upon Me,
Therefore I will deliver him;
I will set him on high,
Because he has known My name.
He shall call upon Me,
And I will answer him;
I will be with him in trouble;
I will deliver him and honor him.
—PS. 91:14–15

This is God talking to his people! Through the words of the psalmist he promises to rescue those who love him. He will set on high, or securely protect, those who acknowledge his name, who confess him as Lord and Savior. He will be with his people when they are in trouble. He will honor those who love him.

These promises are a marvelous encouragement. They speak of the ultimate wholeness God will accomplish in my life, and also of the everyday incidents he will work through with me. When God rescues his child, he doesn't just snatch him or her out of a difficult situation. He walks alongside his children and protects them in experiences that are too difficult or painful for them to endure. The most incredible portion of these promises is that God will honor those who love him. As I learn to love him more, he will *honor* me for allowing him to participate in my life and save me from despair and death!

Father God, thank you for your great love and mercy toward your children. Thank you that you promise to be with me through all my problems and to rescue me despite my shortcomings and sin. Help me to acknowledge you always as my Lord and Savior.

> *Now this is the confidence that we have in Him,*
> *that if we ask anything according to His will, He*
> *hears us. And if we know that He hears us,*
> *whatever we ask, we know that we have the*
> *petitions that we have asked of Him.*
> —1 JOHN 5:14–15

There has been much emphasis in our day to put on the "gospel of prosperity." This false gospel pulls select verses out of context and declares that if we have "enough faith" we can ask God for whatever we want and he is bound to give it to us.

However, these verses set the record straight. We can, the apostle declares, have great confidence in our prayers "*if* we ask according to *His* will." And no prayer delights the heart of our loving Father more than the prayer of a humble believer asking God to do a work of power and grace in his life.

We know that the Lord Jesus delights in answering this prayer because it is in total alignment with his revealed will for our lives—that we abide in him and become more Christ-like.

To overcome codependency, we must turn from trusting in ourselves to trusting and delighting in the power and strength of Jesus alone. This humility opens to us a new door of blessing as the Lord begins to do his wonderful work of grace in our lives.

Lord, I can't overcome my codependent addictions without your help. I humbly ask for your assistance.

Prayer

Strength to overcome codependent addictions comes from a power source greater than ourselves. God is that power source, and he has so ordained prayer as the medium to commune with him. Throughout Scripture, many examples of prayer are shown to us as models for us to emulate. God does respond to prayer as the following devotionals point out.

We conclude the codependent devotionals by studying various insights on prayer as found in Scripture. As we see biblical characters "cry out to God," so we learn that we too can go directly to him, asking for help in the reestablishment of healthy, positive relationships.

Be anxious for nothing, but in everything by prayer and supplication, with thanksgiving, let your requests be made known to God. —PHIL. 4:6

In her book *Each New Day*, Corrie ten Boom wrote, "When we work in God's Kingdom, we work for and with God. If you work *for* God, have a committee. If you work *with* God, have a prayer meeting."

Prayer is the privilege of working with God to see his desires done on earth. Some people ask and ask in prayer, yet nothing in their lives shows they really mean what they pray or really want what they are asking for. If you ask God for answers to your problems, prepare to be part of the solution! Some situations are beyond your reach, and God will move his hand. Other circumstances can be improved only by active obedience on your part, as you seek to do all God directs and implement his answer to your prayers.

God has a special work he wants you to do. And he will work with you, listening to your concerns, giving strength and guidance, and answering your prayers. But you will have to appropriate his strength, trust his unfailing love, and apply his Word. Don't be satisfied to work *for* God. Work *with* Him.

Thank you, Father, for working with us to accomplish your purposes and advance your kingdom. Thank you for the privilege and power of prayer.

This is the day which the L<small>ORD</small> has made.
—PS. 118:24

We are to live one day at a time—and to understand what effect the choices we make today will have upon our lives tomorrow. Each new day can make a difference in our lives.

Today is the only link between what has been and what will be. If you sincerely want God to help you change your life, today is the moment in time when you must act. Not tomorrow. Magical thinking about "someday" will not change your life. Nor will fantasizing about yesterdays help you deal wisely with the reality of today.

What you choose today matters. How you allow other people and their problems to affect you today matters. Do you really want things to be different? Better? Do you sincerely want to improve the quality of your relationships and your character? Then begin *today*. Commit this day to the Lord and obey him in it.

———————

Lord, the past and the future are out of my reach, but I can touch the things of today. Please help me to live one day at a time and to follow you in each new day. I commit this day to you and ask you to work in it.

*I will instruct you and teach you in the way you
   should go;
I will guide you with My eye.
Do not be like the horse or like the mule,
Which have no understanding,
Which must be harnessed with bit and bridle . . .*
—PS. 32:8–9

A missionary couple wrote home about their search to find a new house: "It was a difficult time, struggling with the decision on a practical level and a spiritual level—will God satisfy our desires or ask us to sacrifice? How clearly can we expect him to lead—will he make the decision for us, or subtly guide us as we make the decision?"

After a lengthy search, the couple found a nice home. "So we saw God richly bless above and beyond our desires," they wrote. "But he didn't make the decision for us like we wished he would. Sometimes we think life would be a lot easier if we could let go of any responsibilities and follow God without thinking, like a mule. But instead he wants us to carry out certain responsibilities and trust him through the stretching part."

God will instruct, teach, and guide you. But he will not live your life for you, make your decisions for you, or force you to obey. God will guide you, but your responsibilities are still your responsibility.

Lord, I sometimes want you to rush in and rescue me and make my decisions for me. Please help me understand what you want me to do and then responsibly do my part.

*Thus says the LORD who made you
And formed you from the womb, who
   will help you:
"Fear not . . ."*

                  —ISA. 44:2

Although these words were written to the nation of Israel, they contain heartwarming truth for each of God's children. God made you and formed you in the womb—He knows you inside and out. God knows the shape of your hands and how they were formed, even as He knows your inner scars and how they were formed. God knows your weaknesses and your potential, your sinfulness and your capacity to love. And God accepts you, flaws and all, with tender mercy and enabling grace.

You may feel unlovable. Undeserving. Yet the Lord longs to be gracious to you; he yearns to show mercy to you. You may feel hopeless and helpless, yet God himself has pledged to be your strength. The Lord will bind up your bruises and heal your wounded heart. His message to you today is, "Fear not, for I am with you."

Father, I want to relax in your arms and feel the warmth of your love around me. It seems too wonderful for words that you would stoop to hold my hand, to forgive and love and cherish me. Thank you for your precious promises and unfailing love. Thank you for making me in your image.

*I thank my God upon every remembrance of you,
always in every prayer of mine making request for
you all with joy . . . being confident of this very
thing, that He who has begun a good work in you
will complete it until the day of Jesus Christ.*
—PHIL. 1:3–4, 6

Do you ever wonder how you should pray for yourself
and others? Do you find yourself running down a "gro-
cery list" of present problems or running out of words?
Look at Paul's prayer for the Philippian believers.

First, we note that Paul prayed *thankfully*. As Paul
prayed for others, he thanked God for them. His prayer
was not a gripe session of everything so-and-so needed
to change! Instead, Paul prays for people with joy and
thankfulness, making requests on their behalf.

Second, Paul prayed *fervently*. He remembered the
needs of others "in every prayer." He was diligent and
persistent, not hit-or-miss.

Third, Paul prayed *confidently*. Paul's confidence
wasn't based upon the people he prayed for. His confidence was based upon God's ability to bring people
into conformity with his Son. Paul knew that God could
be counted on to complete the good work he'd started.
Like Paul, we can pray thankfully, fervently, and confidently, knowing God is able to hear and answer.

*Dear God, thank you for creating me and giving me special strengths
to use in your service. I know you won't give up on me and I won't
either because you can be trusted to complete your work in me.*

> *And this I pray, that your love may abound still*
> *more and more in knowledge and all discernment.*
> —PHIL. 1:9

One dictionary gave this definition for *discern:* "to come to know or recognize mentally." Do you mentally know and recognize Christian love? Can you discern or distinguish between healthy, proper love and dysfunctional, misguided love? Do you have a clear mental image of what discerning love is and acts like? Do your friends?

Everyone needs to grow in knowledgeable love. Paul's prayer is a powerful and relevant pattern for our prayers today!

———————

Dear Father, teach me to recognize love that is good for me and good for others and to avoid destructive patterns of relating to those I love in ways that ultimately aren't in anyone's best interest. I need help knowing what healthy love looks like—where its boundaries are, what limits it sets on disclosure, how it maintains complete dignity and respect for both the giver and receiver.

Lord, I want to grow in love, but it's tough. I need your strength; I can't do it alone. Please let my love increase more and more in clear understanding of what love should do and be. Help me recognize healthy love in others and to comprehend your love for me. Teach me to act in loving ways, discerning what is best in each situation.

And, Lord, I pray for my family, that their love may abound.

For if anyone is a hearer of the word and not a doer, he is like a man observing his natural face in a mirror; for he observes himself, goes away, and immediately forgets what kind of man he was.
—JAMES 1:23–24

Dr. Woodrow Kroll, a man with many distinguished university degrees, commented, "To me, education alone is of no value. It is what a person's education leads to that gives it value."

Studying Scripture, learning more about relationships by reading self-help books, or acquiring an understanding of healthy ways to relate to others through counseling are all ways to increase your knowledge of love. But where is your education leading to? A greater knowledge of love should lead to a clear conscience and sincere faith. It should change your life, leading you to live "without offense" until Christ returns.

If you learn what to do and don't do it, you're no better off with the knowledge! As 1 Timothy 1:5 explains, the goal of the instruction is "love from a pure heart, from a good conscience, and from sincere faith." Real love leads to clean living.

Dear Lord, help me learn about love and discern what is good. Then let that knowledge lead me into a life that pleases you. Help me live out what I learn about love.

> *And this I pray, that your love may abound still*
> *more and more in knowledge and all discernment,*
> *that you may approve the things that are*
> *excellent . . .*
> —PHIL. 1:9–10

Kenneth Taylor paraphrases "that you may approve the things that are excellent" as "for I want you always to see clearly the difference between right and wrong." It should be easy to tell the difference between right and wrong, and then give yourself to the excellent path of love. Discerning what is best isn't always so easy as you seek to live a pure and blameless life.

Is it best to overlook an offense or to confront someone about his or her behavior? Are you loving sacrificially or allowing someone to live irresponsibly at your expense by playing the martyr? Are your motives pure, or are you seeking to control others? These are the kinds of questions that require discernment. It is hard to determine the most excellent way in each situation. Pray for the wisdom to know how to act with healthy love in your specific circumstances.

Lord, learning to love and to know right from wrong isn't always easy in the daily give-and-take of my relationships. Help me to see clearly the way you want me to respond—not react—to the circumstances that come up. Help me find the most excellent way to live—the way of love.

*And this I pray . . . that you may be sincere and
without offense till the day of Christ, being filled
with the fruits of righteousness which are by Jesus
Christ, to the glory and praise of God.*
                                        —PHIL. 1:9–11

We can't produce the fruit of righteousness by straining and exerting ourselves. We produce spiritual fruit by abiding in Christ, the Vine.

We can step off the treadmill of performance-based acceptance. The only way we can be filled with fruit the Bible lists elsewhere—things like love, truth, peace, joy, praise, kindness, self-control, and patience—is to be filled and controlled by the Holy Spirit. Willpower alone just won't do it!

God doesn't tell us to bear good fruit or list these qualities just to make us feel guilty. He knows that without Christ we can do nothing. Things like love and self-control are perfected only through God's enabling grace. God never intended for us to attempt it without him.

Lord, thank you for working in me. I'm desperately dependent upon you. Nothing good comes naturally to me; I need your power to resist sin, to do good, to bear good fruit. Thank you for your Holy Spirit to help me live a fruitful life.

> *"Our Father in heaven,*
> *Hallowed be Your name.*
> *Your kingdom come.*
> *Your will be done on earth . . ."*
> —LUKE 11:2

When Jesus wanted to teach us how to pray, he left us this famous model prayer. We have memorized it. And in our first breath we glide smoothly over "Thy will be done," scarcely stopping to think about the implications of the phrase. Just think how "not my will, Lord, but always yours" can impact our lives.

What is God's will? God's will is that all people are treated with respect and dignity. God's will is that people be freed from the suffering and shame of sin by trusting in his Son, our Lord Jesus Christ. We can give ourselves freely and completely to God's will because God's will is always good and perfect.

In heaven, we will someday see God's will perfectly done, "And God will wipe away every tear . . . there shall be no more death, nor sorrow, nor crying; there shall be no more pain" (Rev. 21:4).

God, I eagerly pray that your will be done. There is nothing to fear in your will, for you are the God of love and goodness. Lord, teach me to seek not the easy way, but the right way; not what makes me happy, but what pleases you. Let your will be done in and through me until we meet face to face.

Give us day by day our daily bread.
—LUKE 11:3

In recovery circles "working a program" means sticking to a daily program of recovery. It means examining your feelings each day. It means managing the little day-to-day conflicts calmly but purposefully. It means learning that each day offers the choice of sticking with recovery or acting out of codependent or addictive cycles.

Living a balanced, healthy life is done on a daily basis. Just as we pray that God will give us "day by day our daily bread," we should pray that God will give us daily emotional and volitional help and strength. Don't get stuck reading and thinking about lifelong recovery. Just concentrate on one day. This day.

Lord, it's easy for me to slip into emotional isolation or deny my feelings when the problems I face seem overwhelming. Help me take life as it comes, one day at a time. Let this be the day I learn more about sharing myself with others in a safe way and relearning relational skills. Please give me this day the strength that I need.

> *And forgive us our sins,*
> *For we also forgive everyone*
> *who is indebted to us.*
> —LUKE 11:4

Healing guilt and shame are key issues in recovery. Seeking and receiving forgiveness is part of the cleansing process. Remind yourself often that you are clean and forgiven in God's eyes. When you receive God's forgiveness you can stand before him unashamed and whole in Christ. God has freed you from the bondage of guilt and shame; forgiveness is available to all who ask. And if God does not condemn you, neither should you condemn yourself. Forgive yourself as God has forgiven you.

What about forgiving others? Forgiving others is not only important, it is also commanded. But forgiving others does not mean that you must absolve the people who have hurt you from their responsibility. Forgiveness isn't just pretending that what happened wasn't so bad after all. Forgiveness is no shortcut to feeling better. Forgiving is letting go of the need to get even and releasing the right to judge, leaving that right to God. When you forgive someone who hurt you, you put the responsibility and guilt on their shoulders, where it belongs, but then you give everything—your hurt, their guilt, and the relationship—over to God.

Lord, forgive me for the wrong that I've done. And help me to truly forgive myself. And, Lord, I pray for your help to forgive those who have wronged me.

And do not lead us into temptation,
But deliver us from the evil one.
—MATT. 6:13

When we live in truth and reality, we are less vulnerable to temptation. Why? Because we don't deny that we are tempted. We are to admit that we are powerless over addictions, compulsions, and sinful desires. When we are honest about the reality of temptation, we are honest about our willingness to avoid it. If it's really a painful problem, we mean it when we pray "do not lead us into temptation."

As we experience the leading of God, we begin to recognize his pattern of prompting us to think ahead, to plan, and to persist in following that plan in order to avoid the sinful behavior patterns that have repeatedly snared us in the past. God will deliver us, but not without our involvement. He can't lead us away from temptation if we won't follow him.

God, help me take the initiative to lead my life according to your Word and away from temptation. Remind me that the time to make the choice is before I'm waist deep in troubled waters! Give me the wisdom to listen to your warnings and heed the quiet voice of your Spirit as he leads me away from temptation.

Now this is the confidence that we have in Him,
that if we ask anything according to His will, He
hears us. And if we know that He hears us,
whatever we ask, we know that we have the
petitions that we have asked of Him.
—1 JOHN 5:14–15

It has been said that prayer does not prepare us for the greater works; it *is* the greater work. One woman candidly remarked, "I'd pray more if I thought it mattered more. I know I shouldn't feel that way, but that's the lie I've been acting on." She had lost her confidence in Christ and his willingness to answer prayer.

Don't be trapped in the web of false doctrine that minimizes prayer and encourages only achievement-oriented activities. Don't be deceived into thinking that prayer doesn't matter or isn't worth the time. Prayer is an important matter between you and God. In a sense, it's part of the "work" you've been called to do. In a deeper sense, prayer is the mainspring that winds our relationship with God. And our spiritual life will stop ticking without it.

Spiritual things are accomplished by spiritual means. We can pray with confidence and compassion—that's our part. God can work miracles through our prayers—that's his specialty!

Lord, give me a renewed vision of the power of prayer and the comfort of conversation with you. Help me to pray confidently, trusting in your ability to answer.

In return for my love they are my accusers,
But I give myself to prayer.   —PS. 109:4

When you begin to change and to follow God's ways of responsible love, you can expect some resistance from others around you who were comfortable with the old roles. What should you do if you are unfairly criticized or unjustly accused of being selfish or self-righteous? Give yourself to prayer!

Don't give up if your efforts toward recovery are misunderstood by others. Not everyone will support your efforts all the time, and you cannot keep people perfectly pleased with you. Instead, do what you feel is right in God's eyes, and pray about any resistance you face.

Dear God, you know that I'm trying to do what is right, but things are almost harder than they were before. So much of what I'm doing to try to set things straight in my life is being misunderstood. That makes it tough for me to sort through things and I lose confidence in myself. And I get angry. I can't control people's reactions, Lord; you'll have to handle that. But please help me handle my own responses and stick with making the changes you want me to make.

*The LORD your God, who goes before you, He will
fight for you, according to all He did for you . . . in
the wilderness where you saw how the LORD your
God carried you, as a man carries his son, in all
the way that you went until you came to this place.*
—DEUT. 1:30–31

While they were taking a family walk, a young
mother challenged her three year old to a race. But the
little boy responded dejectedly, "No way, I can't ever
win!" The father overheard the conversation and gave
his wife a mischievous grin. "This time you will win,
son," he announced. "On your marks. Get set. Go!"
With that, he scooped up his young son in his arms and
strode past his wife with ease, as the little boy giggled
with delight.

There are times in life when we're just not up to the
challenge. Like this little boy, we know we can't win,
and we don't feel there's much use in trying. God, as a
tender and compassionate Father, knows just when to
carry us. We can relax in his arms; rely on his strength.

*Heavenly Father, thank you for your loving arms, for your comfort
and strength. Help me rest in your arms of love, secure in your gentle
strength and confident of your ability to handle any difficulty.*

Then you shall call, and the LORD will answer;
You shall cry, and He will say, "Here I am."
—ISA. 58:9

Ideas have consequences. Gordon and Jean had the idea that prayer changes things. "We always had our own time with the Lord, praying for each child," they said. "Many times that was all that was left in our power to do."

When you feel like life is out of control and there's nothing you can do, you can pray. When a loved one is in trouble and it's out of your hands, you can still place it in God's hands. Pray! When you feel lonely or afraid, you can pray. The Lord will answer.

You never know what might happen if you have the notion that prayer changes things. Gordon and Jean saw God work in their lives and in the lives of their children in remarkable ways. So can you. Prayer has consequences.

Father, there are things in my life that I am deeply troubled about that aren't in my power to change. Lord, I give them to you, inviting you to get involved in my life. Nothing is too difficult for you, Lord. I look forward to seeing your work.

> *Open my eyes, that I may see*
> *Wondrous things from Your*
> *law.* —PS. 119:18

There is a beautiful old hymn by Clara H. Scott based upon this verse. The first stanza and chorus are:

> *Open my eyes, that I may see*
> *Glimpses of truth You have for me;*
> *Place in my hands the wonderful key*
> *That shall unlock and set me free.*

> *Silently now I wait for You*
> *Ready my God, Your will to do*
> *Open my eyes, illumine me*
> *Spirit divine!*

The second verse continues, "Open my ears that I may hear, Voices of Truth so sharp and clear." These lines, and the words of other songs, can be a refreshing and helpful prayer guide. Pray through each line, personalizing it and elaborating on the thought it presents.

Lord, open my eyes that I might see the truth I need to live by. So often, Lord, I'm blinded by my past experiences, my fears, or my stubbornness. Help me comprehend the truth, because I know that only truth can set me free from the self-defeating behaviors that are based upon lies I believe, lies like, "I must have everyone's approval and love" or "I must be perfect." Only your truth can counteract my faulty inner messages and unlock the chains of the past and set me free.

*. . . Let not your heart be troubled, neither let it
be afraid.*
—JOHN 14:27

Jesus didn't say, "I will not let your heart be troubled,
not let it be afraid." He said, "Let not your heart be
troubled . . ." It is a command. God will not keep your
heart free from anxiety and doubt—it's up to you. You
must trust God and choose not to have a troubled
heart.

You cannot choose to avoid all trouble. Life includes
ups and downs, good times and stressful ones. Life is
unpredictable and hard sometimes. But we can choose
not to let our hearts be troubled even in the midst of
trials. How? By pouring out our concerns and fears to
God, by casting our cares upon him in prayer.

Let the peace of God rule in your heart. Don't let the
worries and fears take over. Even in days of uncertainty, you can know with certainty that God will never
leave you. Trust him.

*Heavenly Father, when I get worried and upset, help me to rest in
you—to sit tight, to stick to the things you've told me to do, and to
trust you for the rest. I know that you won't let me down.*

> *"Blessed are You, L*ORD *God of Israel, our*
>   *Father, forever and ever.*
> *Yours, O L*ORD*, is the greatness,*
> *The power and the glory,*
> *The victory and the majesty;*
> *For all that is in heaven and in earth is Yours;*
> *Yours is the kingdom, O L*ORD*,*
> *And You are exalted as head over all.*
> —1 CHRON. 29:10–11

Many of the prayers of David are recorded in the Bible, particularly in the Psalms. And the one theme that stands out in his prayers is worship.

Worship takes our eyes off ourselves and turns them to our glorious God. "Yours, O LORD, is the greatness, the power and the glory, the victory and the majesty!" David praises God in prayer, in front of all the people. Can you imagine a modern politician praying like David? Worship is not a natural part of public life in our society.

Our society does a poor job of instructing us in such things. Adoration, reverence, and worship may not feel natural to you. You may not have much practice at it. But worship will deepen your relationship with God and enrich your life. Songs of praise and prayers of praise are a good place to begin practicing the habit of worship.

_____

O Lord, my God, I will praise your name for ever and ever. Your mighty power created everything in heaven and earth; it all belongs to you. How wonderful you are and how worthy of praise!

For unto us a Child is born,
Unto us a Son is given;
And the government will be upon His shoulder.
And His name will be called
Wonderful, Counselor, Mighty God,
Everlasting Father, Prince of Peace.

—ISA. 9:6

On that night long ago when God became a human baby, the world was a harsh place. A favored few lived comfortably, but the vast majority of folks struggled with poor economic conditions, barbaric social standards, and a bankrupt religious system. Pain and deprivation and hopelessness were facts of daily life.

Jesus grew to manhood in that society, keenly aware of how deeply sin had damaged his world. His earthly ministry was imbued with compassion for the suffering multitudes who were "like sheep without a shepherd." Hebrews 2:17–18 tell us that he was "made like his brethren in all things." And not only does he understand our suffering completely, but because he is the all-wise God, he also has the answer for every situation we face—he is the Wonderful Counselor. He has the power to enable us to overcome every struggle—he is Mighty God. He never changes and always desires the best for us—he is our Everlasting Father. As we trust and obey him, he will give our lives the stability we long for—he is the Prince of Peace.

I worship you, Wonderful Lord, and thank you for the gift of Jesus to a sinful world. Let me know you more deeply and trust you more completely.

Both riches and honor come from You,
And You reign over all.
In Your hand is power and might;
In Your hand it is to make great
And to give strength to all.
—1 CHRON. 29:12

David is quick to give God credit in all good things. From God's hand we, too, enjoy many benefits. God is gracious to his children. Over your shame and shortcomings God places his cloak of honor and dignity. He freely gives you good things and lifts you up to a position of worth and esteem in his family.

The problem is that we are used to low living. Like the prodigal son we slip off to the pigpen, wallowing in the indulgent pleasures of sin. But we belong in the exalted place, the dwelling place of the Most High. We are to live in the exaltation of Christ. We are to be part of his family in good standing. Secure. Safe. Accepted. God wants to impart all that we are entitled to as his children. But we must return home to him.

In God's family we have the privilege of being protected, accepted, and directed through life. Good things come to us from the hand of our God.

Lord, how majestic is your name. From your mighty throne in heaven you rule over all. It's hard to imagine myself as the adult child of the reigning King! But you have given me your name and have adopted me into your family.

Now therefore, our God,
We thank You
And praise Your glorious name.
　　　　—1 CHRON. 29:13

One of the conscious choices we make every day is our attitude. Thankfulness is a habit. Praise is a habit. Joy is a habit. If you make a habit of looking at life in an optimistic way, you will have greater energy and hope to work through your problems. Thankfulness and an attitude of gratitude to God can help you turn whatever situation you face to your advantage.

A great place to begin cultivating an attitude of gratitude and praise is in your prayer life. Make a habit of thinking about blessings as well as trials, opportunities as well as disappointments, and progress as well as setbacks. Ask for God to help you improve your attitude toward life.

———————————

Father, you and I both know all about my bad habits, so let's talk about a good habit I can begin today. I can be thankful. Right now I thank you for the many blessings and answers to prayer I've received. Specifically I thank you for . . . and I praise you for . . . Help me make a habit of looking at life in a hopeful, thankful, positive way.

[I pray] that the God of our Lord Jesus Christ, the Father of glory, may give to you the spirit of wisdom and revelation in the knowledge of Him.
—EPH. 1:17

Many paradoxes in the Bible don't make sense according to worldly wisdom: trouble brings joy, weakness brings strength, servitude brings greatness, to die is to live. That is part of the reason we are so completely dependent upon God to reveal himself and his ways to us.

God's thoughts are beyond us. You can't pour an infinite amount of water in a small, finite cup. In the same way, the human mind cannot hold the infinite wonders and vast knowledge of God and his glory. We must pray for wisdom and revelation from above—wisdom to know God as he is revealed through his Son by his Spirit, wisdom to know how to do God's will on earth.

The human mind can not comprehend itself or the complexities of life without the help of God. You need God's wisdom to unravel the tangles in your thinking and your life.

Almighty God, the vastness of your knowledge and the depth of your wisdom is awesome. I come to you admitting my foolishness and ignorance. Please give me wisdom. Reveal the truth to me and enable me to act upon it, that you might be glorified and honored by my life.

> *O God, my heart is steadfast;*
> *I will sing and give praise. . . .*
> *I will praise You, O LORD, among the peoples,*
> *And I will sing praises to You among the nations.*
> *For Your mercy is great above the heavens,*
> *And Your truth reaches to the clouds.*
> —PS. 108:1, 3–4

Sally had a problem. "When things go bad, I get discouraged and depressed. Usually I blame myself," she explained. "Then when things go well for me, I feel like I don't deserve it—I feel guilty for having it so good! I minimize my successes and worry about what's coming next. I can't win!"

Do you, like Sally, have difficulty giving yourself permission to be happy, especially if someone else is unhappy? Do you envision God as a killjoy? He isn't! And you needn't be.

God allows us to enjoy life. He encourages us to sing, give thanks, and rejoice in response to his abundant blessings. It's okay to relax and have fun; to celebrate the goodness of life. When things are going well, let yourself be glad about it!

O Lord, it feels so great to be making progress. I thank you that things are going well. I praise you for your kindness and mercy. Help me learn how to relax and have fun. I'm glad I'm me, and I'm glad you are my God. I have much to be happy about. Show me how to feel and express happiness.

*For I know the thoughts I think toward you, says
the LORD, thoughts of peace and not of evil, to give
you a future and a hope.*　　　　—JER. 29:11

In a "Peanuts" comic strip, Charles Schulz wrote, "I
have a new philosophy. I'm only going to dread one
day at a time."

There is more to life than just survival. For the Christian the future is bright with hope. We don't have to
"dread one day at a time!" Instead, we can say, "This is
the day the Lord has made, I will rejoice and be glad in
it."

In Christ you have help for today and hope for the
future. As you trust in the Lord, he will give you the
desires of your heart. There are no trouble-free
happily-ever-afters, and neither God nor I will promise
you one. But you can look forward to good things in
your life because God is watching over you and will be
with you. God has plans for you. Good plans! Plans for
a future and a hope. As you live your future, one day at
a time, you will find reasons to rejoice in our Lord and
be glad.

———————

*Father, I commit my future to you with faith in your goodness. I thank
you for the work you've already done in my life and look forward to
growing even stronger in the days to come. Thank you for your constant care, for giving me a future and a hope.*

Blessed is the man whose strength is in You,
Whose heart is set on pilgrimage.
As they pass through the valley of Baca,
They make it a spring;
The rain also covers it with pools.
They go from strength to strength;
Every one of them appears before God in Zion. . . .
O LORD of hosts,
Blessed is the man who trusts in You!
—PS. 84:5–7, 12

During Old Testament times, devout Jews made annual pilgrimages to the temple in Jerusalem for worship, prayer and meditation. Today, believers don't make pilgrimages to a specific place. But as we seek to know God better, our lives are pilgrimages.

The strength for our journey does not come from within ourselves. When we are hungry to know God, our hearts become *set* on our pilgrimage; our strength comes from the Lord. We pass through waterless valleys of struggle and discouragement just as the Israelites had to pass through Baca, a valley of parched, dry land. But when the rains came, the land was covered with pools of water symbolizing God's blessing to the faithful. Because they journeyed in spite of all obstacles, their strength was increased—just as ours is when we learn to trust and obey God, no matter what our circumstances.

Lord, provide me with nourishment to keep going, even when times are tough.